Dr. Deming

Dr. Deming

The American Who Taught the Japanese About Quality

Rafael Aguayo

A Lyle Stuart Book
Published by Carol Publishing Group

First Carol Publishing Edition 1990

A Lyle Stuart Book
Published by Carol Publishing Group

Editorial Offices	Sales & Distribution Offices
600 Madison Avenue	120 Enterprise Avenue
New York, NY 10022	Secaucus, NJ 07094

In Canada: Musson Book Company
A division of General Publishing Co., Limited
Don Mills, Ontario

Queries regarding rights and permissions should be addressed:
Carol Publishing Group, 600 Madison Avenue, New York, NY 10022

Manufactured in the United States of America

10 9 8 7 6 5 4 3 2

Figure on pages 120 and 161 reprinted from *Out of the Crisis* by W. Edwards
Deming, by permission of MIT and W. Edwards Deming. Published by MIT,
Center for Advanced Engineering Study, Cambridge, Mass. 02139. Copyright 1982,
1986 by W. Edwards Deming.   Figure on page 164 reprinted from *Guide to Quality
Control* by Dr. Kaoru Ishikawa, by permission of the publisher, the Asian
Productivity Organization.

Library of Congress Cataloging-in-Publication Data

Aguayo, Rafael.
   Dr. Deming : the man who taught the Japanese about quality / by Rafael
Aguayo.
      p. cm.
   "A Lyle Stuart book."
   ISBN 0-8184-0519-8 :
      1. Quality control—United States.   2. Deming, W. Edwards (William
Edwards), 1990–   . I. Title.
TS156.A35   1990
658.5′62′092—dc20
                                                                                      90–47036
                                                                                            CIP

To all my teachers, especially

Aida R. Aguayo
J. Roberto Aguayo
Lincoln Barnett
Eido T'ai Shimano
Kyudo Nakagawa
W. Edwards Deming

To my family,

Alexis, Brendan, Cindia, Peggy, and Hops

Contents

	Introduction	ix
	Acknowledgments	xiv
1	Management and Quality	3
2	Quality Must Come First	19
3	What Is Quality?	35
4	Variation in Management	51
5	Stable Systems	67
6	Cooperation: Suppliers and Divisions	83
7	Cooperation Between Management and Workers	93
8	Cooperation Among Competitors	105
9	The Need for Transformation	113
10	Focus and Philosophy	126
11	Inspection	139
12	Attitudes Toward Suppliers	149
13	Rebirth and Renewal	158
14	The Importance of Training	168
15	Leadership	175
16	Driving Out Fear	183
17	Enhancing Pride and Joy in Work	199
18	Improvement and the Minds of Workers	205
19	Basic Transformation	213
20	Competition	219
21	Where Are We?	235

Appendix A. The Deming Prize   245
Appendix B. William Edward Deming: A Brief
     Biography   251
Appendix C. Some National Implications of the Deming
     View   254
Appendix D. Further Reading   275
Notes   277
Index   281

Introduction

IN 1977 I completed the requirements for my Master of Business Administration (M.B.A.) degree at New York University. I had already been working in the financial sector as a bank executive for seven years and had been disturbed by the management practices I saw. Something was wrong and something was missing, but studying in business school did not seem to provide any additional insight or understanding, much less help alleviate the problem.

At that time, Japan was posing a formidable challenge to the assumed supremacy of American industry and American managerial skills. American multinational firms were big, powerful, and successful; and our assumed superiority in managerial ability, education, and talent led many of us, myself included, to believe smugly that we would continue to dominate and influence the world economy.

Sure, Japan would make inroads and continue to develop. Their cars, especially small cars, were good. Their electronics were good, but they had some special advantages that would soon disappear. As soon as the American automotive firms got serious about building small cars, or the electronics firms got serious about lowering costs, we would reemerge with our pride intact, the masters of world commerce.

The Japanese just could not be as creative, innovative, or hardworking because they did not reward each individual for his or her specific contribution. They did not cherish individual competition the way we did. They did not have management by objectives the way we did. At least that was what I and many others thought. If

I had not been explicitly taught these notions in business school, they certainly were not discouraged or challenged. In fact, they were implied by most of what was called management literature. In America we recognized the superior performers, and these were the ones (we thought) who contributed to progress. By recognizing and rewarding them, we could tap their creativity and force, therefore securing our future position in the world.

But it did not turn out that way. Japanese industry did not fade into the background. Japanese workers did not become lazy as their standard of living and pay increased. Not only did Japanese firms catch up, but they started to surpass American firms in features, innovation, design, and, of course, quality. As American firms became more serious about meeting the competition and instituting rigorous objectives, the situation became worse. As more M.B.A.'s trained in "modern management" entered the corporate ranks and took over the leadership of firms, the situation continued to worsen. What was wrong? What was going on?

You can imagine my surprise, then, when I opened the *Wall Street Journal* one day and saw a full two-page advertisement with the headline, **"The most famous name in Japanese quality control is American."** The text went on to say:

His name is W. Edwards Deming, and he's a quality control expert.

In 1950, the Union of Japanese Scientists and Engineers (JUSE) invited Dr. Deming to lecture several times in Japan, an event that turned out to be overwhelmingly successful.

To commemorate Dr. Deming's visit and to further Japan's development of quality control, JUSE shortly thereafter established the Deming Prizes, to be presented each year to the Japanese companies with the most outstanding achievement in quality control.

Today, Dr. Deming's name is well known within Japan's industrial community, and companies compete fiercely to win the prestigious Demings.

In 1953, Sumitomo Metals was fortunate enough to win the Deming Prize for Application. In retrospect, we believe it may have been the single most important event in the history of quality control at Sumitomo. By inspiring us to even greater efforts, it helped us to eventually become one of the world's largest and most advanced steelmakers.

Sumitomo Metals owes a great deal to the American quality control expert who became one of Japan's greatest inspirations. On that point, the management and employees of Sumitomo Metals would like to take this opportunity to say simply, "Thanks, Dr. Deming, for helping to start it all."

I was shocked. I soon learned that Deming had been a professor since 1946, and was still teaching, at the school where I had obtained my graduate business degree. How could this be? How was it that I had never heard of him? What was so vital about quality control? I resolved to learn more at the first opportunity.

That opportunity came in 1983 when I was toying with the idea of getting another degree. While I was on line for course registration, a sheet announcing a minicourse, given by Deming, caught my eye. I attended that class.

For some reason I sat myself at the front of the class. The students were sitting with an air of anticipation, and in walked a man with a large smile on his face and a wonderfully friendly demeanor. He began his lecture. "What is quality?" he asked.

I had been thinking about similar issues regarding work and management. When is a firm getting the best from its people? I felt brave that day, so I volunteered an answer: "I think people have to be happy for there to be quality."

He looked at me and asked my name. "Rafael," I said. He nodded and then said, "Not a bad answer. Quality is pride of workmanship."

I was stunned. No talk of inspection or of the minimum acceptable level of quality. The one time quality had been mentioned during my previous business education was as a system of inspection of final product to determine when a machine had to be adjusted. I now know this was totally incorrect. If quality is not inspected in but is built in, if quality is integral to the product or service, then quality is a function of management.

In that first course Deming proceeded to destroy every important notion of management I had been taught. He showed me that the important things I had learned in business school were wrong. Not only were they wrong, but they led to inferior results, poor quality, and customer dissatisfaction. Everything that was missing from my business education, everything that should have been taught, was being taught in just one place, in just one course. Why hadn't I heard of Deming? Perhaps because what was being taught in business schools all over the country was at odds with what he was saying about management.

Throughout that first course I kept asking myself, why isn't he better known in the U.S.? Why isn't there a popular book explaining his teachings? At the end of the course I wrote Deming a letter stating that I wanted to write a book on his teachings. I wanted to get his thoughts on the subject and, if he thought it was a good idea, his help. I thought I should spend several years studying before beginning to write. Several months later he wrote back telling me he approved of the project and would help me in whatever way possible. And so began the work on this book.

What I thought would be a three- or four-year project has taken seven years. But I count the extra time as a blessing. It has been my great fortune to have immersed myself in this wonderful body of knowledge. Deming's teachings are rigorous and beautiful, and have application in virtually every field and every area of our lives.

Deming is world-renowned as a statistician, and most of us think of statistics as very dry mathematics. But statistical thinking has been applied to science and technology for over a century. It is not the techniques that are all-important but the inferences and prediction. When statistical thinking was applied to atomic phenomena in the early part of this century, quantum mechanics, which explained phenomena that the classical deterministic theory could not, was formulated. Quantum mechanics made some very strange predictions about an uncertainty principle, electron tunneling, and other strange occurrences. Nevertheless, its predictions turned out to be correct even though they seemed to violate intuitive notions based on past concepts and experiences. Similarly, Deming's theory makes some startling predictions about good management that contradict notions many of us have.

If you have difficulty swallowing some of these results at first, you should know that you're in good company. Albert Einstein hoped that quantum mechanics would eventually be replaced by something else. As he told his friend and associate, the great physicist Niels Bohr, "I can't believe God would play dice with the Universe." Bohr is reputed to have responded, "Albert, if God wants to play dice, let him."

In spite of Einstein's wishes, quantum mechanics has not been replaced. If anything, it is now being applied more broadly.

In this work I de-emphasize techniques in favor of stressing the implications for good management. The test for any set of ideas is how well they predict or how well they work, not how comfortable we are with them initially.

There is something else, equally vital, that has made this book such a great experience and such a great pleasure. I've known too many professors who seem to have trouble getting their heads through the door on their way to a class—professors who grace us with their presence and bring a fixed body of material to teach the students. God help the student who disagrees or even questions the sanctity of the professor's word. After all, students are only students.

But from the very first class Deming was different. Here is a man of international prominence, who in fact has changed the world, but who believes every student has something to offer, something to teach. Deming goes to a class or seminar prepared to learn as well as to teach. He is a true man without rank. Learning with him has been one of the great pleasures of my life.

I hope that this book presents a clear view to others of the teachings of a great man. I hope that some of the power of the man passes through these pages. I hope you enjoy reading it. I certainly enjoyed writing it.

Acknowledgments

THIS part of the book may be the most difficult to write. In some sense this book wrote itself—I was one of many contributors. I have received at odd moments and from totally unexpected sources suggestions and help that greatly contributed to the writing, completion, and publication of this book.

Frankly, I don't remember the names of everyone who helped clarify my thinking (sometimes we were never introduced). Nevertheless, I will do my best to name as many of the people who contributed to this book as I possibly can, recognizing that such a list is necessarily incomplete.

My thanks to Mike Kahann, Nancy Mann, Brian Joiner, Joyce Orsini, Ben Epstein, Ed Baker, Earl Conway, Clare Crawford-Mason, Wendy L. Coles, Barbara Lawton, Karl Haushalter, Thomas Boardman, Louis Schultz, all the participants in all the red bead experiments, Linda Dougherty, John Whitney, Drew Hariss, Marshall Thurber, John Dowling, David Levine, John Lampl, and Donna McCurry.

My thanks to those I never met but whose words and ideas somehow reached me: Pete Peterson, Lloyd Nelson, Norb Keller, William Scherkenbach, Herb Cohen, Joseph Juran, Kaoru Ishikawa, Alfie Kohn, William G. Ouchi, and David Chambers.

Acknowledgment is due to individuals whose names I cannot remember (or never recorded) yet who provided me with essential help: people I met and spoke to during seminar recesses and intermissions or while on the job; individuals whose questions or comments helped clarify my own thinking.

My thanks go out to those individuals whose ideas and writings I criticize in this work as incorrect practice. I hope my criticism is taken in the manner intended—of free and open discussion of ideas so we all may obtain greater clarity. No personal affront is intended or implied.

Special thanks are due those who helped in the production of this book: my agent, Mitch Rose, who understood what this project was about and helped me turn my ideas into a workable proposal; Jane Chelius for her initial help in reading the proposal and introducing me to Mitch; my editor, Carole Stuart, who helped transform my style from one bordering on the unreadable into what I hope is a much more lucid one; Bruce Shostak, who took over where Carole left off as I finished the manuscript.

Especially important are my family, who lived with me while I labored with this labor of love. Thank you, Alexis, Brendan, Cindia, Hops, and my wife, Peggy, who put up with what must have seemed like a madman. Your love nourished me not only in the writing of this book but at all times.

I thank Cecelia S. Kilian, Dr. Deming's secretary, for her friendly help and encouragement. Finally, I thank Dr. W. Edwards Deming himself. Not only are he and his teachings the subject of this book, but his patience, guidance, and encouragement made this book possible. His reading of the earlier versions of the manuscript, his clarifications, corrections, criticisms, praise, and encouragement guided me and rewarded me with great understanding and knowledge that are critical to good management and have application everywhere. Thank you, Dr. Deming.

Any errors, omissions, oversights, or misinterpretations of Deming's theories and philosophy in this book are my responsibility and only mine.

CHAPTER 1

Management and Quality

In 1986 Ford emerged as the darling of the American auto industry. Earnings, for the first time since the 1920s, exceeded those of General Motors, and in fact exceeded GM's and Chrysler's combined. Ford's market share continued to increase at the expense of its two American rivals. Its new Taurus/Sable car line was an unqualified success, commercially and in the eyes of Detroit's critics. *Consumer Reports* magazine, not usually a fan of American automobiles, called the new cars the best American cars it had ever tested and used the Taurus as the standard by which to judge other domestic models. In its press releases and advertisements, however, Ford did not stress sales or marketing but quality. For the sixth year in a row Ford automobiles were rated highest in quality of all the domestic manufacturers.

Subsequent years confirmed that Ford's success was not a fluke as earnings continued to exceed GM's and Chrysler's. Ford announced profit sharing for its hourly employees of over $2,000 per worker in 1987 and $3,700 in 1988. Some estimates of Ford's cost advantage over GM ran as high as $600 per car.

Not bad for a company that in 1980 had seemed on the brink of disaster and which prior to 1980 hadn't enjoyed a reputation for quality, particularly when compared to the Japanese automakers.

Back in 1980, while Chrysler was grabbing headlines with its brush with bankruptcy and the controversy surrounding the federal loan guarantee that kept its doors open, Ford was quietly suffering, hardly in better shape.

But in 1983 a quiet revolution began at Ford. The quality of

3

American cars was the biggest complaint at the time. Ford management knew something had to be done. In 1983 Ford asked the
foremost American expert on quality, the world-renowned Dr. W.
Edwards Deming, for help. To management's surprise, however,
Deming talked not about quality but about management. All of
Ford's top management attended Deming's seminars, and the
company has not been the same since. Among those who attended
was Donald Petersen, who later became chairman and proclaimed
Ford's intent to implement Deming's philosophy throughout the
company.

In a letter to *Autoweek*, Petersen stated, "We are moving toward
building a quality culture at Ford and the many changes that have
been taking place here have their roots directly in Dr. Deming's
teachings."[1]

While other old-line domestic manufacturers have begun imple-
menting quality cultures, few have gone as far as Ford in revamping
their way of doing business. A limited or partial application of the
Deming philosophy doesn't have the dramatic results that a full
application has. An August 18, 1986, article in *Fortune* stated, "By
spreading Deming's philosophy throughout the company, Ford, in
the view of consultants and market researchers who have made
comparisons, has probably taken greater strides in improving
quality than any other U.S. auto manufacturer. . . . A company that
decides to take its quality consultant seriously can take off on a road
that will transform the whole corporate culture. As Ford found out,
following the Deming path leads to a lot more than tinkering with
the assembly line."[2]

Deming is no newcomer to American management or quality
control. One of the founders of the field, he was actively involved in
American quality control efforts during World War II, teaching
engineers and academicians who in turn taught thousands of
others. Many feel this program was integral to the success of the
United States during the war.

After the war, however, many companies that had initiated
quality control programs began to lose their incentive and convic-
tion. The primary goal for most American enterprises was to
produce enough to satisfy the seemingly endless demand for goods
of all kinds. One of the main reasons for the failure of quality
consciousness to take hold in this country was that management

had never been taught its responsibility. The direct relationship between quality and sales, quality and productivity, quality and profit, quality and competitive position, had never been understood by most managers. The quality control courses taught by Deming and others under the auspices of the Department of War were directed primarily at engineers, inspectors, and industrial people who needed to be fully versed in specific methods and techniques. Once the critical push for high quality, low failure rates, and low cost was relaxed, management stopped the vigorous pursuit of quality.

Comparison Shopping

Although Deming is probably the most respected statistician in America, if not the world, his letterhead modestly introduces him as a "Consultant in Statistical Studies." Despite the fact that he has won every major statistical award, is a professor emeritus at New York University, has an American award for quality named in his honor, has written more than 170 scientific papers and several books, and is a management and quality control consultant to major companies throughout the world, he does not distribute a brochure listing his accomplishments. Among his clients are the most successful and quality-conscious American companies, a veritable Who's Who of American Business, such as IBM, AT&T, Hewlett-Packard, Scott Paper, DuPont, and Procter & Gamble, but he steadfastly refuses to promote himself.

Deming is a remarkable man with remarkable credentials, but one must ask how his advice compares with the practices of Japanese companies. After all, Toyota is widely recognized as having the highest quality cars in the world (those who disagree place Nissan or Honda at the top—Honda's customer satisfaction exceeds that of Mercedes-Benz). Perhaps Ford should hire Toyota's quality consultant.

This might seem a reasonable approach, especially since the U.S. trade deficit with Japan exceeded an unprecedented $50 billion in 1986 and, despite the yen's dramatic rise against the dollar since then, stubbornly refuses to shrink. Consumers cite higher quality as the main reason they continue to prefer Japanese goods to American goods. Certainly a comparison of the methods advocated by the United States' premier quality expert and Japanese methods would prove instructive.

A good place to start is Toyota's headquarters in Tokyo. The striking thing one first notices in the main lobby is larger than life pictures of three individuals. One is of Toyota's founder, another of the same size is of Toyota's current chairman, and a third, much larger picture, is of W. Edwards Deming.

Is there some mistake? Has Toyota gone mad? Are they paying homage to the competition? No! The picture is there out of respect for the man they acknowledge as having started it all. W. Edwards Deming is the man who taught Japan quality.

After World War II, Deming visited Japan and at the request of the Japanese Union of Scientists and Engineers (JUSE) gave a series of lectures on quality control to Japanese engineers and to top management on management's tasks and responsibilities. Deming predicted that within five years Japan would be economically competitive and that consumers worldwide would clamor for Japanese goods. While many were skeptical, the presence of an American expert was compelling. In order not to lose face they faithfully followed his instructions. Within eighteen months of the first lecture the Japanese saw tremendous improvements in the quality of their goods and in productivity. They beat Deming's five-year timetable with a year to spare.

Few Americans have to be told of the prowess of Japanese business, as it has come to dominate industry after industry, including consumer electronics, motorcycles, automobiles, watches, cameras, and semiconductors. But few Americans realize that Japanese industrial leaders credit Deming with having initiated that success and that the most prestigious award a Japanese company or industrialist can win is the Deming Prize.

What is also too little understood is the role that management has played. All too often American observers cite cultural differences as the reason for the disparity between American and Japanese business practices. But quality management was born in one of America's premier institutions, the Bell Telephone Laboratories of AT&T. Dr. Walter A. Shewhart, a physicist, worked on the problem of quality and uniformity for AT&T's manufacturing arm, Western Electric. His work was found to have great application not just in manufacturing but in the service end of the phone business. For years the American phone system was the envy of the world, providing a level and quality of service unmatched anywhere else.

Shewhart was Deming's friend and associate. Both men, trained in physics, were working in the new field of statistics. When Shewhart published his second book, *Statistical Method from the Viewpoint of Quality Control*, it was Deming who acted as editor and wrote the foreword.

When Deming joined the U.S. Census Bureau in 1939, he was already the acknowledged world expert in sampling. But the Census Bureau provided an environment in which quality control methods could be employed in a pure service field, with no manufacturing outlet. According to the theory expounded by Shewhart and Deming, as quality improves, costs go down and productivity increases. Quality and productivity can be continually improved. Could the Census Bureau, a government agency, be made ever more efficient and productive? The results were in decades ago. The Census Bureau provided then and provides today a bounty of information of unquestioned integrity at a price that cannot be matched by any other organization in the world, public or private.

Compare this with the Internal Revenue Service, which by its own account has an error rate of more than 25 percent for telephoned inquiries from taxpayers. Congress estimated the error rate at 43 percent. No matter which figure is more accurate, the cost to the IRS and to society is staggering. Are the management styles and methods of the two agencies different? Of course. According to Deming, management is the whole difference. The current predicament we find ourselves in is due to managerial decisions in the public and private sectors at all levels of management.

"Don't blame the Japanese," he says. "We did it to ourselves."

A Busy Schedule

Since 1946 Deming has been a private consultant. While Japan represents the most dramatic, large-scale implementation of his methods and teachings, and Ford is an old-line company transforming itself with startling results, Deming has been helping companies worldwide for decades. Quality has only recently been popularly acknowledged as one of the most pressing issues in business.

In 1980, NBC televised a program called "If Japan Can, Why Can't We?" Deming was prominently featured and his role in Japan was explained. Since that program aired, the demands on his time have greatly increased and his schedule is now booked up to three years in advance.

He gives roughly twenty four-day seminars a year to corporate managers in the United States. Attendance at these seminars ranges from 600 to 4,000. Another dozen or so Deming-trained consultants are reforming the management practices of companies that engage their services.

Before going to Japan in August for the annual presentation of the Deming Prize, Deming visits Australia and New Zealand, where, at the request of government and business groups, he lectures, consults, and encourages change in the practices of those two nations.

Organizations large and small, in manufacturing and in service fields, in the private and public sectors, are slowly changing. In each case, while the actual practices differ, the message is the same. Management is the key difference.

The Source of Profit

Deming's philosophy calls for organizations to produce products and services that help people live better. Providing those goods and services is the raison d'être of an organization. By providing ever-improving services and products, an organization develops loyal customers.

In Deming's philosophy, real profits are generated by loyal customers—not just satisfied customers. Satisfied customers may try a new product from a competitor or switch to an existing product if the price is right. But loyal customers brag about the goods or services they are receiving. They buy the company's new products with little sales effort, and often bring a friend. Profit from the sale to a loyal customer is six to eight times the profit from other customers. Is this the wishful thinking of an idealist? No! This is the conclusion of the most renowned expert on sampling, who has been called on by virtually all the major consumer research organizations to plan surveys on consumer behavior. It is a well-known fact among those who have studied consumer buying that profits from loyal customers are not only of better quality but many times higher than from the average customer. The company that develops loyal customers has much higher earnings than the company that just pushes the product out the door.

Yet in the purely financial approach a sale is a sale, just a number. The level of customer satisfaction isn't believed to impact on profit.

Driving by Looking Out the Rearview Mirror

From a Deming perspective most managers' view of profit is backward. To Deming, a company continually improving the quality of its goods or services improves its productivity and produces loyal customers. Loyal customers are, in turn, the engine producing increased market share, higher profit margins, higher profits, higher stock price, a secure and satisfied work force, and more jobs.

Too many managers, concerned with keeping the stock price up, increase their profit margins by cutting costs and cutting quality. The inevitable results are a loss of customer confidence and decreased market share and profitability. Large amounts must then be spent trying to regain or increase sales. This, of course, results in decreased profitability.

In the Deming view, increasing the quality of goods and services leads to higher productivity and profitability. The converse, however, of artificially increasing profits, does not lead to better quality or productivity or, ironically, profitability. Instead it leads to the decline of the company. If such a company is competing with a Deming-style company, the decline can be quite dramatic.

A Hypothetical Example, Within a Company

A manager who has had no exposure to Deming theory and has been taught to manage by the visible numbers only will define profit as the difference between revenues and expenses. In examining the income statements and the balance sheet, such a manager sees many items that don't seem to have a direct effect on today's profit. When the pressure is on because of a slowdown in sales, such items as training programs, research and development, aftersales service, and engineering staff become candidates for elimination. In order to meet profit goals, which are set in some arbitrary manner, such as 110 percent of last year's profit, it is mandated that costs be cut by some arbitrary amount. The workers find themselves waiting around for supplies or using lower quality supplies.

Invariably, quality suffers and profit declines. When this happens, managers who manage only by visible numbers start clutching at anything. Restructuring becomes a key word. Automation and gadgets, redeployment of assets, streamlining and cost-cutting abound. Much of what is called cost-cutting today is really just disinvestment. These managers don't understand the relationship between quality and profits.

Consider a company with two distinct subsidiaries selling in mutually exclusive geographic areas. One subsidiary's manager is interested in improving the quality of the company's products. The other subsidiary is run by a visible numbers only (VNO) manager. The VNO manager decides he wants to raise profits by 10 percent a year. To accomplish this he cuts training programs the first year. The second year he cuts all spending for development, curtails advertising, and revalues some of his plant and equipment. The next year he cuts dealer support and some of the engineering staff. Earnings, as measured by accountants, have increased by 10 percent per year. Meanwhile, the manager of the other subsidiary has done everything right. He's running a healthy subsidiary, introducing new products, and improving delivery time and customer support. His people are becoming more and more competent. Nothing has been cut; in fact, training programs have been improved and supplemented, and his engineering department has the latest hardware to cut product development time. But earnings as measured by accountants may have increased only 8 percent per year.

Suppose that after three years the president of the firm decides to retire and has to choose a successor between the heads of the two subsidiaries. The VNO manager argues that his division's earnings were up 10 percent whereas his rival's were up only 8 percent. No one on the board suspects how bad things really are at the VNO subsidiary and therefore no additional investigations are done. It's possible that the VNO manager may get the position and even be lauded for the wonderful job he's doing. He goes on to destroy the rest of the company.

Suppose, however, that another company in a different part of the country (or in another country) has been properly run and decides to enter the regional market presently dominated by the VNO company. VNO counters by invading that Deming company's territory. But the VNO's customers are willing, maybe even eager, to try a different source. The Deming company quickly eats into the VNO's customer base. The Deming company's customers can barely be induced to try the other company's products. If customers do try, they quickly switch back, even more loyal than before.

It's possible for a VNO manager to win out over a Deming manager in the numbers-oriented world of corporate politics. But when the two managerial styles clash in the marketplace, the results are always the same. Customers aren't fooled by accounting numbers.

Who's Right?

The management lessons of Deming are in direct opposition to what is currently taught in most business schools and advocated by management consultants and business writers. Even some who call themselves consultants in quality are pushing methods that will only make things worse. Some of the differences are glaring.

Peter Drucker, the well-known business writer and consultant, aggressively advocates a merit system that he calls management by objectives. Other writers, whose excellent company theses have collapsed in the real world, also push for management by objectives (MBO). The idea is so neat and pleasing that it is almost a given among American managers that a merit system is necessary to make people work better or harder and therefore improve productivity and profit. But Deming states unequivocally that merit reviews, by whatever name, including management by objectives, are the single most destructive force in American management today.

The system of management by objectives is appealing because of our own formative experiences. Most of us have had some experience of being coaxed to do better by teachers or coaches or friends.

We may have found that we could do forty or fifty push-ups during football practice or after boot camp, whereas before we could do but ten. We may have had a wonderful teacher who demanded that we read a book every ten days, and we did. Although our intent was to continue the pace when the course was over, we found ourselves slipping back into the old pattern of reading at a much more leisurely pace. Some of our teachers may have talked about giving 110 percent, and this seemed to inspire us. Therefore, when a merit system is proposed whereby we are constantly setting ever higher goals for ourselves, it seems to make sense, and we welcome it. It seems to make sense that everybody's individual improvement in performance is the key to the company's improvement in performance. Everybody doing his or her best is the way out of the crisis, right? Wrong!

What happens when everyone is already giving 110 percent? Management working under an MBO system looks at the goals for the next year and then lowers the costs a little more and increases the goals a little more. But it is not physically possible for humans or machines operating in the same system to produce more with less. In Deming's seminars, the participants are asked to list managerial impediments to doing their best. One item that consistently ranks near the top is being asked to accomplish something without sufficient resources. But determined people can be very persistent and may move mountains to accomplish their objectives, even at the expense of the long-term health of the company. Bank of America had one of the most aggressive merit systems in banking, rewarding "top performers" with up to 50 percent more pay than "average" and "below average performers." They got what they deserved and what they asked for—massive loan problems. Hundreds of millions of dollars of loans had to be written off. Who can best judge the quality of a loan, the loan officer who has intimate contact with the customer or the committee judging employees' worth on the basis of such visible figures as loans generated?

Judging individuals' performance without consideration of such invisible figures as loan quality, risk, or customer loyalty is madness. But asking everyone to work at 110 percent and then 10 percent harder again, each and every year, is even greater madness. The problems with merit systems are deep and fundamental and I will discuss them extensively in later chapters.

Merit Systems in Society

One more example, however, is worth mentioning because it aptly illustrates the damage done by merit systems, not just in the business world but in our society at large. A couple of years ago it came to light that several officers of the New York City Transit Police who reported to the same commander had, over a period of years, systematically made false and illegal arrests. Each police officer's "performance" was evaluated by this commander on the number and types of arrests made. Those with the most arrests, particularly felony and sexual abuse cases, were rewarded with the best assignments and promotions. Four of this unit's officers during one twelve-month period were responsible for 10 percent of the attempted grand larceny arrests and 18 percent of the sexual abuse arrests of the entire transit police force. These same four were the ones who made the false arrests and were rated highest by their commander.[3]

The commander wanted arrests and he got them. To him, the number of arrests was a measure of the performance of an officer and he rated each by that criterion. But the cost to society and to the transit police is immeasurable. Every arrest by the offending officers is now suspect, and indeed every arrest by every officer reporting to this commander must now be questioned. Most of the false arrests were of black and Hispanic men, innocent men charged with serious crimes. What is the cost to everyone of such blatant injustice?

The Price of Quality

Another area about which most individuals in and out of business have an inadequate understanding is the meaning and cost of quality. Most of us believe that quality products cost more to create than defective or inferior products. But that is not true. In fact, quality management produces fewer defects and lower costs. A personal example may help illustrate this point. A number of years ago, before I had studied under Deming, I owned some apartments. To keep costs down, I did some of the work in the building myself. An apartment had just been vacated and I had to clean, repair, and paint it in order to rent it. Since any money saved flowed directly into my own pocket, I went out and bought a large five-gallon container of inexpensive paint that cost about $5.00 a gallon. Normally I used paint that cost almost twice as much.

A 50 percent reduction in cost was just too much of a savings to pass up. But as I started to paint, a curious thing began to happen. When the first coat dried, it appeared streaked, as if large sections hadn't been painted at all. Even after two coats, which was the most I had ever applied before, the job looked unfinished. I eventually went out and bought more paint to make it look satisfactory. I had used twice as much paint as I should have, eliminating any cost advantage, and, what's worse, spent twice as much time as I normally would have. But the problem didn't end there. The first time the walls were washed, some of the paint came off. That paint job never looked good. Years later, when the apartment came on the market again, I confirmed that using higher quality paint, with a careful application, cost much less in time and money and produced a much better result.

In a work environment where some functions are carried on repeatedly, the results of putting quality first are more dramatic. A plant that is producing 5 percent defectives has an immediate increase in productivity of more than 5 percent when the process is improved to produce 0 percent defectives on the first try.

In most plants that are producing 5 percent defectives there is an inspection process that segregates the defectives. Those products judged to be unacceptable are then reworked off the assembly line, at a cost that is very high. Those defectives have already had as much capital, raw material, and labor put into them as the acceptable products. But now they are put aside, adding to the company's inventory, and later reworked, adding to their labor content and raw material costs. But no matter how much they are reworked, they rarely end up as good as those that were right from the start.

The costs continue to accelerate if a defective reaches the customer. No one knows the exact cost of a disgruntled former customer, but we know it's quite high. Market research done by Ford showed that a happy customer tells on average eight people the good news about the product, but a dissatisfied customer tells on average more than twenty people of the ordeal with the product.

Deming and other consultants have been extremely busy helping our companies over the last decade as the Japanese challenge turned into a rout. The quality of American goods has definitely improved, but perceptions die hard and slowly. Whether planned obsolescence was really planned by American manufacturers or just a term coined for what seemed to be happening, too many consumers remember the sinking feeling of having a three-year-old auto that seemed to fall apart all at once. I know people who told their children and their grandchildren never to purchase a Firestone tire because of the poor experience they had with Firestone radials and the subsequent behavior of that company.

A simple response from too many managers is to make workers responsible for quality—if it's not right the first time, let them go. But management by edict doesn't work. It will only make things worse. The belief that the worker is responsible for the poor quality and low productivity of American firms is wrong. That many executives, journalists, and business consultants believe this to be the case doesn't make it so. But their belief leads to dangerous business practices that only make matters worse. Japanese firms that have set up operations in the United States, such as Honda, Toyota, Quasar, and Nissan, have brought the level of productivity in their U.S. plants up to that of their Japanese plants. Those old-line U.S. firms, such as Ford, Burlington Industries, and Scott Paper, that have adopted quality control techniques in their plants and changed their management style have seen enormous improvements in quality and productivity. Those firms that have always been quality conscious, such as AT&T and IBM, have high and improving levels of productivity and enjoy the respect of their customers and competitors.

The workers don't determine the layout of the plant, the room temperature, the amount invested in research, development, and training. They don't buy the equipment, tools, and raw materials or determine the design of the product. They don't develop the reward system or organizational structure. In short, they don't determine 90 percent of the things responsible for the quality of the product. Why then hold them responsible for all of the defects? Workers cannot change the system; only management can change the system. It is management's responsibility to change the system so that quality and productivity improve and workers can experience pride of workmanship. Once that happens, worker input becomes a continual part of the improvement process. Toyota workers on average make about thirty-three suggestions per worker per year, 90 percent of which are implemented within weeks of their submission.

One so-called quality expert tells his clients that all that needs to be done to improve quality is to have everyone meet specifications. All employees must sign statements promising not to make defects. Initially there may be some improvement, since everyone hopes changes will be made. But since management have not been instructed in their responsibility, the system isn't changed and the company finds itself in the same position as before.

It is easy to conclude when seeing a successful plant where workers are enthusiastic and making numerous suggestions that all that is necessary is for management to disappear and let the workers do their jobs. Alas, this conclusion is simplistic and incorrect. Managing the Deming way is much harder than managing by visible numbers only, the way taught by too many business schools. The Deming way requires profound knowledge.

Another obvious difference between Deming and other management consultants is where they believe quality is created. Too many business school–trained managers are busy using visible numbers to justify their actions. That approach considers quality to be created by the worker, in the plant or at the desk. Therefore these managers may hire some quality control people to work in the plants, give them some goals, and then consider their responsibility finished. The quality control people may use control charts and statistical process control, two of Deming's trademarks, to reduce errors at the plant level. But they cannot eliminate errors coming in from suppliers. Company policy may call for the purchasing department to buy supplies based on lowest price. But the supplies that are the lowest priced when they arrive at the plant may be the highest priced when the finished product leaves the plant.

The quality control people are helpless to change this because the purchasing department is judged as a cost center. The lower its costs, the higher the bonuses and promotions. By minimizing their costs, they may be increasing the cost to the company. Only management can change the reward system, the structure of the organization, and the philosophy of doing business. If they do not, any progress toward quality will be limited. As Deming says, "Where is quality made? Quality is made in the boardroom."

Some of the important differences in belief between most conventional organizations and Deming organizations are listed below.

Standard Company	*Deming Company*
Quality is expensive.	Quality leads to lower costs.
Inspection is the key to quality.	Inspection is too late. If workers can produce defect-free goods, eliminate inspections.
Quality control experts and inspectors can assure quality.	Quality is made in the boardroom.
Defects are caused by workers.	Most defects are caused by the system.
The manufacturing process can be optimized by outside experts. No change in system afterward. No input from workers.	Process never optimized; it can always be improved.
Use of work standards, quotas, and goals can help productivity.	Elimination of *all* work standards and quotas is necessary.
Fear and reward are proper ways to motivate.	Fear leads to disaster.
People can be treated like commodities—buying more when needed, laying off when needing less.	People should be made to feel secure in their jobs.
Rewarding the best performers and punishing the worst will lead to greater productivity and creativity.	Most variation is caused by the system. Review systems that judge, punish, and reward above, or below-average performance destroy teamwork and the company.
Buy on lowest cost.	Buy from vendors committed to quality.
Play one supplier off against another.	Work with suppliers.
Switch suppliers frequently based on price only.	Invest time and knowledge to help suppliers improve quality and costs. Develop long-term relationships with suppliers.
Profits are made by keeping revenue high and costs down.	Profits are generated by loyal customers.

Standard Company	*Deming Company*
Profit is the most important indicator of a company.	Running a company by profit alone is like driving a car by looking in the rearview mirror. It tells you where you've been, not where you are going.

Improvement in quality and productivity is not limited to manufacturing operations. The greatest benefit the Deming style of management offers may be to the service industries. The U.S. Census Bureau, where Deming for many years applied his knowledge, is one of the unsung success stories in government service. Municipal agencies, insurance companies, banks, and trucking and freight companies have also successfully implemented Deming systems.

In recent years many of the winners of the Japanese Deming Prize have been service companies. Construction firms have won three Deming Prizes and experienced soaring levels of productivity after initiating transformations to total quality control. Japanese banks, insurance companies, and brokerage houses are quite large and very profitable. Each of the four largest Japanese brokerage houses is about twice as profitable as any American firm. In analyzing this situation, the financial press have sought easy answers, such as protected markets, government help, and so on. But as Japanese financial institutions begin making inroads in world markets, American firms are making news with layoffs and firings. Some of our most prestigious firms, anticipating expanding business, hired heavily in recent years. When their projections proved inaccurate, they retrenched and fired heavily.

In other words, the workers are paying for the errors of management. Some Japanese and some American firms, on the other hand, are taking a longer-term view of business. Which companies have the best long-term prospects? Those that treat their employees as commodities, hiring and firing based on short-term needs, or those who develop their people and their company with a long-term commitment to be in business? Which would you rather work for? Which would you rather own five years from now?

CHAPTER 2

Quality Must Come First

Quality, Productivity, and Profit

One of the most fascinating aspects of Deming's teachings, one that radically departs from conventional thinking, is his treatment of the relationships among quality, costs, productivity, and profit. According to Deming, as quality is increased, costs decrease. This sets in motion a chain reaction. Better quality leads to lower costs and higher productivity. Any firm with lower costs can pass along some of the savings to its customers in the form of lower prices. The company's customers get the best of all worlds, better quality and lower prices. This allows it to capture markets and increase market share, which in turn allows it to stay in business and provide more and more jobs.

This was the basic chain reaction Deming demonstrated to the Japanese in his lectures beginning in 1950. The consequences for Japan as a nation were that increasing the quality of goods led to Japanese companies capturing more markets, creating more jobs, and providing a higher standard of living for all the Japanese people. Everyone benefited.

The consequences for an individual company are that increasing quality leads to higher productivity, lower costs, higher profits, higher share price, and greater security for everyone in the company—the managers, the workers, and the owners.

But isn't increasing profits the main goal of American business? In business schools, we're taught that the object of business is to maximize the wealth of the owners of a company by increasing stock share price. Isn't the best way of doing this increasing profits?

We graduate thousands of accountants, lawyers, and masters of business administration whose main goal in life is supposed to be just that—increasing and maximizing profit. Why are we in such a mess? Why are the Japanese running all over us?

Some Elementary Logic

To see what's wrong, let's recall some basic logic. A statement such as "If A happens, B will follow" may be true. But its converse, "If B happens, A will follow," is not necessarily true.

In other words, increasing quality will lead to increasing productivity and increasing profit, but increasing profit will not necessarily lead to increasing quality. There are many ways of increasing profit. Some have nothing to do with quality, and some lower quality. Some attempts to improve profit by working on the accounting numbers backfire. If quality suffers as a result, profitability soon suffers.

One example was related to me by a former RCA researcher. When he started with RCA, the company was an innovative leader. At one time Robert Sarnoff, Sr., chairman of RCA, was actively engaged in the company's efforts to innovate and improve, and maintained an apartment at the RCA research complex. After he left, however, the firm found a new direction in the pure maximization of profit. At one point, to squeeze a little more profit out of each television set, the company began substituting less expensive parts.

Now any accountant can tell you that if costs decrease, profits increase. So substituting cheaper, but inferior, parts into RCA televisions would naturally mean higher margins on each set and higher profits for the company, right? Wrong! A funny thing happened. Many more televisions failed during the warranty period. These had to be replaced. Between the paperwork and personnel costs, taking back a faulty set is surprisingly expensive. Perhaps 25 percent or more of the cost of manufacturing.

But the cost of repairing the set, which would involve locating the faulty part and replacing it, is prohibitively expensive. It would cost as much or more to fix a defective set as it would to manufacture it in the first place. The defectives accumulated. RCA had ware-houses filled with returns. Every now and then an audit revealed warehouses filled with obsolete merchandise that had to be written off. The write-offs were seen as evidence of poor inventory control or of management's inability to react quickly to technological changes. But the write-offs were quite simply the result of poor quality.

Quality and profits are indeed related. Successful efforts to improve quality lead to higher profitability. But efforts that attempt to raise profitability by tinkering with financial numbers will not improve quality. If quality is sacrificed in trying to increase profitability, the actions will backfire.

One cost that hasn't been mentioned yet is the cost of a lost customer. What about those customers whose sets failed after the warranty period? RCA didn't take a direct loss on those sets, the customers did. But how many of those customers ever bought another RCA product? How many loyal RCA customers who never would have considered a foreign-built set became loyal Sony customers after that experience? How many dissatisfied customers told all their friends about their problems with the set?

When I was fourteen, I received an RCA tape recorder that proceeded to break down in three days. I returned it for a Dutch-made Wollensak. My father liked the Wollensak so much, he bought one for himself. I never considered returning the defective RCA product for another RCA model. It was twenty-four years before I considered another RCA product. Did Americans buy Japanese cars by the millions because we were all unloyal or had a fancy for anything Japanese? No, we bought European and Jap-anese products because we got stung by the quality of domestic goods. Our problem has been quality.

Working Backward Versus Working Forward

Most of what we call American management theory is derived backward from profit. Profit has to be increased. Looking at the financial reports, we can deduce that if sales go up 10 percent and production costs go down 5 percent, profit must improve. To make sure that production costs decline, we'll just allocate less money for wages and create a higher production quota per plant. The plant manager then has the distasteful task of cutting the work force while increasing production. He has to increase the quota of each individual worker. Even though the quota wasn't met last year, he'll take a page out of the wisdom of Pogo, "Having lost sight of our objectives, we redoubled our efforts."

Salespeople also have their quotas, so we'll just raise theirs by 10 percent. Isn't management fun? And clean. No mention of quality, and the managers don't even have any idea what the company makes. All that one has to do to be a good manager is play with the accounting numbers, according to too many managers, consultants, and writers. Brian Joiner, the 1988 winner of the American Deming Prize, calls this management by control. Others call it management by objectives.

But the most important numbers don't even show up on the financial reports. Where are quality and innovation? What's the cost of having a defect reach the customer? How many sales are lost as a result of poor quality? How many potential customers wouldn't buy your product regardless of price? What's the cost to the nation of the *Challenger* disaster, where poor quality led to the deaths of our astronauts and perhaps cost us our leadership in space? What's the cost to Exxon and the nation of Exxon's inability to clean up the oil spill off the coast of Alaska?

How many plants, how many offices, are run by the numbers only, pushing out products, sales, or loans without regard to quality? Pushing out more, while slowly (and in some cases not so slowly) going out of business.

ITT Management

Lest anyone think I'm exaggerating the following quote is taken directly from Harold Geneen's book *Managing*:

> *A three sentence course of business Management: You read a book from the beginning to the end. You run a business the opposite way. You start with the end, and then you do everything you must to reach it.* [1]

Harold Geneen was chairman of ITT, and during his tenure ITT increased in size dramatically. ITT acquired numerous other companies and became a diversified conglomerate. Its management style was studied and emulated by others. According to Geneen, who was trained as an accountant, managing is simple and direct. All one has to do is decide what kind of improved financial result is desired—at ITT he insisted on 15 percent improvement in profit every year—and then look at the financial numbers to see how that could be achieved.

It's all direct and logical. Looking at the financial figures, a manager can see that by increasing sales so much and decreasing cost so much he can meet the desired financial objective. This can be achieved if each department sells more, which means each individual must sell more. Cost must be slashed and production and sales quotas increased.

The analysis is simple; all that remains is to enforce it. Make sure everyone meets or exceeds his or her individual objective for the quarter and for the year and live happily ever after.

Enforcement of goals is simple: provide rewards for meeting the goals and punishment for failure—incentive pay and bonuses for those who succeed and harsh realities for those who fail. Those who don't meet the objectives won't be around for very long.

When Geneen first took over as chairman of the International Telephone and Telegraph Company, later renamed ITT, earnings began to increase. Its stock price rose to a premium over other companies' stock because financial analysts considered it a well-run company. With its stock selling at twenty times its yearly earnings, it was in a position to acquire other companies whose shares only sold at ten times yearly earnings.

If ITT sold $100 million of its stock and invested the proceeds in its business, it needed to earn $5 million to maintain its stock price. But if, instead, it invested the funds in a company that earned $10 million a year, it could increase earnings per share and therefore increase its stock price. If it could also work its "managerial magic" and increase the earnings of the newly purchased subsidiary, it could improve its stock price and grow some more.

This is just what ITT did. Alvin Moscow, coauthor with Geneen of the book *Managing,* writes in his introduction that in 1961, two years after Geneen was made chief executive of ITT, the company had sales of $756.6 million and earnings of $29 million. In 1977, when he stepped down as chief executive, sales had reached $16.7 billion with earnings of $562 million. In those sixteen years ITT "had bought, merged with or absorbed some 350 different businesses in eighty countries."[2] "At its peak," Moscow writes, "ITT was the ninth-largest industrial company on the Fortune 500 list,"[3] putting it in the rarified company of such firms as Ford, GM, IBM, and GE.

But what followed was a most spectacular collapse. The company began to acknowledge problems at some of its major subsidiaries and began selling them off. The government of France and the government of the Commonwealth of Puerto Rico insisted on buying back their respective phone companies. ITT shrank to a fraction of its former size and it is now no longer in the league of IBM or GE. It is doubtful that it ever was in the same category as those firms in any real sense.

I spoke to a family friend shortly after his party won the elections in Puerto Rico and he had been asked by the governor-elect to serve in the new government. He disagreed with some of the actions of the former administration, but the one area where his party had no disagreement with the previous administration was on the need to buy back the phone company. The phone system just didn't work.

The one ITT product I bought was a telephone. I figured that since ITT had been in the phone business for so long it knew how to make a good phone. I was fooled. The phone carried a ninety-day warranty. To my chagrin the phone broke down ninety-one days after it was purchased. Apparently I wasn't the only one to have problems. ITT's problem was quality. While the company reported making a lot of money, no one ever accused ITT of quality.

ITT fooled a lot of people with impressive financial results. In the late sixties and early seventies the Europeans were awed by American managerial know-how, as exemplified by ITT. But as problems with quality became evident, ITT lost all its mystique. Investors were fooled by ITT's financial results, giving it a high price-to-earnings ratio, which in turn enabled it to buy and ruin more operations. A whole nation had been fooled into believing the company's managers knew how to manage. Hundreds of ITT managers went to other companies, bringing their management "know-how" along. Many became chief executives of other firms, and then had an opportunity to import the ITT management style and ruin those operations. The company was studied and used as an example of successful management technique. Geneen's basic lessons underlie much of what we call American management. Some of it seems so obvious that it is accepted without question.

One person who wasn't fooled was Deming. Nor were the Japanese, who were faithfully carrying out the lessons he had taught.

What Went Wrong?

In retrospect we see that what we thought was right didn't work. But why?

Let's put ourselves into the shoes of a bright and well-meaning executive who finds himself working for a firm that uses management by objectives to obtain desired financial results. The analysis of last year's results is done and next year's budget is being formulated. Our illustrious chairman just had lunch with some financial analysts and in a burst of confidence predicted an earnings increase of 10 percent for the coming year. At the budget meeting we find a bound stack of papers, called next year's budget, in front of us when we take our seat. After some pleasantries all the managers begin reviewing the budget. When we come to the section covering our division, the chairman addresses us, "Well, Mr. A, do you think you can reach that 10 percent increase in profits as outlined in the budget?"

"Well, sir, it depends on a number of factors. I'm not sure about the strength of the market for the coming year. One of our prime customers is considering a major order, which will help if..."

We're interrupted by our chairman, "Mr. A., let me remind you of the fate of your predecessor. I hired you to obtain results. I don't want yes-men in my company. I want movers, shakers, doers. Real competent managers."

"Yes, sir, I can do it!"

So we proceed to do our job as best we can. We work with all our salespeople, see what they need, and try to support them. We look for ways to improve sales and operations and to lower costs. If things go our way, we may reach or exceed our targets. Profit may increase 10 percent or more and we become heroes, earning our incentive pay and bonus. We become real believers in management by objectives.

What happens, however, if one of our large customers experiences a strike? The best we can do is increase profit by 8 percent and our chairman's words echo through our mind: "I hired you to get results, not make excuses."

Now we could be honest and do the right thing. We could tell the chairman a 10 percent increase just isn't possible this year. "Mr. Chairman, the original goal was made unrealistic by events beyond our control. However it might be possible to lower costs over the next three years by investing in our people or changing part of the operation." But then we remember that our daughter's tuition is due next month, and our summer vacation is already planned, and our chairman's words ring through our head, "We want results!"

So we resolve to get results. All the salespeople are called in and told to sell more, regardless of what it takes. The plant manager is told to cut the staff and further delay maintenance. Perhaps we cut the training program or research and development, areas that won't contribute to this year's revenue but will contribute to this year's cost. Somehow we find that extra profit.

The message to everyone is clear: Do it. I don't care how, just do it.

People can be very determined. They can move mountains to meet their goals, even to the detriment of the company. One personnel director was given the objective of reducing turnover and increasing use of the training program. She noticed that people with less education and less potential stayed at her firm longer than others. So she made a concerted effort to hire those with the least education and avoided hiring anyone who seemed too creative. She also sent people through the training program two and three times. She met both her objectives and was congratulated for an outstanding job by the chairman. But I think everyone would agree that the company was worse off, not better. This example is typical.

One plant couldn't meet its production quota. But it had to, so the numbers were fudged. But every time inventory was counted, it was lower than it should have been. Management thought it had a problem with theft, so it installed an elaborate security system. The problem persisted. The numbers were being faked because people had to survive. There was no problem with theft, just a problem with management.

The Pressure for Results

When the pressure is on, more and more product gets sent out the door. Inspectors are hardly in a position to stop something from leaving the plant when their boss has a deadline or an objective to meet. Everyone puts pressure on everyone else. Morale drops. Health problems and absenteeism increase. Quality was forgotten long ago.

Oftentimes, to meet a monthly quota, a plant will ship 30 percent of the month's production on the last day. However, much of it gets sent back the next month because it's unfinished, or a service rep is sent out to finish it on the site.

Of course quality suffers. But if the profit objective is still not met, then those aspects of the business that represent the company's future suffer—training programs, development, research. Geneen bragged in his book about how he had several people employed locating the existence of any computer research at the various subsidiaries and eradicating it upon discovery. He felt he couldn't compete against IBM, which, of course, was true, but a telecommunications company cannot possibly provide competitive, quality service without extensive knowledge of computers.

When it gets to this point, the company is really disinvesting, squeezing out the last accounting dollar at the expense of the future.

There is another equally insidious aspect of management by control. Almost invariably the tool used to force compliance is fear. People do not innovate and make real contributions in an environment of fear. The motto soon becomes "Don't rock the boat." Creativity and real productivity are lost. People strive to meet their numerical objective regardless of the consequences to their company.

An Example in Service

I was an international banker until 1977. At that time Brazil had an external debt of $25 billion, and some of the lending officers, myself included, had concerns about Brazil's ability to handle so much debt. At the same time, banks were leaving the field of trade financing. As one banker told me, "Why should we do trade financing, which involves a lot of work with smaller loans and lines of credit. I can have lunch with the head of a Brazilian government agency and lend out $15 million over dessert. It's easy, profitable, and I'm very productive."

Talk about loan quality was countered by some oblique statement that countries don't go bankrupt, only people and corporations do. Today Brazil's debt is about $100 billion. Several banks have taken multibillion-dollar write-offs, and not a single American bank has a triple A credit rating. The final tally on the losses isn't completed yet, but some banks have already written off more than they earned in the last five years.

Who was really the better banker, the one who went along and received his merit pay or the one who questioned the direction of the institution? What would happen to the banker who walked into the chairman's office and said, "You know, Mr. Chairman, I think this is not such a good idea?"

Management by Control Worldwide

How bad is American management? Deming says, "Export anything except American management. At least not to friendly nations."

Some of the worst practices, however, are not unique to American managers. Working backward from a desired end result to derive the necessary inputs has been practiced throughout the world. The Soviet Union, for instance, manages its whole economy this way. Russian bureaucrats formerly set a tonnage quota for each nail manufacturing plant. Russian industry invariably experienced a shortage of small nails and a surplus of large ones. It's easier to make a ton of big nails than a ton of small nails.

One bright bureaucrat noticed this, so he changed the quota. Now each plant was to produce a certain *number* of nails each month. Sure enough, a shortage of large nails developed and a surplus of small ones.

A less comical example involved Soviet health care. The claim often heard was that the Soviet health care system was a model of affordability and efficiency. It provided health care nationwide with everyone able to see a doctor free of charge. To make that possible, however, each doctor had a government-set time limit of seven-and-a-half minutes per patient. How could quality health care be delivered in seven-and-a-half minutes?

Anyone who has watched their gymnasts or ballet stars, listened to their musicians, worn their furs, or drunk their vodka knows that the people of the Soviet Union understand quality. But their present system and style of management will never allow quality to manifest itself in mass-produced goods. In some respects the Soviet Union today is similar to Japan in 1950. There are some highly developed areas, but ignorance about management and the nature of quality prevent the necessary changes from being made.

More of the Same?

There is just one reason for rejecting management by control in whatever form, including management by objectives, merit reviews, and aggressive goal setting. It does not work! Of course, if you believe that things in the United States are great and getting better, that our $100 billion trade deficit is insignificant, and that our inability to compete in whole industries is unimportant, then you'll see no reason to change. But even very bright individuals who admit we are not competitive have difficulty believing it's the way we manage that's at fault. Tom Peters, coauthor of *In Search of Excellence*, advocates more of the same in his newest book, *Thriving on Chaos*. He calls for setting ever-higher goals as the way to make us competitive.

It is not enough to admit that our system of management has failed. We had better understand the conceptual errors involved, and we need an alternative.

One Fallacy: From Result to Cause

As I've already pointed out, working backward has a major logical flaw. Profit is a result of action taken in the past. In management by objectives, however, the cause of profit is seen to be accounting items, such as revenues and costs. Each individual cost is assumed to be a cause. It is assumed that if you eliminate the cost, you eliminate the cause.

My literary agent provided me with one example of this fallacy from his own career. In his first job with a large publishing house he shared, with seven other editors, a directory containing the current phone numbers and addresses of agents, editors, publishers, and others active in the business. One bright manager wanted to cut costs, so he stopped the purchase of the directory and saved his company fifteen dollars. But in a few months several letters came back because the recipients had changed addresses. Some of these letters had to be sent on a rush basis by messengers. High-priced people spent hours tracking down the new addresses and phone numbers of editors who had switched firms or transferred within firms. Fifteen dollars of visible costs were saved, but thousands of dollars of waste were incurred in the bargain. Cutting the cost did not eliminate the cause.

In reality, each cost is not a direct cause. Each is the result of many things and impacts on other costs and revenues. The financial statements are not reality. They are a financial description of the past, a one-dimensional picture of a multidimensional world. They can be a very powerful picture when one knows how to use them. However, the most important thing to know about any tool, including financial reports, is its limitations.

The Fallacy of Independence

The view implied by management by objectives is that the operation of a company is analogous to a river and its tributaries. Each person has control over a certain area. His or her results feed into the results of the department. The department's efforts feed into the results of the division, which feed into the results of the region, which feed into the results of the company.

Salespeople get a product and all they have to do is sell it. Workers are fed materials and all they have to do is assemble according to the design. Each area is compartmentalized and need only perform its function well for the company to perform well. When a company isn't doing well, it is assumed it is because people aren't trying their hardest.

But this is wrong. Every person, every facet in a company is affected by and related to other areas in ways that we cannot see or measure and in some cases can't even imagine. Salespeople's ability to sell in any given year is affected not just by their own effort but by the quality, design, and usefulness of the product or service in prior years as well as this year. Their efforts are affected by the efforts of those who produced the product, the designers, the level of improvement of the product or service this year over last, and all the decisions made by management. Virtually no one's results are independent in a company.

The Fallacy of Best Efforts

This is a most seductive fallacy. All we need, supposedly, is for everyone to give a little more, and all our problems will be solved. The corollary is that our problems arise because people aren't doing their best. They're careless, or they're purposely making mistakes. Deming claims that in his more than sixty years of experience he has yet to find the person who isn't trying his or her hardest. Some people, though, are constrained by the system from doing what they know is best and right.

Let me draw an analogy with a car. If you want your car to accelerate from 50 miles per hour to 60 miles per hour, you step on the accelerator. The engine consumes more gasoline, creating more power. The suspension system and tires handle more bumps, crevices, and potholes each hour, the cooling system works harder to keep the engine at the proper temperature, and the driver has to be more careful. But every car, and likewise every company, has a maximum capacity. Your car may operate safely at 90 miles an hour. But if you want it to travel at 120 miles per hour, you can't just step on the accelerator harder, put in jet fuel, or hire a racing driver. The whole car has to be modified—the suspension, the engine, the tires, the brakes.

Similarly, to improve the output of a company, no matter how that is measured, such as quality, profitability or innovation, the whole company has to be changed, not just some financial numbers, not just the effort or inputs of the individual workers. The financial numbers don't even identify the most important numbers, and the workers are already giving all they can. The workers are powerless to change the system. Only management can do that.

Our competitive problems are not due to the workers in the system. They are due to poor management. More accurately, they are due to our managing under a set of ideas that is outmoded and incorrect.

Improvement in the system is necessary to improve the output. As Deming says, "Let's not talk about working harder. Everyone is already working their hardest. Work smarter."

Sometimes those working in the system are capable of recognizing changes that could improve their performance and the performance of the company. But fear and efforts to meet numerical objectives in many American production lines and offices prevent innovation and improvement.

Motivation?

In every example motivation has not been the problem. If anything, people respond too well to requests from management. In many cases it might be better if people did less. But they respond to the reward system and do exactly what is called for. Management asks for certain numbers and it gets them. But then it has to live with the consequences.

A Better Way

Rather than analyzing what needs to be done by working backward from profit, managers must make quality the first priority of every organization. Quality must come first over considerations of profit, especially short-term profit. Putting quality first will result in better financial performance than will putting short-term profit considerations ahead of quality.

Ford's profit ballooned to close to $6 billion per year after the company made quality its first job. Prior to making the change, it was losing billions. Before, if an executive made a mistake, he was out. That's not the case anymore.

The Old Attitude Versus the New

No matter where it is now, a firm should always be working toward improvement. This is in direct opposition to the conventional view that there is an acceptable level of quality and an unacceptable level. In the view held by Deming and those companies that have adopted his philosophy, meeting the specifications is not good enough. American clichés such as "If it ain't broke, don't fix it" and "Don't tamper with a cash cow" are incorrect.

Attitudes must change. Some specific changes have already been suggested here. Following are some of Deming's 14 points for the transformation of management that have been touched upon so far:

Point 5. Improve constantly and forever the system of production and service.

Point 8. Drive out fear.

Point 10. Eliminate slogans, exhortations, and targets for the work force.

Point 11a. Eliminate numerical quotas for the work force.

Point 11b. Eliminate numerical goals for people in management.

Why Does Quality Improve Profit?

Why do productivity and costs improve with greater quality? The answer is easy enough. Less rework. Defectives are expensive. They cost just as much to produce as perfectly good items.

Suppose you were running a plant that was producing 5 defectives for every 100 items made. Your plant has 95 items to sell but costs associated with producing 100. You revamp the company with a view toward quality. In time the level of defects drops to zero. Let's suppose your costs are $90 for each 100 units made and you sell each unit for $1. Your revenue before was $95, leaving a profit of $5 on each 100 items manufactured (5 of which were defective).

But now, with no defects, productivity has increased about 5 percent. The plant is making 100 usable items for the same cost and in the same time that it made 95. But profit has doubled. Your company now has 100 items to sell at $1 each while your costs are still $90, resulting in a profit of $10 as opposed to $5 before.

No Defects—What Now?

But now that the plant has no defects, should you keep improving quality? After all, what further benefits could accrue? Your plant is already defect free. The surprising answer is that you are now in a position to make even greater strides in quality, productivity, and profit.

Yokohama Hewlett-Packard, the Japanese arm of Hewlett-Packard, won the Japanese Deming Prize for a division in 1982. Before they instituted Deming's methods, their defect rate was four parts per thousand. By the time they won the Deming Prize, the defect rate had fallen to three parts per million. One might wonder what kind of financial benefits can accrue from eliminating four defects out of a thousand. The quality improvements, however, helped make it the most profitable division of Hewlett-Packard.

To understand the effect of improvement of quality on profits once defects and problems are negligible, we have to further explore the meaning of quality.

CHAPTER 3

What Is Quality?

Quality Is...

Quality has to be considered from the point of view of the user. One definition of quality is anything that enhances the product from the viewpoint of the customer. Some aspects of quality are easily identified, such as how well something works, its dependability, and the length of time before failure. But other aspects of quality are not easily identified or measured.

Deming likes to use the example given by his friend Robert Piketty of Paris: "Listen to the Royal Philharmonic Orchestra of London play Beethoven's Fifth Symphony. Now listen to some amateur orchestra play it. Of course, you like both performances: you enjoy home-grown talent. Both orchestras met the specifications: not a mistake. But listen to the difference. Just listen to the difference!"[1]

For those who aren't musically inclined I can provide another example. I was invited by a friend to see his amateur troupe perform *Arsenic and Old Lace*. I had seen the movie version with Cary Grant several times and consider it one funny movie. So naturally I accepted his invitation. At the performance every line was delivered on cue. The actors projected their voices, they left the stage at the proper time, and there wasn't a single forgotten line. But not one belly laugh emanated from any member of the audience during the whole performance.

In either case it is hard to identify or measure quality, but the absence of it stands out like Bermuda shorts worn to a black tie affair.

Rethinking the Definition of Quality

There exists a general conception among most of us that higher quality is always accompanied by higher prices. Our attitude in this regard seems justified by our daily experience. A better suit has a higher price tag. That beautiful, sleek automobile that can cruise at 130 miles per hour on the Autobahn has a much higher price tag than the car we can afford. That beautiful $150 fountain pen we bought to impress the bankers at the closing on our mortgage is certainly a quality product.

But is the fountain pen really of higher quality than the 59¢ disposable we use for everything else? In terms of function they both may be very good. Both serve their purpose. The fountain pen may allow us to sign our name in fancy calligraphy but requires that we perform an elaborate ritual, blowing over the paper and waving it, to dry the ink.

It makes more sense to think of the two pens as two distinctly different products, representing different product categories: one, the expensive status fountain pen, and the other, the disposable pen.

When talking about quality, one fountain pen may be of higher quality than another and one disposable may be better than the other. Depending on the customer's needs, disposability or calligraphic ability may be important. But a customer interested in replacing his 59¢ disposable isn't likely to change his mind at the counter and buy the fountain pen. Very few disposable pens are given as graduation gifts, regardless of their reputations.

Both have a common element of quality from the user's point of view. If either failed to write or left too much ink on the paper, the user would consider it inferior to others that performed better. Similarly for cars. While one car may have leather seats, a titanium engine, and jet engine exhausts and the other has cloth seats, a cast iron engine, and regular car exhausts, none of these differences should be considered differences in quality. As far as I can make out, people who are stuck on the highway in a $50,000 car are just as miserable as those stuck in a $15,000 car.

In either case the buyer expects a certain level of performance. Each car should be dependable, easy to start and handle, to enter and exit, and be designed with comfort and safety in mind.

In service the same applies. The food and service at a fast-food restaurant are different than at a five-star restaurant, but quality can exist or be lacking in either. Service that is too slow or too pushy in either is never appreciated.

Quality Is Not Preference

There may be near universal preference for leather seats over cloth seats, but that does not mean that leather seats are better than cloth seats. It is merely a preference. Americans may prefer sweet oranges over tart oranges, but once again that says nothing about quality. Of course producers have to be aware of the preferences of their customers and tailor their goods accordingly, but they had also better deliver quality to whichever market segments they serve.

Quality Is Not Technology or Features

Managers sometimes confuse quality with new technology, and that is reflected in their advertising and in their products. As an example, I was in the market for a pair of walking shoes. One old-line American shoe manufacturer advertised the quality of its shoes. The company said it had the latest and best waterproofing and claimed its shoes would last forever. When I tried on a pair, size 10½ was a little snug, so I tried on a size 11, which was even smaller. Size 10 was the same as 10½. That indicated to me a problem with quality.

Quality Is Not Backup Systems or Overdesign

In the early 1970s, just after graduating from college and in my first management position, I was reading voraciously about management. One piece was a presentation to Congress given by an American executive of a high-technology firm. He was discussing safety and quality. Why things break down, how failures could be avoided, and at what cost. He very eloquently argued that any product could be made to operate without failure during its lifetime if it were designed with backup systems or with the most expensive materials. Quality to him meant fail-safe designs, a secondary system duplicating the function, and swinging into action, should the primary system fail. Naturally quality to him meant higher cost.

But his arguments also implied, and he stated outright, that in the absence of these backup systems there was a limit to any product's dependability. We had to learn to live with a certain level of defects, unless we were willing to pay more for the goods and services in our lives.

At the time, this reasoning made sense to me, and it justified the level of American quality. But it also prevented me and other managers from working continually to improve quality. As Henry Ford, Sr., said, "If you think you can't, you're right, you can't." If there is a perceived upper limit to quality and you're almost there, it seems you are justified in attending to other matters, such as increasing profit exclusively.

Needless to say, this attitude is wrong. But it has been taught and practiced by educators and managers. Peter Drucker, sometimes billed as the Dean of American Management, states in one of his best-selling books: "Inventory controls or quality control are already handled this way in a good many businesses. Acceptable limits of nonperformance are set. How poor can customer acceptance of the product, minimum fulfillment of delivery promises, or of manufacturing schedules be before it endangers desired business results?"[2] He is not criticizing the practice but lauding it as a great contribution of management science.

Harold Geneen, in his book *Managing,* writes: "In quality control, you are controlling the down side. You are stipulating how many defects, how many minus numbers, are acceptable."[3]

No wonder we are in trouble. Our managers have been taught either that quality is unimportant or that it comes at the expense of profit. When quality is discussed, we are taught that once an acceptable level is reached, our work is over. As long as we believe that, we will be at a disadvantage.

Our managers have been ignorant of the principle, stated in Chapter 1 and taught by Deming to the Japanese since 1950, that improving quality leads to lower costs and higher profit. But ambiguous definitions of quality have also clouded the picture.

All the characteristics mentioned above, fail-safe systems, features such as leather seats, and sophisticated technology, may be called quality by some consumers; but it makes more sense to view these as items defining the product category. Other characteristics or ingredients of quality apply to all products and services, regardless of price. Let's consider some of them.

Quality by Increasing Uniformity

One important ingredient of quality is uniformity. It seems almost too simple and insignificant.

But consider any item. A car piston in a cylinder in the engine block is a common example. The piston should fit the cylinder. If the piston is too small, power will escape, resulting in poor mileage and sluggishness. If the piston is too large, it will rub on the inside of the cylinder and eventually damage the cylinder or the crankshaft. In either case the car's engine won't run smoothly, and performance will suffer.

The same is true of virtually every part or service. If a door is too large or too small, it won't close right. The suit that is too large or too small is not acceptable. Not just physical dimensions require greater uniformity. The heating element that heats at the wrong temperature, too high or too low, causes problems.

The delivery system that is twenty minutes early one day and two hours late the next causes substantial problems. An unreliable train system is virtually worthless, regardless of how new and fancy the train cars, or the seats upon which the customers sit and fume.

Specifications

We know from experience that every product or service we purchase will vary from item to item. Small differences from item to item may be acceptable, while large differences may wreak havoc.

The way we deal at present with variation in business is to specify an acceptable limit of variation. Thus business ordering is always accompanied by specifications. The ideal measurement for a part may be 3 inches, but one quarter inch either way may be good enough to work with. The specification would then allow for any item that measures from $2^{3}/_{4}$ inch to $3^{1}/_{4}$ inch to be acceptable. When greater precision is required, the specifications are narrower.

Specifications are a statement of what we wish, want, or need from our inputs to make an acceptable end product. If all the parts cannot be made according to specifications, then we have some measurable waste. If only 95 percent of the parts were made according to specifications and we improved our production process so that 100 percent were made to specifications, then our costs would improve a little over 5 percent with a substantial increase in profits.

But what happens when all the parts are within specifications? Where is the improvement in costs from making even better quality, that is to say, getting the parts to be more and more uniform?

The answer is everywhere, but it can't always be measured directly. A more uniform part lowers the cost downstream because it is easier to handle and install, and leads to fewer problems in the rest of the system.

The Cost of Lack of Quality

The cost of a defect increases dramatically as it moves along the production line. If it gets out to the customer, the cost, although unmeasurable, is at its greatest. But what is called a defect is somewhat arbitrary. Specifications are somewhat arbitrary. The closer a part is to the ideal, the better it is, and the less it costs to handle. The last step in the production line is the customers. They notice quality. Even though two products perform satisfactorily, if one is exceptional the customer's attitude toward it, and the company that produced it, is markedly different from his or her attitude toward the other product.

At one point Ford had cars equipped with transmissions from two different sources. One source was its own plant and the other was a Japanese manufacturer. It found that customers were requesting the Japanese transmissions. People were waiting for these cars and paying a premium for them over those equipped with Ford's own transmissions. The incidence of repair on cars equipped with Japanese transmissions was lower and the cars were noticeably quieter. Ford engineers decided to investigate. They took apart the transmissions of several cars of each type. They measured all parts on their own transmissions and found that the parts varied in size from car to car but all were within specifications. But when they measured the parts on the Japanese transmissions, they couldn't find any differences in the dimensions of the parts from one transmission to another with the instruments at hand. They had to be sent to a scientific lab for measurement.

The Japanese producer was delivering transmissions of much higher quality than called for in the specs. Why was he delivering better quality than needed to make the sale? Because by constantly improving the process and the product, he was lowering his own costs and serving his customers better. The customers were lining up and waiting for his product.

This was just what Deming taught the Japanese. An all too prevalent attitude in American business was expressed by an individual who attended a Deming seminar. He told Deming, "I need to know the minimum level of quality necessary to satisfy the customer."

As Deming said, "So much misunderstanding was conveyed in such few words."

Quality Audits

The idea of stopping any effort toward improvement once everything is within specifications seems logical. Shouldn't everything pay for itself, including quality? If every expense has to be justified in light of alternative investments, then why not perform a cost-benefit analysis on every attempt to improve quality? Most of the quality control texts in our country have several chapters on quality audits. The idea is to put scarce corporate resources to their best use. It seems logical but it's wrong.

Many of the most important benefits of improved quality can't be measured or sometimes even identified. The benefit of loyal customers and happy employees is unknown and unknowable. The improvement in costs because of better quality is also rarely measurable in full.

But more important, improvements of any kind are cumulative. A 2 percent improvement in productivity in any given year doesn't sound like much, but if it is repeated every year, it may lead to dominance in an industry. No one can predict in advance the effects of continual improvement.

A Different Attitude

The difference in the attitude toward quality and improvement between Japanese industry and American industry is highlighted in a letter sent Deming by his friend Dr. Yoshikasu Tsuda of Rikkyo University of Tokyo, dated March 1980:

> I have just spent a year in the northern hemisphere, in twenty-three countries, in which I visited many industrial plants, and talked with many industrialists.
>
> In Europe and in America, people are now more interested in cost of quality and in systems of quality-audit. But in Japan, we are keeping very strong interest to improve quality by use of methods which you started.... when we improve quality we also improve productivity, just as you told us in 1950 would happen.[4]

Consequences of Better Quality in the Marketplace

From everything I've said so far, it seems possible we might see some products of higher quality being offered in the marketplace for less money than those of poorer quality. In fact that does occur from time to time. But the lower-quality, higher-priced item is soon driven off the market. When Japanese electronics were introduced into the American marketplace, the conventional wisdom was that they were cheaper because of lower wages and were of lower quality than their American counterparts. As American consumers discovered that there was nothing wrong with the quality, and then realized that the quality was better than that of domestic goods, they began preferring Japanese goods. Eventually the American producers had to withdraw from these markets. Ironically some of our top management consultants praised the decisions of these companies to withdraw from these markets. The rationale was, "Those were yesterday's products." They were mature products. The cold, hard analysis of the numbers indicated that sufficient profit could not be generated from mature products. The so-called hard decisions were made, and defeat was painted as a victory—a triumph of American management.

Not Just Japan

Positive examples are not limited to Japanese firms. IBM, for instance, has introduced a new generation of computers roughly every five years. Typically, a new generation of computers has resulted in two to four times the functionality of the old for the same price. As a result IBM achieved world dominance in the computer industry even when competing against giant firms such as GE and RCA.

I don't mean to imply that all of Japan has adopted Deming's methods. Some of the worst practices possible are still to be found among Japanese firms. But they have instituted a vigorous program of education, open to all industry, which is administered by JUSE, the Union of Japanese Scientists and Engineers. Classes teaching Deming's methods are fully booked, with a nine-month waiting list.

Here in the United States, Deming gives about twenty four-day seminars to corporate managers every year. Up to four thousand people attend each seminar. But this is just a beginning.

We are hampered by long-held attitudes and beliefs of our executives and political leaders. A group of American executives visited plants of Japanese suppliers to the auto industry. They were shown everything in the plants and all their questions were answered. At the end of the tour one of the Americans asked why their hosts were so open about all their methods. The Japanese executive replied, "We know you won't adopt what you have seen here today, and even if you did, by the time you instituted everything, we will be ten years ahead of where we are now."

An article in the May 14, 1989, Sunday *New York Times* starts, "For many companies, the good news is that they have finally managed to improve the quality of their products."[5] One business editor told me, "Quality is passé. It is no longer an issue."

As long as our attitude toward quality is that we just need to meet the competition or obtain a certain level of quality, we are going to be in trouble.

Another Ingredient of Quality: Pride of Workmanship or Joy in Work

While still a monopoly, the Bell System conducted an experiment. Their telephone repair people were required to do four jobs a day, every day. One group of repair people was given a different mandate. They were told to stay with a job until they were personally satisfied, regardless of the time involved. The two groups were tracked and compared. The results? Profitability was higher by every measure, including profitability per employee, when the repair person did the job to his satisfaction.

Of course it would be. Who can arbitrarily determine that a job will take a quarter of a day. Some jobs require more time, some less. Why was profitability greater without the constraints of a quota? Less rework. The company didn't have to send out another repair person days or weeks later to repair the job again. What about customer satisfaction and loyalty? That was an added benefit which cost the Bell system nothing.

Another example involves service operators who explain to customers all the intricacies, schedules, and rates of their company, a well-known air-freight company. The company has imposed a rule that each operator must talk to twenty customers a day and that the maximum time allowed for any single phone conversation is twenty minutes. The rationale is understandable. The company wants to assure high productivity. The more calls each operator handles, the lower their cost; the more customers dealt with, the better the customers are served and the higher the company's profit, right? Wrong!

The operators have become extremely adept at meeting their goals. Place yourself in the position of a customer who is talking to a service operator about a fairly complex routing. Nineteen-and-a-half minutes into the conversation the line disconnects in the middle of the operator's sentence. You call back, muttering under your breath about the lousy phone system, and speak with a new operator, reiterating the background information.

What happened is the operator, aware of his time limit, hung up on himself as the conversation approached the twenty-minute time limit. Another technique is to put the customer on permanent hold. In one IRS office with a similar rule, any customer who called with a particularly complex question was given the phone number of an out-of-state office, which, he was told, specialized in that type of question.

When quotas are used, the workers do exactly what management demands from them, but the company, the workers, and the customers all suffer. Customers with complex questions are greatly inconvenienced. They must call back several times. Whereas one service operator may be able to answer all the questions in thirty-five minutes, it might take three operators fifty-five minutes over three phone calls to do the same. The company's resources are poorly utilized, the customers are frustrated and angry, and the workers are unhappy. The workers are prevented from experiencing the intrinsic rewards of doing a good job by the very system management believes is helping.

An alternative to the quota system is to put quality first. In some instances quality cannot be measured by uniformity and isn't easily quantified. Quality is pride of workmanship or joy of work. By allowing and even urging workers to experience the intrinsic rewards that come from doing something well, using their innate and acquired abilities, productivity improves, quality improves, and customer satisfaction improves.

Quality and Job Security

Lynn Townsend, a respected accountant, took over as chief executive of Chrysler when the industry was in the midst of a sales slump and the company was experiencing financial difficulties. He examined the financial statements and noticed a large overhead. He cut costs by firing the engineering staff. Earnings rebounded. Wall Street declared him a hero. But a few years later Chrysler was in worse trouble. Eventually Chrysler was saved from bankruptcy by massive government aid and new management.

Mazda also experienced financial difficulties. The company's main product, rotary engine cars, was perceived by the public as a gas guzzler and made instantly obsolete by the energy crunch of 1974–75. Mazda was faced with problems similar to Chrysler's and needed to cut production, lower costs, and restructure itself. But it didn't fire a single worker. Instead, engineers were reassigned. Many staff people became part of the sales force and everyone in the company, including top management, took a pay cut. Some of the reassigned engineers became top salespeople. When the company recovered and they returned to engineering, they had a perspective on customer needs that few staff people in other companies ever acquire. Within a few years Mazda became one of several Japanese car companies from which Ford, GM, and Chrysler were petitioning the federal government for relief.

Virtually every American company claims that its most important resource is its people, yet when trouble strikes, the first thing
to go is its people. First it lays off production workers, then it lays
off middle managers, then cuts pay for middle managers, then cuts
dividends, and finally cuts pay for top management.

Compare this with the attitude of IBM, which, in a series of
advertisements, brags about the continual retraining of its people as
skills are made obsolete by technological change. Compare this
with the Japanese attitude as outlined by Yoshi Tsurumi in his
article "American Management Has Missed the Point—The Point
Is Management Itself." He states:

> In Japan, when a company has to absorb a sudden economic hardship,
> such as a 25 percent decline in sales, the sacrificial pecking order is
> firmly set. First the corporate dividends are cut. Then the salaries
> and the bonuses of top management are reduced. Next, management
> salaries are trimmed from the top to the middle of the hierarchy.
> Lastly, the rank and file are asked to accept pay cuts or a reduction in
> the work force through attrition or voluntary discharge. In the United
> States, a typical firm would probably do the opposite under similar
> circumstances....As long as management is quick to take credit for a
> firm's successes but equally swift to blame its workers for its failures,
> no surefire remedy for low productivity can be expected in American
> manufacturing and service industries.[6]

Tsurumi quotes "one Japanese plant manager who turned an
unproductive U.S. factory into a profitable venture in less than
three months" as saying: "'It is simple. You treat American workers
as human beings with ordinary human needs and values. They
react like human beings.' Once the superficial, adversarial relationship between managers and workers is eliminated, they are more
likely to pull together during difficult times and to defend their
common interest in the firm's health."

Can a company whose workers are despondent, insecure about
their future, and uncertain of management's commitment to getting the job done right possibly compete with a company whose
workers know management stands with them? The historical
record seems to strongly indicate that it cannot. In making a good
product or service in a company, cooperation is key—cooperation
between management and workers, worker and worker. This is best

achieved when workers and managers feel secure in their jobs. That is to say, without fear.

The actions of contemporary managers too often reflect the thinking of a portfolio manager rather than that of an industrialist—and a mediocre portfolio manager at that. Aren't shareholders interested in tomorrow's dividend as well as today's? Shareholders and portfolio managers have responsibilities also. But as long as they are ignorant of the relationship between quality and profit, between workers experiencing pride of workmanship (or joy of work) and profit, they will be unable to fully exercise their rights and take the proper action.

Job Security and Improvement

As quality and productivity are improved, a product's price may be lowered, resulting in greater market share and more jobs. But as growth levels off and productivity increases still further, it is expected that fewer workers will be required for that product.

Are people commodities to be taken on as needed and released when no longer needed? Such a view is inconsistent with continual improvement. As fewer people are needed on one product, they must be trained and retrained for new areas within the company.

Naturally workers will resist changes toward improvement when in the past improvement has meant higher returns for managers and shareholders but fewer jobs and less security for everyone else.

In a company that has adopted the Deming philosophy the company's fate and its workers' fate are tied together. This is a win-win philosophy as opposed to the more common "I win, you lose" philosophy. As productivity improves and costs decrease, profits rise. With high quality the workers can experience pride in their work and job security is enhanced. Shareholders win, managers win, and workers win.

Knowledge and Quality

General Motors, anxious to learn the Japanese secret, invited Toyota into a joint venture to produce cars in one of GM's most troublesome plants in California. GM had assumed that automation and high technology were the Japanese secret and would be the company's route to higher productivity and higher quality. They had spent a fortune publicizing and preparing for their highly automated and technologically advanced Saturn subsidiary.

GM was not disappointed with their joint venture with Toyota. When the Toyota plant began operating, the quality was the best in the whole GM system. When it reached full production, productivity was 50 percent higher than at a comparable plant producing the same car. But when GM executives visited the plant, they were shocked. There was no new equipment. In fact, some of the new automated equipment that GM had installed had been ripped out in favor of older technology. The same plant with the same workers and the same equipment was producing 50 percent more and with much higher quality than ever before.

The whole difference was five Toyota managers and the knowledge they brought with them. The senior member of Toyota's staff had studied with Deming.

The Toyota managers appreciated the value of knowledge and skills. In a typical plant in this country production for a new model reaches full capacity within about six months of retooling. The plant run by Toyota was producing fewer cars than the American counterpart for the first six to twelve months. Full capacity wasn't reached until eighteen months after retooling. But when it was, more cars were produced at lower cost and higher quality.

During the first eighteen months management's primary concern was that everyone understand his or her job. Numbers took a back seat to training. After eighteen months each worker knew his or her job and the plant was able to produce a very high output. In a sense, management during the first eighteen months invested not in equipment but in people and their training.

Knowledge is a key ingredient of quality. Economic theory states there are two primary elements of production, capital and labor. Most economists recognize another aspect, usually in the form of technology. Given the same capital and labor, a firm with better technology can produce more and better. Deming's theory, however, calls for the recognition of another element, which he calls profound knowledge. Given the same capital, labor, and technology, one firm can produce better quality with higher and continually improving productivity than another if it possesses profound knowledge and the other does not.

Profound Knowledge

What Deming calls profound knowledge is knowledge universal to all businesses, large or small, in service or manufacturing, profit-making or not-for-profit. Several aspects of profound knowledge have been discussed in the text: Clarity in the definition of quality and knowledge of the principle that increasing quality leads to increased productivity and higher profit are two elements. Other aspects include knowledge of variation, some psychology, and knowledge of the need for cooperation.

When Shewhart first began to attack the problem of quality in the Bell Laboratories during the 1920s, he emphasized the need for minimizing variation and understanding the sources of variation. An extensive theory and a set of techniques called statistical process control were developed. A class of specialists was born. The assumption among managers was that quality control could be installed like an air conditioner, just by hiring some quality control experts.

But the actions and policies set by management can put an upper limit on quality, in some cases guaranteeing problems. The specialist is helpless to improve quality when managerial policy forces the purchasing department to buy supplies on the basis of lowest cost. She is helpless to improve quality from poor design because designers ignore consumer research or the needs of the engineers who have to build the product.

Management policies that treat employees like commodities, institute quotas and use fear to enforce them, push for greater numbers at the expense of quality, foster competition among departments that must cooperate to produce quality, and mandate that tools and equipment be bought on the basis of lowest cost prevent quality from ever improving, regardless of the number of specialists hired.

Quality is not the responsibility of the quality control department or any other specialist. Quality is everyone's responsibility, but top management have more leverage in their decisions than anyone else. Their policies can limit quality or encourage continual improvement. Quality is made in the boardroom.

The people who are most in need of profound knowledge are the managers, particularly top managers.

Summary

Quality defined from the user's point of view is anything that enhances satisfaction. Some quality characteristics, such as reliability and time before failure, are more easily defined and measured than others. Attempts to improve these quality characteristics by using expensive, exotic materials and backup systems are not improvement in quality but the design and creation of a different product.

Important quality characteristics such as reliability, time before failure, and ease of use are improved by improving uniformity. Uniformity can be increased and costs lowered for any product or service by improving the production process. Statistical process control is a very powerful method for improving the process. But management policies designed to lower costs often lead to policies that hamper improvement of the process and make improvement of quality all but impossible.

Quality is only possible when the people in the system feel secure and experience joy in what they do. Any policy that prevents people from experiencing this is dysfunctional and leads to poor quality and loss for the company.

Knowledge of variation is important in understanding good management and will be covered in the next chapter.

CHAPTER 4

Variation in Management

It comes as a real surprise to most people, as it did to me, to realize that the roots of Japanese management are in the Bell Laboratories, where Walter Shewhart, the founder of quality control, worked during the 1920s and developed insight into the nature of variation and ways to minimize it. His work was first published in his book *Economic Control of Quality of Manufactured Product* in 1931. Deming, his friend and associate, served as editor for Shewhart's second book, *Statistical Methods from the Viewpoint of Quality Control.* Both men held doctorates in physics and were actively engaged in the emerging science of statistics.

While the methods used to analyze variation and the sources of quality are quite sophisticated, the implications are in many cases quite simple. Deming over the last sixty years has extended the analysis to all parts of commerce, including management policies.

Application to a Common Practice

But what is so different about one style of management over the other? How do statistics and insight into variation lead to different policies, and why do different policies have such different results?

Let's put ourselves in the shoes of a manager confronted with a typical problem at the end of the year. It seems reasonable to believe that if everyone worked a little better or harder, the group would be better off. One way in which many executives feel this might be accomplished is to provide incentives by rewarding exceptional individual performance and punishing below-average results. This is the idea behind merit pay and incentive pay, but we find it in all aspects of our society—grading, for instance.

But this very practice, even the belief that incentives lead to better results for the group, or the individual, is going to be challenged in the next few pages.

It's promotion time and Mr. A is reviewing the results of his group. His company measures performance by the number of defects produced per quarter. Naturally, fewer defects indicate better performance. Below is a table with the results for the six individuals in the group, along with their ranking for the year.

Defects per Worker per Quarter

Name	Quarter 1	2	3	4	Total	Rank
Ken	8	10	12	9	39	5
Barbara	6	4	11	7	28	1
Lenny	11	11	11	8	41	6
Noboru	8	11	8	11	38	4
Cathy	15	5	12	4	36	3
Steve	5	9	9	10	33	2

The results are straightforward and objective. Mr. A doesn't like subjective ratings because they are too "unscientific," but he knows how to analyze performance by ranking people from first to last. This year Barbara was the star performer and Lenny was the worst, with an unacceptable level of 41 defects. In no quarter did Barbara's level of defects exceed Lenny's. Barbara is in line for a promotion to manager. She certainly earned her merit pay. Lenny, on the other hand, appears to have been goofing off. Whatever the reason, his work wasn't good enough. Some organizations would let him go. Imagine what the group could do if it had five more people just like Barbara.

The Red Bead Experiment

One of Deming's best-known lectures is his Parable of the Red Beads. Using a simple example, he is able to demonstrate much of what is wrong with American management.

In a typical session Deming asks for volunteers from his audience. He needs six willing workers, no experience necessary. The company will train them. After some coaxing, six members of the audience step forward. Now some additional personnel are needed to ensure quality. Two inspectors are recruited. The only requirement is an ability to count to twenty. Finally, a chief inspector and a recorder are chosen. Deming acts as foreman.

Six workers, one foreman, and an administrative staff of four are now about to mimic a typical work environment. This is a modern factory employing the latest and best in management methods. The factory makes white beads. But some times it turns out red beads, which are defects. The customers pay only for white beads.

The production equipment includes two plastic rectangular pans. One is larger than the other and contains 4,000 beads, 3,200 whites and 800 reds. A rectangular paddle with fifty holes is part of the equipment. The paddle is dipped into the beads and, when raised, should be filled with beads. Preferably white beads. A factory goal of only two red beads per paddle has been established by a very concerned management.

Deming, acting as the serious foreman, demonstrates the production technique. "Pay attention. I want everyone to pay attention," he begins. "There is no variation in the method; therefore there should be no variation in the results. Grab the larger container in the right hand and slowly pour the beads into the smaller container. Now grab the smaller container in the right hand and pour the beads back into the larger container. Now angle the paddle and immerse it into the beads so that it's fully submerged and draw it out. Careful, don't shake it."

After drawing the paddle out, he points out eight red beads among the fifty it holds. "As you can see, I intentionally made a few red beads so you can see what they look like. Now walk over to the inspectors and show them your paddles. Each inspector counts the number of red beads. The chief inspector compares his count with the other two inspectors. If there are no discrepancies, the chief inspector announces the count."

"Eight," is announced by the chief inspector.

"Now dismiss the willing worker."

"Dismissed."

"Very good. We do everything wrong in this company," Deming says, "except one thing. The inspectors are independent."

Now the willing workers begin their training with one practice run apiece. As they proceed, Deming shouts slogans and clichés one would expect from a crusty foreman.

"Not that way, you weren't watching me. Like this!"

"Don't shake the paddle, just angle it out."

"We want only the best workers. We constantly strive for improvement."

"There will be no quitting. You can be fired but you can't quit."

After the foreman has trained his workers, he asks for an average worker. Ken volunteers to be the average worker. "Good. Now Ken is our average worker, and he'll go first. Everyone else is above average."

Ken begins his first day's production under the watchful eye of our foreman. He pours the beads from one container into the other. "Don't tilt it. Weren't you watching me? That's better."

When he finishes, the chief inspector announces the count. "Eight. Dismissed."

"Well, Ken, I suppose that's not too bad for a first try, but you're going to have to do better."

Next Barbara tries her hand. She produces six red beads on her first try. Our foreman booms out, "Now Barbara made only six red beads. If she can make only six, no one should make more than six."

Lenny on his first try produces eleven, Noboru makes eight, and Cathy makes fifteen, producing an outcry from our foreman.

"Now hold on a minute. Cathy, don't you understand? Weren't you paying attention? That kind of performance just isn't acceptable. Our goal is two red beads at most and you're not even close."

Steve on his turn produces five red beads.

After the first quarter a performance review is conducted. "Steve was our best worker. He gets the highest pay increase and earns merit pay. He's in line for a promotion. Poor Cathy, we all like her but she can't do the job. She's not living up to her ability. We may have to let her go."

And so it goes for three more quarters. Each quarter a personnel review is conducted, and each quarter a different individual is at the top and a different individual is at the bottom. But the overall results don't change much. Deming gets to utter every cliché known to man, dumps on a worker whenever his or her red bead count is very high and praises him or her whenever it's very low. At the end of four runs the results are as follows:

Full Year Results

Name	Quarter				Total	Rank
	1	2	3	4		
Ken	8	10	12	9	39	5
Barbara	6	4	11	7	28	1
Lenny	11	11	11	8	41	6
Noboru	8	11	8	11	38	4
Cathy	15	5	12	4	36	3
Steve	5	9	9	10	33	2
Total	53	50	63	49		

The results are exactly those first used at the beginning of this chapter to demonstrate a performance review. Of course, from the nature of the red bead production technique we know that the performance of each individual on any given day and, in fact, for any length of time is due entirely to chance. But what is surprising is the amount of variation from person to person. The best quarterly performance in our experiment is four red beads, repeated by both Barbara and Cathy, while the worst is fifteen by Cathy in the first quarter.

We all acknowledge the existence of chance in everyday life. Yet most of us assume that chance is not responsible for differences in individual performance. But here we encounter a situation where chance is responsible for 100 percent of the difference in performance. Surprisingly, in many commercial situations where one might believe that the results are controlled by the individual, all or almost all the variation from person to person and from quarter to quarter is due to chance.

Let's return to Deming's demonstration. The results for the four quarters are in, and the foreman who has been complaining about quality and touting management's commitment to quality throughout the year now has a tough task to face. "Management has asked me to inform you that although you improved, it was not enough. We were prepared to close the plant but someone in management has come up with a brilliant idea. This is a stunning breakthrough in management technique. We'll keep the plant open with the three best workers. All the above-average performers will stay on, while the laggards will be let go. Barbara, Cathy, and Steve will stay on. As for Ken, Lenny, and Noboru, we're sorry. We all like you. Please pick up your last paycheck as you leave."

The "best" workers must do two runs each. On her first run Barbara produces eight red beads and on her second try thirteen. Cathy makes fifteen and thirteen. Steve has eight then seven. Using the best workers, the plant has sixty-four red beads, the worst quarter ever. Of course, we knew that there was no reason for the plant to operate any better or worse using the best workers. The three workers were chosen because they were the best workers in the past, but management should be interested in the future. However, when all the variation in performance is due to chance, past performance is neither a guarantee nor an indication of future performance.

The management of the bead factory held the workers responsible for their individual production. They blamed the workers for the problems of the system. This kind of mistaken thinking is aptly demonstrated by the following memo taken from a Navy yard bulletin.

I want to reemphasize that improved quality of work is critical to every one of our jobs. True productivity should translate into increased production of an acceptable professional product. Shoddy work does not improve productivity no matter how quickly [sic] or in what quantity it is completed. We would only discredit ourselves and disserve the public by turning out poor quality work.

The importance of the concept of accountability of individuals, and the power of a pervasive human knowledge among the workers,

supervisors, managers and that each individual will be held accountable for his work products cannot be overstressed. Audit trails must
be maintained that document completed work and the supervisors
responsible for such work. People generally want to do the right
thing, but in a large organization they frequently don't really
understand what is the right thing. Management must make crystal
clear what is expected from each employee and that personal
performance is essential to holding a job or to being promoted. When
instructions and expectations are made absolutely clear, and follow-up
action is taken swiftly where failures occur, compliance will result.
Proper managerial conduct will result in a loyal, highly motivated and
very capable work force with tremendous surge capability. The
managerial ability to pull all of this together in a manner that
supports human development is a vital ingredient in our shipyards.
We should intensively and analytically evaluate how to handle compliance (holding workmen, supervisor, and managers accountable)
and to deal with failure in a manner that will have the highest payoff
in improving quality and productivity.[1]

How do we know whether or not the differences are due to
chance?

When management looks at information on output or performance, it is confronted with a bunch of numbers. The usual
assumption is that each number is due to one specific cause, such as
the effort or lack of effort of an individual. But in a system like the
bead factory all the variation is due to chance, which means it is
caused by the system not the workers. Management is responsible
for the system. Why then blame the workers?

How do we determine if the variation in a system is due to chance
or individual causes?

Control Limits

This was the problem confronted by Shewhart. After much
theorizing and experimentation, he devised a set of limits that could
be calculated from the data. In the bead factory the average number
of red beads per person is nine. The upper control limit and the
lower control limit calculated for the red bead factory are respec-

tively eighteen and one. As long as the number of red beads on each tray is between eighteen and one and there are no trends in the data, we are confident in saying that all the variation from person to person is due to chance. In other words, the variation is inherent in the system and will persist regardless of who the workers are.

The idea behind control limits is fairly simple. When chance is responsible for all the differences in a measured quantity, such as production output or the number of defects, almost all the data will fall within three common measures of variation (standard deviation) from the average. Shewhart devised a function similar to the standard deviation that could be applied to any situation. In all kinds of different situations the control limits were shown to be effective. When all the data fall within the control limits and there are no trends or cycles, we have achieved what he called statistical control or stability. All the variation is best explained by chance.

When, however, a point falls outside the control limits, either above the upper limit or below the lower limit, then it is worth our while to hunt for the cause of that variation. Anything that causes a point to fall outside the control limits is probably a special cause. Special causes can be found and often eliminated.

A system that is operating in the state of statistical control is not necessarily defect-free. In the red bead factory, for instance, the average level of defects was more than 18 percent. But what it does mean is that at this point there can be no further improvement by looking for individual causes of defects. Only by working on the whole system can we achieve improvement. The system must be altered in some fundamental way, and that only management can do.

A Practical Example of Statistical Control

Although the term may seem imposing, we all have some familiarity with the idea of achieving statistical control. Suppose, for instance, you are assigned the task of starting up a completely new department. At first everything seems chaotic. Every problem is new and special. To deal with the problems and day-to-day tasks you establish routines and procedures. As you learn to handle a certain type of situation, it becomes more routine, and can be easily delegated.

Gradually most of the special problems are eliminated and things begin to run smoothly. New situations are constantly cropping up, but much of the business on hand is handled in routine fashion.

No business can operate for long unless a certain amount of stability has been achieved. Deming estimates that, based on his experience, in most business situations 94 percent of the problems are problems of the system while only 6 percent are special in nature.

Some Commonly Proposed Solutions

With this in mind let's examine some of the solutions to our quality problems proposed by business consultants, political leaders, and editorialists.

Hold the workers accountable for their work

Sounds wonderful. But the workers are helpless to improve. They haven't chosen the equipment, the suppliers, the lighting, the order of tasks, or the layout of the plant. Changing the workers may have no effect on the results in a stable system. Workers are constrained by the existing system. Working twice as hard, if that were possible, would have no effect.

Merit reviews, incentive pay

Once again, sounds wonderful but this will only produce strife and tension. If all workers were to have their pay doubled, the results would not change. Some workers will, of course, perform "better," that is to say, he or she will have fewer red beads. Giving them higher pay will not improve quality but will cause resentment among those who do not receive incentive pay. Holding a lottery and giving the winners more money may be harmless, and even fun, but call the results of a lottery merit and deep trouble will result.

A former president of the United States and his secretary of education were urging merit pay among schoolteachers as being the way to improve the quality of education. Would teaching or learning improve with merit pay? Could the students learn more in the same environment, with the same books, in the same classes just because some teachers earned more? Doubtful.

Let the workers compete against one another

Competition in this and analogous situations is totally inappropriate and harmful.

New technology, automation, mechanization

Suppose someone from management convinced the board that the problem lay in the lazy and inefficient workers. After much research and analysis, management purchases new mechanical dippers, which could replace the workers. But quality does not improve. It stays the same or deteriorates while a host of new problems have to be dealt with. Many companies that embraced automated plants as their solution to problems of quality and productivity are quickly retreating from them.

Quotas, piecework, work standards

Quotas double the cost of production. Quotas may result in more items being shoved out the door, but the cost to the company increases as returns increase. As quality declines, inventory increases, waste soars, and the customer's perception of product quality declines.

But quotas have a more insidious characteristic. If everyone is meeting the quota, someone must be capable of exceeding it on a given day. But once she reaches the quota, she stops for fear that the quota will be raised. It is not unusual to find workers stopping an hour before the whistle blows. Great peer pressure is exerted to keep production down so that all can meet the quota. No one makes suggestions that may improve production. The workers in such an environment are unhappy, but from management's point of view the quota is being met and that is all that counts.

Meeting specifications, conformance

The goal in the red bead parable is two red beads at most. How was this decided? At a meeting someone looked at the results and decided the firm could do better. A goal was set as a target. In other words, like most goals, it was invented. Is it possible to meet the goal? Only by working outside the system. Outside of bribing the inspectors, however, most workers are bound by the system.

Everyone doing his best; working harder

Everyone is already doing his or her best, working his or her hardest.

Excessive testing of new employees

In this system there will be problems regardless of who the workers are. If the workers all had IQs of 200 and were master craftspeople as well, it would make no difference. They are all constrained by the capability of the system.

Management by walking around

Just imagine all the damage that can be done by allowing bright young individuals who are ignorant of the nature and sources of variation walking around the plant floor, or office, and making changes and suggestions on the basis of three-minute observations. In the next chapter we'll cover the harm that can be done by constant changes to a system.

What Will Help

In our bead factory nothing can be done at the factory level to improve quality. Neither the workers nor the foreman are capable of making the necessary changes. Even the quality control expert might be helpless if he does not have the authority to change policy. Holding the workers, the foreman, or the quality control expert responsible for quality would be futile and senseless.

The problem's source is the supply of beads. If we could eliminate all the red beads from the incoming source, we would eliminate all the red beads from the end product. The problem begins well upstream from the factory. But why are so many red beads being delivered? It could be for any number of reasons. The specifications may call for no more than 20 percent defective beads being delivered, which guarantees exactly 20 percent defectives.

The supplier may have been chosen on the basis of lowest price, without much regard to quality. Management may be on a cost-cutting binge or just unaware of the effect on the bottom line of inferior quality.

It's possible that the supplier's production method produces 20 percent red beads but that a few modifications may eliminate all red beads. The company should join forces with the supplier, sharing knowledge to improve the supplier's production methods.

The changes necessary to improve the quality of the incoming materials are changes in policy that only management can authorize.

Common Causes

When all the special causes of problems and variation have been eliminated and statistical control or stability has been established, variation and problems will still exist. The variation at this point is said to be caused by common causes.

Common causes are interactive in nature. Let's consider a hypothetical example. Suppose we have a plant assembling a flywheel that will rotate at very high speeds during operation. Each worker arranges three plates on a rod. Now in the real world every plate is not totally uniform; variation exists, and every plate has one section that is slightly heavier than the rest. The difference is very small and can't be seen or felt without sophisticated equipment. But if the heavy parts of all three plates are aligned, the flywheel will wobble at high speeds and have a greater tendency to fail.

Most of the time the heavy sides of each plate are aligned in different directions so that they counterbalance. But once in a while, strictly by chance, the three plates will be perfectly aligned and the mechanism will fail. The failure is not caused by any single cause but rather is a chance occurrence of the system. Several factors have to occur for the failure to occur. Plate 1 *and* Plate 2 *and* Plate 3 have to be aligned, *and* the mechanism has to be spinning at high speeds for a long period of time. No matter how hard you searched for a cause of the breakage, you couldn't find one. Everything in the system is working as it should. The workers place the plates on the rods in exactly the same manner for the mechanisms that fail and for those that don't. The plates and rods are equally good in each case, but every once in a while, strictly by chance, a mechanism that is prone to failure will be produced. The same system that produces the good products produces the bad products in exactly the same way.

Management, through their words and actions, act as if there were two systems working side by side—one producing good

products and one producing defects. Management often act as if all
the good products are produced by the system when everyone does
his or her job while defects must be caused by someone doing
something different, outside of prescribed fashion. As a result, they
are quick to take credit for success but blame those working in the
system for failures. But this attitude not only causes friction and
dissension with their own work force, it also prohibits improvement
because their view of the cause of problems and failures is
inaccurate.

Oftentimes when a failure or problem occurs, the organization is
sent into a frenzy searching for the cause. One tire manufacturer
had all the day's defective products segregated and stored in a room
until their engineers could dissect all the defectives and search for
the cause of failure. This was the case for years, with the level of
defectives remaining the same.

A Cure for the Problem

Let's suppose the engineers of our hypothetical plant producing
the flywheel figure out that random alignment of the heavy sides of
all three plates could cause the mechanism to become unstable
when spinning at very high speeds. How could they prevent further
failures from occurring in the future? One way would be to
determine the bias of each plate, using sophisticated equipment,
before it is assembled onto the rods and mark the heavy side with a
red dot. The workers would then be instructed to assemble the
mechanism so that the red dot on each plate is turned 120 degrees
clockwise from the one before it.

Another method would be to inspect all the finished, assembled
mechanisms for any wobble by testing each one at high speeds
before it is sent out. In both cases the cost of eliminating a possible
failure would be very high, requiring extensive inspection, new
procedures, and new equipment.

But suppose, on the other hand, the company is constantly
improving quality by lessening variation. The company works with
the supplier of the plates and constantly strives to make the plates
more uniform by improving the platemaking process. In time the
plates become so uniform that, even if all three are perfectly
aligned, the wobble even at high speed is minimal. The problem

goes away without being attacked directly. And the cost is not higher and may be less.

Comparing the Two Methods of Improving Quality

These two methods of improving quality, one by inspection and the other by constant improvement of the process and the products, highlight the difference in attitudes and understanding between conventional companies and those companies that have taken Deming's lessons to heart. The companies that rely on inspection to improve quality believe that quality is expensive (because of the way they believe improvements are made). The Deming companies, on the other hand, are constantly improving the process and the product without justifying every improvement, confident that higher productivity, lower costs, and higher profits will result.

A Real-Life Example

Nashua Corporation began applying quality control to the manufacture of carbonless paper in 1979. Before the institution of quality control, their production process was marked with many interruptions for adjustments. While the process was running, technicians would take samples of the paper and make tests to determine if the quality of the copy was satisfactory. When the mark was too dark, or too faint, the process would be stopped to readjust the amount of coating being applied. When quality control was applied, the control charts indicated that the process was in fairly good statistical control. Some special causes of variation indicated by the control charts were tracked down and eliminated.

Realizing the nature of the remaining variation, the engineers then experimented with different settings, and different formulations for the coating and brought down the amount of coating needed by 17 percent, resulting in a cost saving of more then $800,000 yearly, all with better quality. Improvements continued to be made every year thereafter, with quality improving and substantial cost savings accruing.

Two Kinds of Mistakes

In analyzing variation there are two kinds of mistakes we could make:

1. We could mistake the cause of variation as being special in nature, when in fact it is random and caused by the system (common causes).

2. We could mistake the source of variation as being systemic in nature (common causes), when in fact it is special in nature (a special cause) and can and should be identified and, if possible, eliminated.

If you ignore a new rattle in your car, continue driving, and the crankshaft breaks, you have made a type two mistake. If the quality in your plant or office is gradually getting worse, and you ignore it, you may be committing a type two error. When a new employee enters the work force and the number of mistakes of the department increases significantly, that may be a special cause due to the employee not knowing his job. If management disregards the problem, they are committing a type two error. Incidentally, who is responsible for making sure the employee is properly trained for his new job? That is management's responsibility.

Type one errors are more common. Ask most managers at plants that are experiencing difficulty how many of the problems are due to the workers and the answer is almost always, "All the problems are caused by the work force." Soviet leader Mikhail Gorbachev made a type one mistake when he blamed a blast in a gas pipeline on the lax behavior of the workers. He blamed the workers at the nuclear plant at Chernobyl as being the culprits in the nuclear disaster there. When top management blame every accident on the lax behavior of the workers, they are admitting their ignorance and abdicating their responsibility. It is not really clear that improper training or lax behavior is the cause, but it is almost certain that we are confronting a common cause. If the training of everyone is indeed at fault, it is only management that can institute the proper training systemwide.

Our Federal Aviation Administration tracks down the "cause" of every airline accident and ends up blaming someone or something for every accident.

At most companies customer complaints are individually tracked down and brought to the attention of the individual thought to be responsible. One firm began drawing control charts of customer complaints after taking a Deming seminar and realized they had been chasing phantom problems for years. All their efforts in the past had been wasted. More importantly, now that they understood the nature of common causes, they were in a position to make genuine improvements.

One plant manager told Deming, "Our engineers never rest until they have found the cause of every defect." According to the plant manager, quality control was not needed because they understood every problem. But for years the level of defectives had remained the same, a sure sign that defectives were due to common causes.

The plant engineers were wasting their time and probably making things worse.

The reader may protest, "Perhaps they were wasting their effort but no real harm was done." But there is another surprise in store. Great damage may be done by chasing down phantom problems. In fact, a perfectly good system can be ruined by overadjustment and trying too hard. To understand this, we have to examine some additional properties of a stable system.

CHAPTER 5

Stable Systems

I mentioned in the previous chapter that adjusting or interfering in a stable system instead of improving it could do considerable damage. Let me show you how with a simple mechanical system first demonstrated by Lloyd Nelson, the 1987 winner of the American Deming Prize. All we need are a funnel, a stand, a ball small enough to pass through the funnel, and a square piece of carpet at least two feet by two feet.

The funnel is mounted on the stand with its nozzle a few inches off the ground. We mark a large X in the center of the carpet and aim the funnel at it. We then drop the ball through the funnel, observe where it stops, and mark and measure that spot. Our objective is to have the ball end up right in the center of our target. We drop the ball through the funnel fifty times with the funnel stationary and mark the final resting place each time.

Let me tell you what I observed when I tried this. Once in a while the ball stopped on or very near the target, but most of the time the ball rolled off in one direction. The marks indicating the final resting spot of the ball formed a rough circle. A picture of what this looks like after five hundred drops is shown in Figure 5-1 (see page 69). When I did it for fifty drops, all but one point were within seven inches of the target and that point was nine inches from the target. If we were to keep trying, we would see the blank areas of the circle filled.

This is a stable system. It is in statistical control with no special causes of problems. The markings are randomly distributed, and if we tried to predict whether on the next try the ball would end up north or south of the target, we would have a one-in-two chance of being right.

Attempts at Improvement—Modest Adjustments

Let's try to improve our accuracy and get more of our drops closer to the target. No one is going to blame us for trying. In fact, in the real world a boss or a board of directors may be looking over our shoulder. Almost invariably we're asked what we're doing to improve results, and from experience we know we had better have an answer.

One possible solution is to adjust the funnel, whenever we miss the target, by an amount equal to the miss but in the opposite direction. If the ball ends up south of the target by two inches, we will move the funnel two inches north of its present position for the next attempt. Our reasoning is that with this adjustment the ball would have hit the target on the last try.

Let's call the first method with the funnel stationary Rule 1 and our new procedure of adjusting the funnel Rule 2, or the rule of modest adjustments.

Now we retry the experiment, making modest adjustments whenever we miss. The results for five hundred tries are shown in Figure 5-2. What has happened? The results are worse! Once again a rough circle is formed by the scatter of the marks, but the radius is larger. When I tried it for fifty drops, most of the points fell within ten inches of the target but one point was thirteen inches from the target.

Once again the system is in statistical control, but now the area of the circle is roughly double the area of the previous one, when we did nothing.

Examples from Real Life of Adjustments Using Rule 2

Let's look at some real-life situations where modest adjustments like those we just performed are done as a matter of course. You may find these examples funny or disturbing, but keep in mind that the people performing or authorizing the adjustments are completely unaware of the ill effects of their actions.

Simulations of the Nelson Funnel

Performed by Professors Thomas J. Boardman and Harry Iyer, Colorado State University.

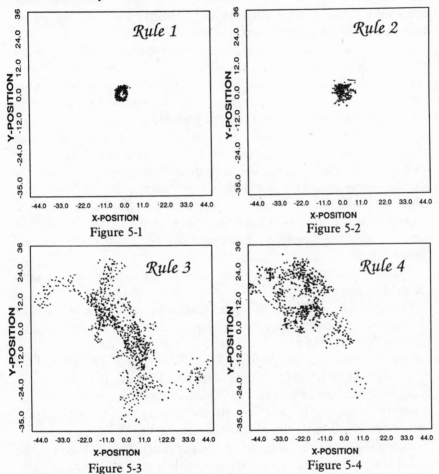

Figure 5-1

Figure 5-2

Figure 5-3

Figure 5-4

Example I. In the military it is common practice to test a gun in the morning. If the target isn't hit, then the gun or the sighting mechanism is readjusted so that it would have hit the target on the last try. Does this improve the accuracy or lessen it?

Prior to seeing the results of modest adjustments of the funnel, most of us would have answered automatically that adjusting helps the accuracy. But remember there are many things that can cause a gun to miss its target. Each bullet has a slightly different shape.

The gunpowder in each bullet is packed differently. Constantly changing air currents could cause a difference in the bullet's trajectory. There are untold sources of variation. Adjusting after one shot is doing exactly what we did when we adjusted the funnel each time it missed the target.

If you're like me, this example is hard to swallow. All of us have adjusted something to bring it back in line. We have taken it as a matter of faith that this would make things better. But the lesson here is that it does not; it only makes things worse if the system is stable. If you don't believe it, try it yourself.

But there is another point to consider. When some American observers went to Japan to find out the Japanese secret, they came back disappointed because the only difference they could find was the Japanese penchant for boisterous singing in the morning. Objective observers will only see what they're trained to see. Few people would notice that certain things *aren't* done. Subtle differences will be completely overlooked if one isn't aware of their importance.

But let's look at some other situations where modest adjustments are taking place.

Example II. William W. Scherkenbach, who studied under Deming at NYU and is now in charge of statistical methods at General Motors, investigated a mechanism that guaranteed that a part would be made to specifications. The mechanism worked all right. But when he shut the mechanism off, he found that everything was still made within specifications but with less variation, closer to the ideal. In other words the quality was better and the costs were lower with the mechanism turned off.

Example III. In the example of the previous chapter Nashua was doing the same thing manually, but with a modified form of our rule for modest adjustments. They didn't adjust their mechanisms after every miss, only when the miss was "large enough." But the results were the same. They were making the system worse by over-adjusting.

Example IV. A manager looks at the sales figures for his group. He's elated to see that almost half his staff performed above average last year, undoubtedly due to his superior leadership and management skills. Unfortunately, about half are below average, and there are a few laggards in the bottom 15 percent who haven't responded to his leadership.

To help the laggards and encourage the superachievers, he sets up an incentive program. Anyone selling over a certain dollar amount next year will earn a bonus. Anyone selling below a certain level is penalized.

Of course next year some will earn the bonus and some will be penalized, but will the company be better off or worse off because of this merit system?

Example V. The Federal Reserve Board is charged with regulating the nation's money supply. It looks at current data on the money supply or inflation, depending on what it is trying to regulate this year, and decides that money supply is "too high" or "too low" and takes steps to compensate for the amount it is off target.

I think if you're reading this for the first time, it must be a bit of a shock to realize that some of our best efforts to make things better are making things worse. But wait, there's more.

Rule 3—More Extreme Action

Clearly there is a lot of adjusting going on in business, but our funnel experiment suggests much of this effort makes matters worse, rather than improves it. But let's go back to the funnel and try something else. Perhaps we weren't trying hard enough with Rule 2. Let's try some other rules to see if we can't improve upon the results.

We can devise a new adjustment procedure, which we'll call Rule 3, or the rule of extreme adjustments. Now we'll move the funnel relative to the target instead of relative to its last position. Using our new rule, if the ball ends up three inches south of the target, we move the funnel to a position three inches north of the target for the next drop. Under Rule 2 we would have moved the funnel three inches north of its previous position. The results for Rule 3 are shown in Figure 5-3.

Remarkably, the results are worse than ever. The system is exploding in two directions, getting progressively worse. It is no longer stable. We have taken a perfectly good system (that was stable) and through our efforts to make it better (less variable) made it much worse, to the extent that it is now unstable. The situation is getting out of control. To keep the system from exploding, we have to shut it down.

When we tried modest adjustments, we took a system that had a certain level of natural variation and through our efforts to lessen the variation increased it. In effect we added another source of variation, our movement of the funnel. But the variation we introduced by moving the funnel didn't cancel the natural variation of the funnel. Instead it combined with it, giving us a system with greater variation. But with the extreme adjustments of Rule 3 the variation is cumulative, gradually pushing the results farther and farther from the target.

Examples of Rule 3—Extreme Adjustments

Let's look at a few cases of extreme adjustment.

Example I. A company's personnel policy calls for it to pay competitive salaries. Each year it orders a survey of compensation for its industry and adjusts its pay scale so salaries are 10 percent higher than industry average. One year sales and profits decline. The company looks at its personnel expense and decides it's too high. The policy is now changed so that salaries are 10 percent below the average. When the economy turns around, it finds itself short of people. It reverts to its old policy.

Example II. The federal government collects money through various revenue collecting measures, including the federal income tax. It redistributes money back to the states in the form of revenue sharing based upon a formula negotiated in Congress—the idea being to help those areas of the country that are poorer (or below average). In the past the formula favored the South and Southwest because the median income of those areas was below that of the Northeast. During the 1970s the Northeast became one of the nation's most distressed areas, and the formula was changed so that funds would flow back into the Northeast and away from the South and Southwest.

Senators and representatives from outside the Northeast are now complaining that the system is unfair because incomes in the Northeast are among the highest in the nation. The more they try to make it "fair," the more unfair it seems to become.

In general, shifts in policy based on results are examples of the rule of extreme adjustments. Rather than stabilizing the situation, these frequent and extreme adjustments make the situation more volatile and more "unfair."

Rule 4—Just Like the Last

So far our efforts directed at obtaining better results haven't been successful. For better results we could substitute other phrases, such as greater accuracy, more fairness, greater uniformity, or fewer defects. However we describe the desired result, the Nelson funnel has helped us see the folly in several courses of action. But we can try one more rule.

In our final attempt we devise Rule 4, which I'll call the rule of just like the last. Under this rule we re-aim the funnel after each drop so that it is directly over the spot where the previous drop ended up. The results for five hundred tries using Rule 4 are shown in Figure 5-4.

If you weren't totally discouraged before, this should do the trick. Now the system is exploding in a manner similar to the situation under the rule of extreme adjustments, but in just one direction.

Examples of Rule 4—Just Like the Last Adjustment

Just-like-the-last adjustments are extremely common. Let's start with one obvious example:

Example I. Most of us at one time played a game called Telephone or Post Office. Someone starts by whispering a message into the ear of the adjacent person. That person in turn whispers the same message into someone else's ear. After passing this way through thirty people, the message is completely transformed. Every third or fourth person in the chain heard a different message.

Example II. The chain of command is an example of Rule 4. Whether communications are flowing up or down the chain of command in an organization, after going through five different people, the original message and intent are altered. The message after twelve people may be just the opposite of the original.

This example makes a strong case against management systems with many levels. When it comes to layers of management, less is more. It also indicates that pushing the level of authority and expertise closer to the scene of the action cuts down on the amount of misunderstanding and leads to better results.

Example III. A devastating example of Rule 4 is worker training worker. A worker comes on the job and is told to learn from another. After three weeks she's an old-timer, a pro. When someone new comes on the job, she is told to teach him. Soon the new worker is also a pro. Each has a different idea of what the job is. Some will admit not really knowing what the job is. None is properly trained. If everyone has a different idea of what the job is, how can quality possibly be achieved? Think back to the number of jobs you've started in a new company or department where one person was responsible for training everyone. I doubt most of us will remember many instances. But I'll bet almost everyone who has held a job was told at least once, "You'll pick it up," or "Learn from those around you."

Some firms have all kinds of teaching materials and manuals but much of it is incomprehensible. Whose obligation is it to see that workers are properly trained? Management's.

Example IV. Rule 4 was followed when a Japanese car manufacturer sent DuPont a paint sample with instructions to match it. When that batch was used up, they sent a sample of the new batch of paint to DuPont with instructions to match this batch. They continued ordering and using paint in this manner. After a while a noticeable difference developed between the first batch and the most recent.

To assure the same color, the manufacturer should have left a sample of the original batch with DuPont with instructions to match the original whenever more paint was required.

Example V. Legal precedent is an obvious but frightening example of just-like-the-last adjustment. Each judge interprets a case based on her understanding of the law. Her decision is then the platform from which other judges interpret the law. Their decisions then serve as the basis for future decisions. After a while a law can be interpreted in a way that is unrelated to its original meaning.

Example VI. Languages are another example of Rule 4, just like the last. After several hundred years American English had developed many distinct accents and drawls. National television, on the other hand, has brought the accents of the various regions much closer together, since children now learn to speak English as much from television as from their parents. International television will undoubtedly bring the English spoken in the various English-speaking nations much closer together.

Real Improvement

With all these attempts at improvement backfiring, you've got to wonder if there is any way we could improve the results. The answer is, yes, there is, but not by constant adjustment. The urge to do something, to do anything, can make things worse if one proceeds in ignorance.

Only changes of the system, not adjustments of the existing system (which is already in control), can lessen variation and volatility. Change the funnel, the length of the funnel's barrel, the ball, the size or texture of the ball, the surface on which the ball lands, or any combination of these, and you change the system. These changes are all fundamental changes to the system. Not all changes in the system will make things better. The only way of being certain is to try it—on a small scale, if possible.

Overadjustment of a stable system invariably makes things worse. This deserves a special name—tampering. There are three ways of acting on a stable system. One is a change in the system leading to improvement, the second is a change in the system making things worse, and the third is tampering, which also makes things worse. Only one of the three, a change in the system leading to improvement, will make things better. Only management is in a position to make any of these changes, but making changes in the system without the benefit of profound knowledge can result in tampering—worsening, even ruining, a system.

But remember, when we say a system is stable, that means there is variation. Some systems can have a lot of variation and some display little, but all systems vary.

The funnel may be a lot of fun to play with, but the reason it's being used here is that the conclusions we draw based on our experiment with the funnel hold true for any system in statistical control, whether that system is mechanical or human.

An example of tampering in a human system is when someone is overseeing the work of or second-guessing someone who is perfectly capable of doing the job correctly. Have you ever been in a situation where the inspector or boss knew less than you? You knew the job, knew what had to be done, and were perfectly capable of doing it, but you had to get your work checked out or approved by the boss. There are few things as demeaning. Basically the firm is telling you that in their eyes you're incapable of doing the job; you're an idiot or, incompetent or can't be trusted.

Tampering in a Small System

Having someone look over your shoulder when you're perfectly capable of doing the job robs you of pride of workmanship. It's demeaning and will worsen the output. You develop the attitude, "Well, the supervisor will catch the error anyway, so why bother."

The supervisor develops the attitude of, "I know his or her work is good. I really don't have to look it over." Neither person has a job, and the results are worse than with someone doing the job unsupervised.

Some inspectors in such a situation give themselves a job by finding problems that don't exist. This is even more extreme tampering, making things progressively worse. One experience of this kind is enough to make most people swear off corporate America. I think that's one reason why we have so many entrepreneurs in this country.

The situation is completely different if a worker is incapable of doing the job. The worker who hasn't yet mastered the job should be supervised and helped. A worker may be new to the job, in which case he should be trained; he may be an experienced worker whose work has fallen out of statistical control, in which case he is in need of special help; or his work may be in statistical control, but unsatisfactory, in which case he should be reassigned and taught new skills.

When a worker whose work was formerly acceptable deteriorates below the lower control limit for the group, it indicates he is in need of special help. But management shouldn't blame him. Fault is not the issue. Solutions and improvement are. Management should consider this as information about the system's shortcomings, which they can use to improve the system for everyone who works in it.

It is a fact of life that people's performance can decline. Management has to be able to distinguish which of the workers are really in need of special help and which just have a tray filled with more red beads than average. The former is a special case and can be addressed; the latter is due to chance, and trying to address it directly will only make things worse. You had better have some way of distinguishing one from the other.

Control limits and knowledge of variation are the best ways we have of making that distinction. Once management determines who is in need of special help, they have an obligation and a responsibility to provide that help. They have a chance and an opportunity to help one worker improve his output, which in turn raises the output of the group and in the process bolsters the morale of everyone in the company.

Wrong Ways of Dealing with Variation—Tampering 101

Let me tell you of some of the funny ways we humans have of dealing with variation when we don't really have the answer, or in some cases the question. Deming tells of a plant that was consistently producing a high level of defects. Using the information on hand, he drew a control chart and calculated the average defect rate of 4 percent, an upper control limit of 6½ percent, and a lower control limit of 1½ percent.

All the week-to-week data were within the control limits, indicating that the system was stable. Stable, but with a high defect rate.

Showing this to the manager, he asked what measures the manager felt were appropriate to improve the situation. The manager proceeded to redraw the control limits, making them narrower and lower.

Would redrawing the control limits change the reality of the system? Of course not. Would it change anything? Yes, it could make things worse. It could lead to the mistaken assumption that stability hadn't been reached, leading one to mistake common causes of defects for special causes. This could lead management to interfere when it wasn't appropriate, or, once again, tampering.

Another Example—Tampering Course 102

Dr. Joyce Orsini, a respected consultant who obtained her doctorate under Deming's guidance, told me the following all too typical story. One perpetual problem among bank tellers is the daily differences between the cash they should have according to the accounting records and the cash they actually have at the end of the day. They may end up with more cash or less cash than indicated by the books. Normally the difference is quite small, although occasionally the amount is substantial. This is a common and persistent problem in all banks.

A chief executive of a New York bank noticed the problem and decided he would eliminate it the old-fashioned way. He just wouldn't tolerate it. He issued an edict that any teller with more than two differences a month would be placed on probation. Any teller on probation for three months would be terminated.

Most of the differences disappeared. The chief executive was elated. He reported the results to his board along with an explanation of his form of management. All that was necessary, according to him, was for him to put his foot down and not accept errors. The board of directors were also elated. This was obviously sound management. But why tolerate two differences a month? No one could think of a good reason, so the rule was changed. Just one difference placed a teller on probation. All the differences disappeared.

How could differences disappear so quickly and so completely? In fact, a simple but sophisticated system had been developed by the tellers to deal with the problem that management denied existed. The tellers began operating their own pools of money when the new policy was initiated. When overages occurred, instead of being reported, they were saved. When a teller came up short on a given day, he would withdraw from the funds saved on the days he was over. Those who needed funds borrowed from those with excess funds. A sophisticated system of borrowing and lending had evolved.

This was, of course, contrary to bank policy, but it was the only way of surviving in the bank. Everyone in the bank knew of the existence of these pools of funds except management. Whenever management uses fear, they will get incorrect numbers and misleading information.

This went on for ten months before management discovered its existence. The president was enraged and took it out on middle management. For weeks life was hell for them.

But who was really responsible? Simple knowledge of variation indicated that day-to-day differences were in statistical control. No special causes were at work. Only changes in the system could improve the performance of the tellers as a whole. The workers were powerless to (improve) make any changes in the system. They could not change the lighting, the room temperature, the time between breaks, the monotony of the job. They could not change or improve the training, the frequency of job changes, or any other significant aspect of the system. Only management could make these changes. But management had abdicated its responsibility because of ignorance.

Symptoms or Causes?

In both of the above examples we can categorize the position of management as one of ignorance of the nature and sources of variation, perhaps even of the existence of variation. But another way to look at their action is to realize that they were dealing with the symptoms of the problem and responding to them, rather than dealing with the causes of the problem.

But the causes of common problems cannot be attacked directly. It is a mistake to believe that one is improving quality when an inspector recognizes and rejects a defective product or when a major quality flaw is found. That is just recognizing a defect being produced by the system. It is not improving quality. It is not improving the system.

Love Those Problems

Every system has some problems. Someone is busy solving these problems. Problem solving is fun, it gives many people meaning, and the results are measurable. "I solved fifteen major problems this week." "Without me the plant would have shut down." "I saved the company a lot of headaches by stopping that shipment." When there are lots of problems, people can easily measure their value to the company. Problem solving is necessary, no doubt about it. Good problem solvers are important. But solving all the problems that come up does not improve quality. The source of the problems is left intact when we recognize defective products and prevent them from reaching the customer.

Improving the operation and lessening the number of problems that are created by the system doesn't have the instant gratification associated with problem solving. A lot of thinking and study of theory and current circumstances is often required. Improvements are sometimes small. But improvements, large or small, are cumulative. In a short while there are fewer day-to-day problems. Improvement can be a threat to many people. People who are busy solving problems will become threatened by improvement and resist it. Their attitude is understandable and justified if management maintains an us-versus-them attitude and views people as commodities to be discarded when their present job categories become obsolete.

The problem is compounded when people are judged based on how many problems they solve. Anyone who takes the time to truly improve the system lowers not only his own rating but the rating of everyone in his group as well. He not only will put himself out of work but will hurt his peers as well.

A company that operates using fear, positioning top management against workers and middle management against both, cannot produce the continual improvement in quality necessary to compete in the marketplace.

A Short Course in Statistics

Let's consider variation in a different context. Imagine that we recruit fifty people who have tested very high on some test, say an IQ test. We sit all of them in a room and give them another standardized test. We then rank them from one to fifty, based on the results of that test. Twenty-five of these people are below average for this group. So what? Are they in need of special help, or is this just another case of the red beads? How could you tell? One could draw a control chart and calculate control limits, although on just one test even this would carry some risk. It is unlikely that twenty-five individuals are in need of special help. Most likely this is just another red bead example.

But all too often it is assumed that those below average or those in the bottom 10 percent have done something wrong. A merit system, for instance, may reprimand, punish, or place on probation those who are in the "bottom 10 percent" of the work force. Reprimand the bottom 10 percent and you'll quickly destroy their self-image. Do it on a regular basis, and you'll quickly destroy the morale of the group. Eventually, almost everyone ends up at the bottom at some point. Will reprimanding the bottom 10 percent make them achieve any better in the future? No! But it will destroy teamwork and any chance for improvement. No one is going to help someone else when doing so may help put the other person ahead of him in the review and give the helper a bigger chance of ending up in the bottom of the group.

The president of a well-known business school beseeched his faculty: Please help those students who are below average do better so they can also be above average. Some corporations only hired the top 10 percent of the graduating class of M.B.A.'s. As Deming says, "They got what they deserved."

The Nuclear Regulatory Commission spends extra time monitoring those nuclear plants that are below average. Historians rank our presidents every ten years or so. Last time, they made a startling discovery. Half of our presidents were above average. Lucky for us. Imagine if all had been below average.

In placing special regulatory emphasis on those plants that are below average the Nuclear Regulatory Commission is tampering. If the faculty complied with the request of the president of the business school, and gave special help to those below average, they would be tampering. Harmless tampering? Isn't it better to do something, do anything, than to do nothing? Acting without knowledge, particularly profound knowledge, can quickly ruin a perfectly good system.

One part of profound knowledge is obvious to children but not to some college presidents. In any group, close to half will be below average.

Improvement and Effort

Asking people who work in a system to do better without providing a plan by which this can be accomplished will do no good. If they could improve quality or profits by 10 percent without a plan, they would already have done so.

A corporation is a highly interactive environment and the results in one area impact on many other areas. Asking everyone to work harder will not help results. The system has to be worked on, people have to work smarter not harder, and that requires intense cooperation. It requires equal cooperation of those in the "top half" and those in the "bottom half" without distinction, because there is no real distinction.

But one of the problems with existing management systems is that they destroy the very teamwork and cooperation that are absolutely essential to improvement. Those companies and those societies that cooperate most effectively in the complex industrial environment of today will see the greatest improvements in productivity and quality. Cooperation is one of the key ingredients of improvement. With cooperation everyone wins—all the employees, the customers, and management—so it is called win-win. But what is most often practiced in the United States are systems of extreme differentiation, where for every winner there is at least one loser, so they are called win-lose systems.

The need for cooperation as an inherent element of management is one of Deming's key messages to corporations and to our society at large. So let's focus on some areas of cooperation considered by him to be of prime importance.

CHAPTER 6

Cooperation: Suppliers and Divisions

In 1950, when Deming went to Japan, that nation had a reputation for cheap goods and shoddy workmanship. During his visits he predicted a complete turnaround in the quality of manufactured goods of the nation if they followed his methods consistently and shared knowledge with suppliers, customers, and competitors.

Japan, he predicted, would become an economic powerhouse and consumers from all over the world would seek out its goods. Japan already had many ingredients necessary to become a great producing nation. It had an educated and hardworking populace, an infrastructure, and leadership. But one element that Deming added was a view of management. As discussed in the earlier chapters, this view has several important aspects that differentiate it from other management theories. Clarification of the meaning of quality, knowledge of variation, and the need to put quality first are fundamental axioms of the Deming view of management. But an equally important axiom is the need for cooperation.

Quality cannot be obtained, and improvement is impossible, without cooperation: cooperation among workers, among managers, between workers and managers, between the company and its suppliers, and even between the company and its competitors. Cooperation between competitors does not imply the absence of competition. In fact competition may be irrelevant in many instances. Competition that most benefits the consumer occurs in a framework of cooperation.

83

In effect, we have been conducting an experiment since 1950 between two very different management styles. This is as close as we could possibly come to conducting a controlled experiment on an international scale. Japan has followed one style of management and the United States another. According to Deming's predictions, Japan would prosper while the United States and other nations following other methods wouldn't be able to compete.

People are free to interpret Japan's rise in whatever way they wish. The power of Deming's prediction about Japan, which he made in 1950 and which has since proved accurate, is that he made it before the results were known. Many experts have chosen to interpret Japan's new prosperity in a way that vindicates their pet theory. These experts look to the Japanese as good examples, but the Japanese look to Deming for guidance in theory and practice. No nation, Japan included, is perfect. When Deming visits Japan, he often severely criticizes practices that have crept into their methods. And they listen.

The problem with interpreting something after the fact is that many reasons for the success or failure of a system can be inferred. Saying I told you so, when no prediction was made beforehand, is not a very convincing argument.

One aspect of the theory of quality management that Japan has embraced, and to which they may have had a cultural predisposition, is the need for cooperation. It just isn't possible for 120 million people to occupy a few islands equal in area to California without a great deal of cooperation. Of course, we in the United States have a tradition of cooperation as well. In the West and Midwest, neighbors cooperated in putting up a new barn. Our phone network under the old Bell System was one coordinated enterprise. But we also have a love affair with the idea that competition is the cure-all for our problems.

With 250 million Americans living in over 3 million square miles of rich land, cooperation has not been essential to our survival. We have formed some habits and methods of thinking that worked fine in the past but have to be reexamined in light of present circumstances and recent events. Some of our ideas were formed when free land was available and whoever got there first took title to it. But things are different now.

A Japanese Example

Competition is everywhere. Deming is not preaching an end to competition but more cooperation—competition in the framework of greater cooperation. One example is in the Japanese effort toward a new technology. Initially all the Japanese companies pool their resources to develop the technology. Rather than having several teams of researchers exploring the same subjects in their respective companies, their efforts are coordinated. The same work isn't duplicated by the various companies. As a result, the technology gets developed more quickly and thoroughly at lower cost. But when the products go to market, there is intense competition in price, features, and performances.

A European-American Example of Cooperation

Americans and Europeans practice cooperation to some extent. But not enough. One example comes from Heathrow Airport in London, where British Airways does all the airplane handling and is contracted by other airlines for the maintenance and servicing of their planes. If each airline had separate maintenance facilities, each would have to employ a crew and maintain docking space, spare parts inventory, and expensive diagnostic tools to service their planes. Much of this would lie idle, since no one airline has enough traffic to keep a crew constantly employed. By pooling resources and allowing one airline to handle all planes and provide maintenance services, there is minimal waste of time and money and no needless duplication. One airline can handle planes and provide maintenance at a lower price to everyone than if each maintained separate facilities. Everyone wins by such an arrangement. Valuable space isn't used up with duplicated facilities, the cost to each airline is less, quality is better, and the cost to the customer is also less.

Cooperation is something that can occur everywhere. But to compare Deming's views with other management theories, let's look at four areas commonly dealt with in management literature. These are a company's relations with its suppliers; intracompany relations, for instance, among divisions; a company's relations with its employees; and a company's interactions with other companies in the same industry.

A Different View

To highlight the difference between Deming's position and others', let's consider the view espoused by Michael Porter, a business professor formerly at Harvard and now at Columbia, in his book *Competitive Strategy: Techniques for Analyzing Industries and Competitors*.[1] On purchasing strategy Porter writes:

> Spread Purchases. Purchases of an item can be spread among alternate suppliers in such a way as to improve the firm's bargaining position. The business given to each individual supplier must be large enough to cause the supplier concern over losing it—spreading purchases too widely does not take advantage of structural bargaining position. However, purchasing everything from one supplier may yield that supplier too much of an opportunity to exercise power or build switching costs. Cutting across these considerations is the purchaser's ability to negotiate volume discounts, which is partly a matter of bargaining power and partly a matter of supplier economics. Balancing these factors, the purchaser would seek to create as much supplier dependence on its business as possible and reap the maximum volume discounts without exposing itself to too great a risk of falling prey to switching costs.[2]
>
> Create a threat of Backward Integration. Whether or not the purchaser actually desires to backward integrate into an item, its bargaining position is helped by the presence of a credible threat. This threat can be created through statement, leaked word or internal studies of the feasibility of integration, creation of contingency plans for integration with consultants or engineering firms, and so on.[3]

Unfortunately, this is representative of what is being done in American business and taught at American business schools. This represents a view common among managers who lack business degrees as well, indicating that similar ideas and practices may have preceded Porter's book by decades. Business schools may have only perpetuated and reinforced what Deming calls wrong practice. If we keep teaching our managers practices that only weaken American business, the result will be a decline in the ability of our companies to compete internationally and a declining standard of living for Americans.

Porter calls for spreading out purchasing as a means of maintaining leverage and playing one supplier off against another. By using the proper strategy, according to Porter, the lowest possible price of supply is obtained. No mention is made of quality, reliability or improvement. Implicit in this view is a win-lose view of the business process. If the purchaser is successful, he can keep his costs down, thus winning, while the supplier is losing. This is a zero-sum game view. There are only so many marbles. If one person grabs one, there is one less for someone else to grab.

Deming's view is distinctly different. According to him, price is meaningless without any reference to quality. What appears cheapest in price when coming in the door may actually end up being most expensive at the end. The point should be to lower total cost. Total cost can't always be measured accurately, but we know that quality makes a big difference in total cost.

One measure of quality and therefore total cost is the amount of variation in the incoming supply. Two products from two different sources may have acceptable quality, but one may be significantly superior for the purpose at hand. Each is different to the machines, and to the people who have to handle and process them. The same assembly process may have to be substantially adjusted when suppliers are switched.

Even if the quality of two products from different suppliers is equal, they are still substantially different products. Agricultural products are one example of great variability. Wheat from different fields is substantially different and behaves differently when being processed into flour. The wheat from each field is perfectly good, but a mill must be adjusted whenever the source of wheat changes. In manufactured goods, also, variability may not be evident to the naked eye, but to the machinery with which it interacts there are vast differences. Ford found that switching its assembly line to accept a foreign piston instead of a domestic piston required six hours of adjustment. Switching back also required six hours. But what would happen if they didn't make the adjustments but indiscriminately changed suppliers? Disaster. Waste would soar and quality would be destroyed. But that's exactly what many companies do.

Single Sourcing

Understandably, Deming urges companies to work toward using one supplier for each part purchased. This will lessen the variation for each part and improve overall quality and costs. But the benefits to both buyer and supplier don't end there. The supplier has large long-term customers and can commit resources to satisfying them. His production runs are longer, his costs are lower. By investing in his facilities, he can further lower costs. He can devote time to working with the buyer, understand the buyer's needs, and find out how his product is being used, which allows him to continually improve his quality and lower the costs for both of them. Through mutual cooperation they both win. Competitive strategy offers no such possibility.

The supplier needs to fully understand how his product fits into the overall scheme of things. He should fully understand how his product or service is being used today and how it may be used in the future. Written specifications, written bids, and an arm's length approach to suppliers are simply insufficient. They don't tell the supplier everything he needs to know in order to make the highest quality input at the lowest total cost.

A portion of the supplier's savings is passed on to the buyer and the customer. Everyone benefits from higher quality. Customers, producers, suppliers. Everyone benefits through cooperation.

Naturally suppliers have to be chosen with care. They need to be informed of the company's intent and they should be chosen based on their commitment to continual improvement of quality. The quality of the individuals is important. One should only deal with honorable people.

An Objection

One objection I hear from time to time is that although this sounds very nice in theory, it won't work in practice. The world isn't like that, according to some. Americans would never work that way, according to others. The reality is that this has been adopted by some of our largest and best firms, and they will never go back to the old way of spreading out purchases. They can't afford to.

Ford is now purchasing 95 percent of its parts from single sources! GM is moving quickly in the same direction. Ninety-five percent may be the upper limit for single sourcing. There are some items that can't be obtained from just one source: No single tire manufacturer can supply either GM or Ford with all the tires it needs.

Another Objection

Some students and managers, on hearing Deming discuss the benefits of single sourcing, argue that a second source of supply serves as insurance. Should their main supplier suffer a fire or other calamity, they have a backup source. But not having single sourcing when your competitor does makes you uncompetitive. Going out of business is a heavy price to pay for insurance.

But there is another aspect to consider. Having two suppliers instead of one doubles the risk of calamity that might disrupt supplies. With two suppliers there are twice as many plants, doubling the risk; with three suppliers there is three times the risk.

When a calamity strikes, management has to revert to solving lots of day-to-day problems. But crisis management should be reserved for real crises. During other times problem solving and improving should be balanced.

Having a cooperative relationship with suppliers means a complete change in attitude toward them. Everything changes. Suppliers have to be told well in advance of new and planned products so they in turn can plan and prepare. They have to be shown how their product is being used. Knowledge of the company's and the supplier's process has to be exchanged so that each can adjust and coordinate its methods. But working like this with one supplier is hard enough. With two it would be twice as time consuming, making it prohibitive. As Deming says, "No one has the resources to work with one supplier fully. How could you possible work with two?"

One Supplier for Each Part

Just to clarify, by one supplier is meant one supplier for each part or service, but the company will have different suppliers for different items. All the screws of a certain type may be supplied by one company, but the chemical solution to clean them may come from another.

Cooperation, a Source of Strength

Deming's view of company-supplier relations is called win-win because the company and its supplier are working together; if one wins, the other wins, and so do the ultimate customers. The company and its suppliers recognize a common stake and work together instead of at cross purposes. Competition is often better than the cooperation found among divisions of companies that are run along conventional lines.

Close cooperation is a source of strength leading to greater competitiveness. But Americans who first observed such relationships in Japan often considered it a handicap that the Japanese would have to overcome in order to compete with the United States.

Intra-Company Cooperation

A second area where cooperation is called for by Deming is in intra-company policy. Competition within a company is often fostered by setting up divisions and departments as profit centers. Profit center managers are judged by their profit numbers only, the idea being that such competition will keep the division managers on their toes, all constantly giving their best. Since each manager has control over her own profit, each will maximize her profit. Profit for the firm as a whole is just the sum total of profit of the individual parts so the reasoning goes; if each part is maximized, the whole will be maximized.

This would be the case if each unit were truly independent of the others. But as I emphasize repeatedly, in any complex process, whether in service or manufacturing, that is not the case. A company is a highly interdependent operation. A small defect may be easy and inexpensive to correct early in the process but very expensive to correct elsewhere.

One company Deming visited had six separate divisions, each of which was judged separately. The company was profitable and resisted any suggestion for change. But as he pointed out, with greater cooperation it could be six to ten times more profitable. Each division made parts or provided services for the others. But they had developed a fortress mentality: design or manufacture the item and throw it over the fence to the next division.

If one division were to spend a little more time and effort to ensure that their product or service was optimal for the next division, it would be penalized with lower short-term profits and lower ratings and bonuses for its managers.

Each division has no incentive to find out what the next division really needs. Each division is maximizing its own position in the current system, but profit and quality for the whole company suffer.

Sub-optimization

When maximizing the parts leads to less than optimal results for the whole, we have sub-optimization. Sub-optimization will occur whenever the individual parts of a process are not truly independent. Even the slightest form of interdependence among departments will lead to sub-optimization if we try to maximize the results of each department.

Deming calls for a distinctly different policy toward intra-company relations. Departments and divisions must cooperate to maximize the return to the firm and the firm's customers. Cooperation among divisions and departments has to replace competition and the fortress mentality that results. Market research, design, engineering, manufacturing, marketing all have to cooperate from the beginning.

Quality Control Circles

It's not surprising, then, that Deming advocates breaking down barriers between departments. Each department has to learn what the others need and what the others can provide. One method successfully employed in Japan, but with little success in the United States, is quality control circles. QC circles are nothing more than formalized meetings of workers, foremen, and engineers from various departments. By pooling their knowledge of a process, they are better able to tackle problems of quality.

In the United States most of the attempts to create QC circles have been failures. American management have been more interested in determining who deserves credit or blame than in instituting improvement. Management turned a deaf ear toward policy changes because they were ignorant of the impact that cooperation can have on quality. Quality control circles were installed like air conditioners and were expected to improve quality at the turn of a switch. But the real work necessary to improve quality belongs to management. The way our companies are run has to change if we are to compete effectively.

CHAPTER 7

Cooperation Between Management and Workers

A third area where Deming calls for greater cooperation is in relations between a company and its employees. Much of the literature on management calls for competition and differentiation among workers as the best way of bringing out the best in them and achieving desired results. A past president of the United States has advocated merit pay for teachers as being the best way to ensure improvement in the reading scores of our children. Some writers call for greater accountability. The computer is seen as the sure way out of our problems by providing management with intricate details about each person's performance. All these views are wrong!

The idea of fostering as much competition as possible has part of its roots in the belief that competition and reward systems cull the strong from the weak, the worker from the drone. I suspect that a mistaken notion of Darwin's theory of evolution is at least subconsciously part of the intellectual justification for the views that dominate American management.

When Darwin spoke of survival of the fittest, he was contemplating the origins of species—survival of the fittest species, not the fittest individual. One of the distinguishing characteristics of human beings, in addition to their intellectual prowess and their manual dexterity, is their cooperative ability. Through cooperative gathering, hunting, and farming, humans have become numerically superior to animals that were stronger and swifter than they.

Nature doesn't operate through merit reviews, as one simple example should illustrate.

An Example of Merit Pay

One group of workers in the customs department is responsible for finding and confiscating an average of $124,000 in illegal drugs each year. Another group on average finds and confiscates $3 million of illegal drugs each year. The second group is obviously better at the job and deserves merit increases. The problem is that the first group comprises humans and the second group trained dogs.

Forcing competition into situations that require cooperation for successful completion is counterproductive. Another way of saying the same thing is that forcing competition between workers wherever the dominant cause of variation in performance is due to the system will lead to conflict, not competition, and certainly not improvement.

In the red bead experiment we had a system that was truly in statistical control. All the differences in performance between individuals (the variation) were due to common causes (the system). There were no special causes. This is not an unrealistic situation. Most ongoing operations have a high level of stability. Variation may be due to both common and special causes, to both the system and individuals. But a typical operation may have only 6 percent of the differences among individuals due to the individuals themselves and 94 percent due to the system. But if management assumes that all the differences among people are due to the individuals and none are inherent in the system, as most managers do, then they would be wrong 94 percent of the time.

Further, if people are penalized for being below some arbitrary level, when their performance is due in large measure to factors beyond their control, they will be demoralized, as will the whole company. Eventually almost everyone will be below that arbitrary level. Obviously, when the variation is due to chance, penalizing those below average or in the bottom 10 percent will not improve the performance of any individual or of the company. It will destroy those individuals who receive a poor rating in any given year. It will destroy the desire to help anyone else because the help one gives may allow the other to receive a higher rating than the helper.

The fundamental problem of American management is that we are systematically destroying the people who work in the system, both hourly workers and managers alike. Our reward system destroys any possibility of teamwork by incorrectly distinguishing the above average from the below average when the difference is due to chance. There are two types of mistakes that management can make.

1. Management can distinguish individuals based on differences in measured performance when in fact no real distinction exists, a type one mistake. Another way of saying this is that a common cause is mistaken for a special cause.

2. Management can fail to distinguish real differences in performance, a type two error. Here a special cause is mistaken for a common cause.

The biggest mistake of American management has been type one errors, assuming that each difference in the performance of individuals is due entirely to the individual when in fact most of the variation is due to chance.

This still leaves room for individual differences. If someone is performing not just better than average, but better than the system as measured by the control limits, then something unusual is going on and is worth investigating. There is nothing wrong with rewarding workers who are outside the system.

But more important than any consideration of additional compensation is the prospect of adopting the methods employed by those outside the system to everyone else. If in fact they are doing something different, then it may be applicable elsewhere. But no rational person will divulge techniques that lead to superior results in an environment of fear. If divulging his methods may lead to someone else getting a higher rating at his expense, he would have to be a fool to cooperate.

Some people may be performing below the capability of the system. Management should find out who is below the system and help them. Some may need training. Training is management's responsibility. Some may need a change of assignment. Fear will not bring them into the system. Knowledge will.

In the Deming view, a leader's job is not to judge people but to determine who is in need of special help and make sure he receives it. A leader should not differentiate the above average from the below average or recite pithy statements, but actively work to determine the real causes of problems and then work to eliminate the real causes. A leader forgives mistakes. A leader fosters cooperation by eliminating barriers to cooperation and barriers to enjoyment of work. A leader fosters the continual development of all those who work for him.

A Personal Example from the Little Leagues

Several years after I began studying with Deming, I had the privilege of coaching a Little League soccer team comprised of my son and twelve other six-year-olds.

As I was coaching, I realized that none of the coaches I had played for really understood teamwork. I had played three sports in high school, so I had had ample exposure to coaching styles.

My own coaching methods began to differ radically from those of any coach I knew personally. I was applying Deming's teachings. My job as coach was not to criticize or distinguish between above-average players and below-average players. My job was to teach the skills, the game, and physical discipline; to make sure that every player had a really good time at each practice and at each game; to encourage continual improvement (which of course meant risk taking and occasional failure); and to encourage teamwork.

I did everything I could to make practices fun and to turn the athletes on to soccer in particular and sports in general. Each practice ended with a scrimmage. I would pick two captains, who would then choose sides. Each captain would then assign positions to each player on his scrimmage squad, and we would play for the balance of the practice.

Each athlete received a turn at being captain. No one had a second turn until everyone had been captain at least once. Many players looked forward to the practices as much as or more than the games. My thinking was that if they loved playing and practicing, they would do it often, and improve.

Before the games I would emphasize that I didn't care about scoring goals or winning, I just wanted them to have fun, to improve, and to play like a team, not a mob of unrelated individuals. For someone like myself, brought up under a system that constantly emphasized winning, this was not an easy thing to do.

After the games I would ask a question like, "Who scored that first goal?" Initially one boy would raise his hand and I would respond, "No! We all scored that goal. Every person on a team is responsible for scoring a goal. The individual who touches it last is the one who may get the statistic, but scoring a goal starts with the goalie passing to a defender, who passes to a midfielder, who passes to a forward. If the forward scores, it is because of everyone else on the team, not just him.

"Now, who scored that goal?" All the athletes would raise their hands. All of them received credit for each goal scored. Unbeknownst to them, they had received their first lecture on common causes.

In our league we presented participation trophies to all the players. In addition, each coach had three trophies that he could present as he saw fit. All of the coaches, except for myself, found some way to single out three players as more outstanding. This, of course, clashed with my view of teamwork, so I had the best-player trophy duplicated and presented one to each player on my team.

Initially there was some resentment from some parents. From what I could tell, the children didn't mind.

It should be mentioned that in the four years I coached, my teams had the best record in the league each of the four years. In fact, in four years we lost all of one game. But more important, from my point of view, is that I turned on a lot of good athletes to team sports, soccer in particular. They were motivated by intrinsic motivation, the love of the game, the desire to play well, not higher pay or bigger trophies. My athletes improved considerably each year, to the point that each was a desirable player from any coach's point of view.

An Example from the Big Leagues

One example doesn't prove one method is better than another. Little League may not translate well into the big leagues. But the following advertisement by Panhandle Eastern Corporation, which appeared in the *Wall Street Journal* and other newspapers in 1986, indicates that a similar coaching philosophy has had enormous success over a long period of time in college athletics. The text is reproduced below in its entirety.

JOHN WOODEN, ON STAYING POWER

John Wooden is the only man ever enshrined in the basketball Hall of Fame as both player and coach. He retired after 40 years of coaching, leaving a record unparalleled in American sport.

During his 27 years as coach of UCLA, his teams never had a losing season. In his last 12 years there, they won ten national championships, seven of those in succession, and still hold the world's record for the longest winning streak in any major sport—88 games bridging four seasons.

Although retired now, he still conducts coaching clinics and basketball camps, and lectures widely.

"Like most coaches, my program revolved around fundamentals, conditioning, and teamwork. But I differed radically in several respects. I never worried about how our opponents would play us, and I never talked about winning.

Peaks create valleys

"I believe that for every artificial peak you create, you also create valleys. When you get too high for anything, emotion takes over and consistency of performance is lost and you will be unduly affected when adversity comes. I emphasized constant improvement and steady performance.

"I have often said, 'The mark of a true champion is to always perform near your own level of competency.' We were able to do that by never being satisfied with the past and always planning for what was to come. I believe that failure to prepare is preparing to fail. This constant focus on the future is one reason we continued staying near the top once we got there.

Develop yourself, don't worry about opponents

"I probably scouted opponents less than any coach in the country. Less than most high school coaches. I don't need to know that this forward likes to drive the outside. You're not supposed to give the outside to any forward whenever he tries it. Sound offensive and defensive principles apply to any style of play.

"Rather than having my teams prepare to play a certain team each week, I prepared to play anybody. I didn't want my players worrying about the other fellows. I wanted them executing the sound offensive and defensive principles we taught in practice.

There's no pillow as soft as
a clear conscience

"To me, success isn't outscoring someone, it's the peace of mind that comes from self-satisfaction in knowing you did your best. That's something each individual must determine for himself. You can fool others, but you can't fool yourself.

"Many people are surprised to learn that in 27 years at UCLA, I never once talked about winning. Instead I would tell my players before games, 'When it's over, I want your head up. And there's only one way your head can be up, that's for you to know, not me, that you gave the best effort of which you're capable. If you do that, then the score doesn't really matter, although I have a feeling that if you do that, the score will be to your liking.' I honestly, deeply believe that in not stressing winning as such, we won more than we would have if I'd stressed outscoring opponents.

Why do so many people dread adversity,
when it is only through adversity that
we grow stronger?

"There's no great fun, satisfaction or joy derived from doing something that's easy. Failure is never fatal, but failure to change might be.

Your strength as an individual depends on, and will be in direct proportion to, how you react to both praise and criticism. If you become too concerned about either, the effect on you is certain to be adverse.

The main ingredient of stardom

"I always taught players that the main ingredient of stardom is the rest of the team. It's amazing how much can be accomplished if no one cares who gets the credit. That's why I was as concerned with a player's character as I was with his ability.

> "While it may be possible to reach the top of one's profession on sheer ability, it is impossible to stay there without hard work and character. One's character may be quite different from one's reputation.
>
> "Your character is what you really are. Your reputation is only what others think you are. I made a determined effort to evaluate character. I looked for young men who would play the game hard, but clean, and who would always be trying to improve themselves to help the team. Then, if their ability warranted it, the championships would take care of themselves."

One sentence from Mr. Wooden's essay helps illuminate some of the ill effects of merit systems and incentive pay plans that foster competition among people who should be working together. "It's amazing how much can be accomplished if no one cares who gets the credit."

A Personal Example from the Banking League

My own experience in banking long ago led me to a similar conclusion. I had joined the New York branch of a foreign bank that in a few years had developed a reputation as a very professional organization. The bank had hired some very talented American bankers and become a major underwriter of international loans and a respected international lender. There was no scorecard on individual performance. The individual bankers were well compensated, but their efforts seemed to be driven by a sense of professionalism: a desire to excel and do what they enjoyed doing—making and syndicating high-quality loans.

Some time after I joined the bank, a Brazilian arrived from the home office. He couldn't speak English and knew nothing about international banking, so no one could figure out his function.

We soon learned that this man was keeping detailed records of costs and revenues by hand, and every loan had been assigned to someone. Arbitrarily? No, the loans seemed to have been assigned based on one's relationship with Mr. Bastos. Within a week of the new system becoming common knowledge, the nature of the bank changed forever. Now everyone became concerned with who owned which loan. Cooperation went out the window. We all had to concentrate on getting our assigned loans up. Fully 30 percent of our time went to internal politics, with each person vying for each existing loan and each new loan. In one stroke management had changed our jobs from making high-quality loans to competing internally for credit. Within two years most of the individuals who had built up the branch left.

When everyone is out for himself, to help his own rating, people who should be working together are fighting one another. Greater effort on everyone's part may only mean a greater attempt to get credit or expand one's turf. Greater effort may produce poorer results for the company. Just as in any team sport, a business that operates like a mob of unrelated individuals will get clobbered when it is up against an organization where the individuals work for a common goal without concern for who gets credit.

Motivation?

Executives and business students often feel lost after hearing Deming rail against merit plans and the annual performance review. It seems to some that he is asking them to give up control of the work force. Questions like the following are often asked: "But how does one motivate people without plans that distinguish and rank performance?" "How does one keep the workers honest?"

The answer is to tap intrinsic motivation. This goes by many names. People do a good job because of pride in their work, a sense of professionalism, love for their work, self-respect. The list of names used to describe intrinsic motivation could be quite long.

Modern management literature since the end of World War II has laid heavy stress on questions such as these: "How does management motivate its people to produce at maximum?" "How does management control its people so that they work hard and don't sluff off or make mistakes?" The answers that have emerged over the last forty years reflect each writer's underlying assumptions about the causes of productivity and the causes of defects. As long as writers of books on management are ignorant of the interactive nature of common causes—in fact even ignorant of the existence of common causes—they will lay all blame at the feet of the hourly worker and middle management.

Our so-called modern management methods have maintained that the vast majority of the problems that arise are caused by those working in the system. It follows that the emphasis in modern management would be determining accountability for each piece of production and each defect. Merit systems, holding the worker accountable, competition at every turn, and culling the strong from the weak all stem from mistaken assumptions about the nature of reality. Cooperation, when it does have a role in modern management literature, is often incidental to the efforts of the individuals toiling in the system.

The very questions that are asked in management literature reflect a mistaken view of reality. While most writers will insist they are cognizant that humans are not machines, in one important respect much of modern management literature does not distinguish between the two. To get a machine to work harder, one just turns up the inputs. Step on the accelerator and a car moves faster. Turn up the thermostat and a boiler heats more. The corresponding analogy toward humans is tangible rewards or extrinsic motivation. Offer someone more money and he'll work harder, according to this thinking. Punish someone for errors and he'll make less. Let each individual know how many widgets he's making and he'll work to make as many as he can, according to conventional thinking.

Two fundamental faults with this type of thinking have already been thoroughly discussed in previous chapters:

1. More is not necessarily better. In fact, if quality suffers, more may be much less. Compaq Computer Company developed a whole new plant to produce its computers. They hung from the ceiling large monitors, visible to all the plant workers, displaying current production numbers. The workers kept watching the figures. Production was increasing, but quality was falling. Management decided to turn the monitors off and told the workers they cared about quality first and foremost. Production levels declined a bit but quality improved. The turned-off monitors were left up as a reminder that numbers were not the key.

2. No matter how much pressure, no matter what the rewards, individuals working in the system are helpless to change things beyond their control. When the system is the major cause of problems, as happens most often, only action on the system can make real improvements. Only management is in a position to work

on the system. That is its responsibility. Quality is made in the boardroom. People working in the system can only produce at the level inherent in the system. They may do worse, but they cannot exceed the capability of the system while working in it.

But there is a third fundamental problem with the questions posed in management literature. It is the assumption that people are *only* motivated by external rewards. As a result we have, in most American firms, killed intrinsic motivation.

In the Deming view, intrinsic motivation is the engine for improvement. If it is kept alive and nourished, quality can and will occur. If it is killed, quality dies with it. One of management's main jobs in the Deming point of view is to foster intrinsic motivation. One way management can judge how well it has done its job is to find out if the people working in the system experience pride of workmanship or if they love their work.

How many people today experience joy and real fulfillment in their work? Deming estimates that perhaps 10 percent of the hourly workers and 2 percent of middle management really enjoy their work. By this measure, at least, American management has failed.

Value of Extrinsic Motivation

This does not mean to say that extrinsic motivation isn't important. It is difficult to experience pride of workmanship or to enjoy your work if you don't earn enough to feed your family or if you always have to worry about being able to meet the mortgage. For most of us, the initial motivation may be extrinsic in nature. But if you hate your work, all the money in the world can't make it a better job.

After a point, extrinsic motivation won't help and may even backfire. But joy in one's work can provide unlimited motivation. People who love their work have to be pulled away from it.

Norb Keller of General Motors, at a meeting of managers with Deming, said, "If GM were to double everybody's pay beginning next month, nobody would do a better job and no one would be happier. If you were able to rank people, the company would not be better off. What could you do with that information? Nothing."

The difference between Deming's view of management and those of others can be stated in the following way. Most other management theories recommend that in trying to tap and direct people's creative energies management put their efforts into judging people—rewarding the above average and punishing the below average—as the way to improve and become competitive. In Deming's view, management should look for problems and the real causes of problems and work to eliminate them. To unleash the creative efforts of people, management must work to eliminate the barriers to joy of work for its people. Among some of the causes of problems are ignorance of variation, poor training, poor supplies, the design of the product, the design of the production facilities, poor equipment and tools, lack of cooperation between departments. Among some of the barriers to joy of work are the reward system; having to produce inferior products or services, because the number of units produced is management's sole concern; waste occurring because of poor planning or poor supplies.

CHAPTER 8

Cooperation Among Competitors

An Obvious Example

Let's consider for the moment the mathematics of a utility. Suppose it cost $100 million to build and install all the underground pipes and equipment necessary to service a community of 100,000 homes with natural gas for heating and cooking. For the sake of argument, let's say this is the total cost for a company to enter the business. The investment per household is $1,000, and the business has to recover this amount through the rates it charges its customers.

One day one of the customers decides to establish a competitor. The new firm has to build a new pipe system costing $100 million. The consumer now has a choice, but the cost that the industry has to recover is $200 million, or $2,000 per household, twice as much as with just one gas company. Any presumed efficiency gained from additional competition cannot make up for the inefficiency inherent in duplicating the delivery system and doubling the cost to the industry, which, of course, is eventually borne by the customers.

We already recognize the logic of this situation and have established laws and procedures allowing one company and only one company to operate the delivery systems for telephone service, natural gas, electricity, or video cable services.

An Example with Foreign Competition

Let's look at another hypothetical example. The ten leading technological companies of country A are all interested in the super-duper computer vial, a remarkable technology allowing them to create intelligent robots capable of cleaning house and uttering sincere-sounding compliments to its owners, helping them through life's harder moments. Everyone would want such a robot. I've already ordered two.

Unfortunately, to perfect the super-duper computer vial device, the industry must develop and perfect several unrelated technologies at a cost of about $1 billion. Nevertheless, the prospects for the device are phenomenal, so all ten companies pursue the project and invest the $1 billion necessary. The development cost to the industry is $10 billion. Each firm duplicates the effort of the others. There are roughly one billion people worldwide who might want the product, so the development cost to the industry is $10 per customer.

Far away on another continent, the four most technologically advanced companies of country B are also aware of the possibilities of the device, which is here known by its acronym, the SDC vial. They decide to develop the device. But their approach is different. They combine and coordinate their efforts. Researchers from the four companies gather together, split the work, and then share all knowledge among themselves. The total cost to the industry is $1 billion. The total cost to each company, if the costs are evenly divided, is $250 million, or one-fourth of the cost to each company in the other country.

The industry of country B is looking at the same market of one billion people, but the cost of developing the technology, which we'll assume dwarfs the cost of producing the device, is only $1 billion, or $1 per customer—one-tenth the cost of that for country A. The companies of country B assault the market with an excellent high-quality SDC device costing $1.25 and make enormous profits, while the companies of A have to charge at least $10 just to recover their research and development costs.

Meanwhile the companies of country B compete ferociously in the marketplace against the companies of country A and each other. The relative positions of the four companies of country B haven't been helped or hurt by their cooperative effort. Each of the four is eager to offer the best device and vies aggressively for market share. While there was cooperation to overcome the large hurdle of development, they now compete vigorously.

The companies of A, on the other hand, just aren't competitive. The irony is that because of excessive competition they have been left unable to compete! They start calling for government investigations into the pricing policies of the gang of four companies from abroad. Rather than adopting some of the more successful methods and ideas, they call for country B to change its ways.

In this example the companies of country A may be forced to change because of the competition from country B. But there is an intrinsic reason why they should cooperate among themselves, at least in the development stage. Their customers are better served through cooperation. The costs of development are much lower, and the price charged can accordingly be lower. The customers benefit from lower cost while receiving quality that is at least equal, if not better.

An Example Without Foreign Competition

Let's look at one more case. Three long-distance phone companies are confronted with the same problem. They must lay a transatlantic cable to upgrade service to Europe. The cost of laying the cable is $100 million, and one cable can service the needs of all three for the foreseeable future. The companies collectively could build one, two, or three cables, but, clearly, from the point of view of lower costs to the consumer, some form of cooperation where all three share a cable network is preferable.

In the common lexicon, cooperation among competitors is a dirty phrase, implying the absence of competition and the existence of collusion on price. But in the last two examples, competition isn't weakened through cooperation; if anything, it's strengthened. With cooperation more competitors, not fewer, can survive, making for a stronger market. Notice that Japan, with its roughly 120 million people, has nine car companies, while the United States, with over 250 million people, has three.

What is being suggested is not totally radical or difficult to comprehend. It is common sense. We need more cooperation. Companies should be open to and actively search out areas of cooperation.

Standards

Industrial standards are another form of cooperation that may seem mundane but are very important. Life would be substantially more difficult without standards. Just consider some of the simple but essential standards. International time or Greenwich mean time is one example. We take it for granted that anywhere in the world an hour has sixty minutes and 2:30 P.M. means the same thing in Calcutta as in New York, but such a convention only came about because of worldwide cooperation and agreement.

Radio batteries are standardized. AA batteries bought in Europe will fit the alarm clock you bought in Atlanta and the radio from Asia. You may prefer one brand over all others, but each will fit.

When standards don't exist, even a simple replacement can be a major problem. Watch batteries are one example. I was painfully made aware of the fact that there are more than thirty different kinds of watch batteries. Most are so similar that visual inspection is not enough. You must try them to see if they fit. Very few stores carry them.

Our corporations use standards and still establish new ones, but guess who has taken the lead in standard setting?

Golf, Anyone?

Dr. William G. Ouchi, a noted author and professor of business at the Graduate School of Management at UCLA, was the guest speaker at a meeting of a U.S. trade association held in Florida. The participants attended meetings from nine in the morning until noon, then broke for lunch. The afternoon sessions included several activities such as golf and fishing. On the third day Dr. Ouchi addressed all the participants and gave this talk:

> While you are out on the golf course this afternoon, waiting for your partner to tee up, I want you to think about something. Last month I was in Tokyo, where I visited your trade association counterpart. It represents the roughly two hundred Japanese companies who are your direct competitors. They are now holding meetings from eight each morning until nine each night, five days a week, for three months straight, so that one company's oscilloscope will connect to another company's analyzer, so that they can agree on product safety

standards to recommend to the government (to speed up getting to the marketplace), so that they can agree on their needs for changes in regulations, export policy, and financing and then approach their government with one voice to ask for cooperation. Tell me who you think is going to be in better shape five years from now.[1]

Problems When Standards Don't Exist

It is not unusual for new technologies to fail because of a lack of standards. Quadraphonic sound is one example. Several competing standards confused the consumer and prevented any single standard from reaching critical mass. The companies were competing on the basis of standards. Consumers didn't give a hoot which standard prevailed; they were only interested in the better sound associated with the new technologies. But because of the confusion, no company was able to garner sufficient business. The record companies didn't know which standard to support, so their efforts were fragmented. Consumers were confused so they held back until the smoke cleared. When the smoke cleared, no one was left.

Competing Standards

Japanese companies have also competed on the basis of standards to their regret, and at great loss to consumers and producers alike. When home video recorders first became available, two incompatible systems were introduced by two large consortiums. One was the Beta system led by Sony and the other was the VHS system led by Panasonic's corporate parent Matsushita. Both standards were directed toward the same consumers for the same purpose. Neither had any significant advantage over the other. Eventually one won out, but only after great loss to consumers who had tapes they couldn't play on the new machines and machines that couldn't play the newer tapes. The market developed more slowly than it could have. Movie companies lost, having to produce two versions of each movie. This kept their costs up and prices higher than would have been the case if only one standard existed.

The lesson wasn't lost on the manufacturers. Recently Matsushita and Sony joined N.V. Philips, the large Dutch electronics firm, to establish a standard format for the new sound, data, graphics, and video information technology called compact disk interactive.

Competition among U.S. computer companies over standards for the next generation of personal computers based on the Intel microprocessor has led to confusion among users and split the efforts of the numerous firms that produce additional hardware and software for the machines. IBM unilaterally adopted a new standard and simultaneously raised its royalty fees for the use of its patents. Several of the other major computer manufacturers have refused to go along and have adopted a different standard.

More than one standard is sometimes appropriate. Home electronics may require different standards than professional electronic equipment. Computers for an engineer's use may require a different standard than computers for financial professionals. Sometimes two standards for the same market are appropriate. Certainly two standards are better than five—and better than none.

But in the case of personal computers based on the same microprocessor, using the same software and aimed at the same market, one standard is better for the consumer and allows the technology to develop faster. When two standards exist where one will do, we have waste.

Room for Voluntary Standards

Standards don't have to be formal. An executive from Bethlehem Steel pointed out to James Bakken, vice president at Ford Motor Company, that Ford buys forty-one different thicknesses of steel between .027 and .045 inches thick from them. "How can any steel company give you precision and economy with so many thicknesses?" he asked Bakken.

A good solution would be for all the domestic auto manufacturers to mutually decide on five different thicknesses of steel in this range. This would be a voluntary standard. If one of the manufacturers wanted to innovate with a different thickness of steel, it would be free to do so. If it turned out five thicknesses were not enough or the thicknesses were not optimal, they could be changed. The standard could be reviewed every few years. Everyone would win with five standard thicknesses, instead of forty-one for Ford, fifty for GM, and thirty for Chrysler. The steel manufacturers could have longer runs. They could produce greater precision at greater economy. The auto manufacturers would have lower retooling costs. Less waste, higher quality. Would such cooperation between the producers help or hurt the consumer? Would competition be lessened in any way by such cooperation? Of course not! Still some will point to this as a form of collusion between producers.

Many executives fear possible repercussions from government enforcement of antitrust laws. In some cases they are justified in their fears. But industry has to take the lead. When it doesn't cooperate and speak to government with one voice, the result is regulation, which can be extremely restrictive and less than optimal.

There is nothing particularly difficult or profound in the notion that greater cooperation would help the productivity, quality, and competitive position of our industry. It is common sense. But if nothing is done to foster more cooperation, our position will not improve.

To revert to a sports analogy for a moment, imagine how our national pastime would be played if there weren't a great deal of cooperation and agreement before the first pitch was thrown. When two teams meet to play, they have already agreed on the time and place of the game, the rules of play, and the standards for the balls, bats, and uniforms. Financial arrangements have already been worked out regarding compensation to the teams and the players. If all this cooperation hadn't been worked out in advance, the result would be chaos. While this may seem trivial, I point it out just to remind the reader that even in the most competitive situations a great deal of cooperation is necessary. Without cooperation there couldn't be competition.

When duplication of effort and excessive conflict are a way of life, the results may be very much less than the sum of the parts. Two plus two may not equal four; they may equal zero or anything in between. Two steps forward followed by two steps back means a net movement of zero. Doubling the effort, doubling the resources directed at a problem, won't double the results if it's ill conceived or if waste, duplicity, and conflict are a way of life.

Compare and Shop

Suppose visitors from a distant star system come to Earth and have to replace some parts for their spaceship. They observe two societies. In one, everyone at every level is fighting and arguing. It's worker versus worker, workers versus managers, managers versus managers, companies versus companies, companies versus their suppliers, and government versus everyone else.

In the other society, harmony and cooperation are stressed. Workers work together. Management is on their side. Companies cooperate at times. They actively seek areas of cooperation. Companies and their suppliers plan and work together. And the government looks for and fosters cooperation, at least on important matters.

Where are they going to buy the replacement parts for their spaceship, knowing the parts have to perform over several hundred light-years of space travel, and that they can ill afford a faulty part?

Deming isn't asking Americans to wear kimonos and use chopsticks or anything particularly exotic—just urging us to use some common sense and cooperate more. Doing so, according to him, will take us a long way in becoming more competitive internationally. The ultimate test of any system is in the marketplace. Can we afford not to listen?

CHAPTER 9

The Need for Transformation

Let's summarize what we've covered so far. Understanding Deming's philosophy of management requires that we comprehend four important axioms:

1. Quality and cost are not opposites or trade-offs, with one being improved at the expense of the other. Instead both can be constantly improved.
2. The meaning of quality is different from conventional views that mistake exotic materials and fail-safe designs for quality. In Deming's view, quality is best understood from the point of view of the customer, but one important component of quality is improving uniformity.
3. Variation is a naturally occurring phenomenon. It is not an exception or fault. Variation is treated differently depending on whether we are dealing with a stable or unstable system. A stable system creates both successes and failures. Lowering the number of defects in a stable system can only be achieved by working on the system.
4. Cooperation is a fundamental ingredient that leads to improvement. Competition is often at work and helps determine which products and which companies survive, but there are times when competition is irrelevant and times when competition is inappropriate.

In conventional thinking, competition is always preferred over cooperation.

There is another fundamental point pervading Deming's teachings. Why is anyone interested in his theories and ideas of management? Because they work!

The only reason anyone should be interested in any scientific theory, whether it be of business or astronomy, is because of its ability to predict.

Now, this may seem obvious, but consider how rarely in business a prediction or plan is compared with its results. In my first job at a major New York bank, for instance, a five-year plan was drawn up every year. The problem was that a new five-year plan was drawn up each year without any reference to the last five-year plan. In fact, no one ever looked at the plan once it was approved and filed away.

A scarier example comes from the field of economics. When I first met Deming, I was considering studying for an advanced degree in economics. In the very first class the professor had me dizzy with rules of calculus required to understand new economic theory. But when a student asked about the comparison of results to prediction, he drew a blank. The new theory had little or no predictive value, no relation to this world.

Now good theory is important—we can't progress without it; but a theory with no predictive ability is of no value. Too many people believe that if a theory is complicated or rife with mathematics, it is science. In most cases it is neither good mathematics nor good science.

I have the distinct impression that business writers refer to conventional management as management science because a lot of measuring and numerical analysis is part of the method. If we have a heavy reliance on computer analysis, we have good scientific method, right? NONSENSE!

You have to ask yourself, with all the M.B.A.'s entering management ranks, with the massive amount of management literature generated since the end of World War II, with the new methods of management and the conspicuous use of computers in management, has our competitive situation improved or deteriorated?

The Deming-Shewhart Cycle of Continual Improvement

One of the most powerful ideas that Deming presented in his lectures on quality control in Japan, beginning in 1950, was the cycle of continual improvement, based on ideas first expounded by Shewhart. The cycle has four steps. The first is to plan a change of whatever you're trying to improve. The second is to carry out the change on a small scale. The third step is to observe the results. The fourth step is to study the results and decide what you've learned from the change.

The cycle is then repeated again and again. One doesn't make a change in one cycle and then undo it in the next cycle—that's just a waste of time. When you plan a change, you are saying, "I believe this change will make things better." If it doesn't, you've learned a great deal.

As you improve your process, you improve your knowledge of the process at the same time. Improvement of the product and process goes hand in hand with greater understanding and better theory.

Maybe this is nothing more than the application of the scientific method to business, but it's the only place where I have seen it done.

Small but Powerful

Deming's theory represents a fundamentally different way of viewing management. One's initial inclination, when first encountering it, is to adopt those of his methods that are to one's liking and to avoid those that clash with the old view. But this fails to capture the true power of his way.

We can draw an analogy from the field of medicine. Hospitals used to be considered places where you went to die. Once you went in, you were a goner for sure. Surgeons used to jump from one patient to the next without washing their hands or changing their garments. Somebody made the implausible and unintuitive suggestion that they were actually spreading diseases from one patient to another because disease was caused by microscopic entities, or germs, which were too small to be seen by the unaided eye. When surgeons simply washed thoroughly, cleaned all their tools, and changed their aprons after each patient, the number of patients who lived improved dramatically. But established surgeons didn't rush to change their ways. They liked the tried and true. The new way caught on as younger surgeons trained in the new theory replaced the older ones who retired.

Individual doctors could improve their success rates by adopting the new techniques. But when the new way was fully adopted and understood throughout the medical profession, real progress became a way of life.

Similarly, managers can adopt some of Deming's methods with good success, but by their fully understanding his theory and embracing it, real and continual progress becomes a way of life.

Deming has been accused of being obscure by some, but as I have tried to point out, his ideas are quite straightforward and clear.

Imagine a hypothetical conversation between a chief executive officer of a company experiencing competitive problems and Deming:

CHIEF: Dr. Deming, I need your help. Until a few years ago our company was prosperous and our shareholders were happy. Recently our competitors have started to come out with new products at lower costs than ours *and* with better quality. How could they do it? They say you have something to do with it. I'd like to send my head of quality control to attend your seminar. Oh, and, by the way, do you have a pamphlet I can read on what it takes to make better quality?

DEMING: No, I don't have a pamphlet and sending the head of your so-called quality control department won't help. Save your money and his time. Don't come.

CHIEF: But we need help. What will help?

DEMING: You're going to have to change the way you operate. Eliminate the annual review of people, merit review, Management By Objectives or whatever you call it. Stop worrying about ranking and rating.

Your relationships with suppliers will have to change. Instead of cutthroat price competition, work with your suppliers on quality. Bring the number of suppliers down to just one for each individual item purchased.

Stop worrying about quarterly profit, and concentrate on improving quality in all its manifestations. Products should be designed from the beginning with quality in mind.

Constantly improve quality and cost by working on the process. No matter how good, any process can always be improved. Forget about quality audits.

Stop relying on mass inspection for quality. Instead work on improving the process. Inspection is just a stopgap measure until real improvement can take place.

Eliminate fear in your organization...

CHIEF: Wait a minute, you're telling me to completely change the way I manage. I didn't come here for that. We don't have a problem with management. Our managers are fine, our management system is fine. I observe and am personally responsible for that. We just have a little problem with quality and cost.

DEMING: If you want to change your results, you have to change your company. You can't keep looking to the past, hoping to copy your competitors. Do you think they are going to stand still and wait for you to catch up and bring out new products? Not if they have been trained by me, they won't. You're aiming at a moving target, and the only way to hit it is to bring out and encourage all the creativity of your people. Fear won't do that, courage and love of their work will.

CHIEF: Okay, okay, we've got to change, but where do we start?

DEMING: Send all your top executives, yourself included, to my seminar. Keep sending as many people as possible to my seminars. Distribute a copy of my book and Mr. Aguayo's book to everyone in your company. I'll give you names of some consultants to work with in transforming your company.

CHIEF: No problem. I'll send all my top people who are in charge of quality, but quality is not my responsibility and I'm very busy with other important issues and problems so I won't be able to attend.

DEMING: What do you mean! Don't you know that quality is made in the boardroom? You have the most important job of all when it comes to quality. If you can't come yourself, send no one.

And so it goes. There's no middle ground. Transforming entails changes in some of our most fundamental beliefs.

Example of the Difficulty of Change

Deming began consulting with Ford and General Motors around the same time. But some of us who are converts to his philosophy were pulling our hair out trying to figure out what GM was up to. GM was constantly emphasizing the wrong things in its advertising, its press releases, and its actions. While Ford was talking about quality and recognizing outstanding quality from suppliers, GM was spending billions on new equipment, claiming that new technology and new equipment were the road to salvation and high productivity. GM acquired an aerospace company and a computer software company, bought all kinds of new equipment, and planned for a new subsidiary that would produce new automobiles in a highly automated plant. All of this was contrary, or irrelevant, to what Deming was saying. GM's management had made quality one issue and management another.

GM had no problem getting people to support and praise its strategy. Professors from the top business schools claimed Saturn, GM's fully automated plant, would be the salvation of American industry. Financial consultants were sure the payoff of high investment in technology was right around the corner. In some sense GM did make progress in quality. The number of defects in the cars was declining. But that is not enough: quality means more than just the number of defects.

GM attempted to graft new techniques onto its management system. But as Harry Belafonte sings in an old Calypso song, "House built on a weak foundation will not stand, oh no." GM continued to lose market share, and dissatisfaction with the handling and feel of its cars was widespread.

Luckily that has changed, and they have now embraced the new philosophy.

But even Ford has made only a fraction of the necessary changes. One example is its reliance on merit reviews. In some areas of the company people are still rated and ranked above or below average. Such a system only destroys the people and kills improvement. Deming's advice is quite explicit: eliminate all annual reviews of people in whatever form, including merit review, Management By Objective, and performance incentive. There's nothing obscure about it. But the idea cuts at the core of our way of doing business since the end of World War II—and at the core of our problems.

Rethink Quality

When quality is viewed as being the number of products that conform to specifications, a company is already behind the eight ball. A product can meet all specifications and still be of poor quality. Workmanship can be excellent, but the product can fail. If there's no market for a product, what's the sense? If the design is obsolete or ineffective, good workmanship can't make up the difference.

A number of banks have failed in the United States during the last decade, but I have yet to read of one that failed because of too many mistakes by the tellers. In most cases the operations of the failed banks were extremely good.

I rented and drove a new car recently and didn't find a single mechanical problem. Everything about it seemed fine, but when it rained and I turned on the windshield wipers, I found my left shoulder was the beneficiary of an involuntary shower if the window was open. Finding the odometer and the gauges seemed to require a manual. They were in illogical and hard-to-find spots. There was something about the feel of the car that I can't name or describe. The net effect is that, even though there were no quality problems per se, the car wasn't good enough. In other words, I wouldn't buy it.

Importance of Design

Once a product is 15 percent designed, it's too late. Problems are already built in that can't be changed or compensated for anywhere down the line. The Deming-Shewhart cycle can be applied to new product introduction. Once a product is produced, even a prototype, it can be tested in the lab. Once it's sold, even in a test market, it can be observed in actual use and the customer's reaction can be used to redesign and improve it.

But what we find in many corporations is that the design area won't talk to engineering, manufacturing, or consumer research. Each area is a separate fiefdom, supposedly competent in its own field. Each is unaware of the problems of the others. Why is it this way? One major reason is the reward system. Each department is judged on numbers and goals that are specific to itself. Maximize the parts and you maximize the whole, right? NONSENSE!

The Big Picture

The following flow diagram was prominently displayed by Deming at every conference with top management and every day at every class with engineers in Japan beginning in 1950.

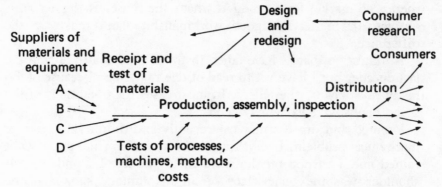

From Deming, *Out of the Crisis*

Recently Deming told me,

I think now, as I look back, that the flow diagram was the most powerful individual piece in Japan. Why was I there? Because top management asked me to come. They had knowledge, little bits and pieces of it. But the flow diagram and my lectures gave an overall view. I put the customer into the production line. I think that helped Japan to forge ahead.

I predicted in 1950 that in five years manufacturers the world over would be screaming for protection. It took only four years. Years later I was told by top management that I was the only man in Japan who believed it in 1950.

The flow diagram introduced the customer into the manufacturing process and introduced the idea of continually refining knowledge, design, and inputs to the process so as to constantly increase customer satisfaction. As one Toshiba executive said, "In the U.S. the customer is king. But in Japan, the customer is God."

The diagram shows the whole process as an integrated operation. From the first input to actual use of the finished product, it's one process. A problem at the beginning will impact on the whole and the end product.

There are no barriers between the company and the customer, between the customer and its suppliers, between the company and its people. The process is unified: the greater the harmony, the better the results.

There is another important lesson in this diagram. People who work with computers have an expression, "Garbage in, garbage out." Perhaps even more appropriate is the expression, "You are what you eat."

The question we all have to ask is, "Is it possible to produce quality when all the inputs are junk; when supplies are chosen on the basis of lowest cost instead of their overall effect; when the people working in the system and those responsible for the system are living and working in fear?"

The Need for Transformation

Deming has developed a number of guidelines for the transformation of management, which he calls the fourteen points. It is an almost instinctive reaction to try and pick out those of the fourteen points that seem most applicable to a company in its present state. This is a mistake. The fourteen points are guidelines for the transformation of a company from one state into another, in the same way that a caterpillar can metamorphose into a butterfly. A butterfly can't maintain a hundred legs and still fly properly.

A company or organization that wants to transform has to change completely, including fundamental beliefs and practices. This is a fundamental point of this chapter and of the entire book.

Transformation Versus Change

Nancy Mann, a noted statistician, and author of *The Keys to Excellence*, applied some statistical methods to understanding drug use and rehabilitation.[1] In studying rehabilitation, she found there existed three different groups. The first and least successful group was forced to stop by some outside pressure, such as being confined to a jail cell. As soon as the exterior pressure was lifted or they found a way of getting around it, they reverted to their drug habit.

The second group had a genuine desire to kick the habit and tried it on their own. But most reverted to drug use within two years when some crisis proved too much to cope with.

The third group, which Mann calls the transformed group, had found something to replace their habit. Some had found religion, some had fallen in love, and some had found a new drug. Many described an individual experience, an awakening or realization that transformed their lives. This group of people lasted more than eight years on average before reverting to their habits, and some never went back.

Similarly, for a company to change, there are three ways. Pressure can be applied from outside. This is the way much of current management operates, with rewards for good behavior and punishment for bad behavior. It works on the body, not the mind. This is how virtually every government program and mandate is approached by our legislators and administrators.

The second route to change is often with the best intentions. If you were to query the chief executives of organizations and our politicians "Are you in favor of quality?" they would answer yes. Everyone wants quality and everyone has a prescription, almost all of which are wrong. Most prescriptions for improvement call for best efforts. Everyone doing his best. Making people accountable for their work, rewarding excellence, and so on. It is time to introduce Deming's theorem number 2: "We are ruined by best efforts." Best efforts without guidance from profound knowledge are oftentimes tampering, ruining perfectly good systems.

If we are to kick the management habits formed over the last forty years, we had better have something to replace them with. A transformation. An entirely different view. It is not unusual for managers who have embraced the Deming philosophy to sound like religious converts. "We have been doing everything wrong for years" is a common refrain when emerging from a Deming seminar. There's no worse critic of smokers, as most of us have found out, than a former smoker.

Even some of the language used often sounds as if it were coming from a preacher. In response to the question, what has to be done, Deming says, "We have to restore the individual."

Yes, the Individual

What does it mean to restore the individual? A surprising number of breakthroughs and major innovations have come from monopolies and giant companies with huge resources. Shewhart's work on quality control, the transistor, and other major contributions came from the Bell Laboratories, the research arm of a monopoly. Nylon came from DuPont, and the most recent breakthrough in superconductor technology started at an IBM laboratory.

Of course, there is a more romantic vision of inventors working in their kitchens or garages. The developers of the personal computer, xerography, and photographic film fit into these categories. What is it that all these individuals, in big companies and working alone, have in common? One common element is a certain amount of economic independence, which gave all these inventors time to pursue their ideas. A successful company is in a position to provide this because it has the resources to think about tomorrow. Some individuals, because of youth or personal wealth, also can give themselves the necessary time and resources.

But all the individuals who made major breakthroughs had one other thing in common. They were all responsible only to themselves! They pursued their visions the way they felt was right.

Breakthroughs by definition are not obvious or determined by a vote or survey. They are real breaks with the past and often strongly resisted. Xerography was turned down by virtually every major company, such as IBM, Kodak, and RCA. A small Rochester, N.Y., company decided to take a chance and became the giant corporation now called Xerox as a result. The personal computer was neglected by all the major computer makers until an upstart company with the funny name Apple developed the industry. When Harvey Firestone brought out his pneumatic tire, people thought he was nuts, riding around on tires with air in them. Now you have to be nuts to do otherwise.

For any enterprise to improve, the individual has to be alive and well, working and living without fear, loving his work. What is it that destroys the individuals in corporations, schools, and government? It is those collective policies that we call modern management. Most often the reward system is the biggest individual culprit. It provokes fear for any nonconforming behavior. It punishes any form of risk taking or spontaneity. We treat our people like children or criminals or, even worse, like machines. Rather than risk failure, people in many corporations, become yes-men and -women. They give the corporation what is rewarded—lots of loans, high production, short-term profit, lower costs—and destroy the company, and sometimes the whole industry, in the process.

All this must change. With this we can now talk about the fourteen points. I list them here without any comment. Most of the rest of the book will cover them in depth.

The Fourteen Points for the Transformation of Management

1. Create constancy of purpose toward improvement of product and service, with the aim to become competitive and to stay in business, and to provide jobs.
2. Adopt the new philosophy. We are in a new economic age. Western management must awaken to the challenge, learn their responsibilities, and take on leadership for change.
3. Cease reliance on mass inspection to achieve quality. Eliminate the need for inspection on a mass basis by building quality into the product in the first place.
4. End the practice of awarding business on the basis of price tag. Instead, minimize total cost. Move toward a single supplier for any one item, on a long-term relationship of loyalty and trust.
5. Improve constantly and forever the system of production and service, to improve quality and productivity, and thus constantly decrease costs.
6. Institute training on the job.
7. Institute leadership. The aim of supervision should be to help people and machines and gadgets to do a better job. Supervision of management is in need of overhaul, as well as supervision of production workers.
8. Drive out fear, so that everyone may work effectively for the company.
9. Break down barriers between departments. People in research, design, sales, and production must work as a team, to foresee problems of production and in use that may be encountered with the product or service.
10. Eliminate slogans, exhortations, and targets for the work force asking for zero defects and new levels of productivity. Such exhortations only create adversarial relationships, since the bulk of the causes of low quality and low productivity belong to the system and thus lie beyond the power of the work force.

11a. Eliminate work standards (quotas) on the factory floor. Substitute leadership.

11b. Eliminate management by objectives. Eliminate management by numbers, numerical goals. Substitute leadership.

12a. Remove barriers that rob the hourly workers of their right to pride of workmanship. The responsibility of supervisors must be changed from mere numbers to quality.

12b. Remove barriers that rob people in management and in engineering of their right to pride of workmanship. This means, *inter alia*, abolishment of the annual review or merit rating and of management by objectives.

13. Institute a vigorous program of education and self-improvement.

14. Put everybody in the company to work to accomplish the transformation. The transformation is everybody's job.

CHAPTER 10

Focus and Philosophy

Point 1. Create constancy of purpose toward improvement of product and service, with the aim to become competitive and to stay in business, and to provide jobs.

In the early 1950s, American coffee roasters faced a dilemma. The price of coffee beans had risen dramatically, and they were faced with two distasteful choices: either absorb the increased price, partially or totally, hurting profitability; or pass the cost on to their customers and risk losing market share or having customers switch to other beverages.

They came up with an innovative alternative. The coffee roasters' business consists of buying, aging, roasting, and blending coffee beans to achieve the desired taste and smell. Coffee beans, like all agricultural commodities, are highly variable. Two beans can be quite distinct. Even beans picked at the same time from the same tree can be different. A bean picked from the top of tree, which receives more sunshine, tastes different than a bean from the bottom of the tree.

Blending is a critical part of the process. The leading roaster of the time tried experimenting with different formulations. It found that gradually changing the formulation, substituting lower quality beans, was unnoticeable to the consumer. It began to slowly change the blend. Every two weeks a few more of the less expensive beans were substituted for the heartier, more expensive ones.

Most consumers couldn't notice the difference in coffees bought two weeks apart. But if they had tasted, side by side, two batches made six weeks apart, they would have noticed a slight difference.

In effect, the roaster started training customers to accept an inferior blend of coffee.

The other roasters noticed what was going on and responded in kind to avoid losing market share. In a few years the American consumer's standards for a decent cup of coffee were radically altered. The managers did their jobs and enjoyed their bonuses. At the time this response was viewed as a triumph of ingenuity. But a funny thing began to happen.

Per capita consumption of coffee began a slow but steady decline. The business stopped growing. The roaster that started it all began to experience profitability problems. It is now part of a huge conglomerate and is still experiencing problems in its coffee business. Consumers have discovered gourmet coffees. But ironically, the coffee drunk by Americans during the 1940s was on a par with what we now call gourmet coffees.

When I first head this story, it explained so much. Why was it so difficult to find a decent cup of coffee in the United States? Sure, some restaurants served better-tasting coffee than others, but in almost any restaurant in any European or South American city one could always get a decent cup of coffee. I am not even talking about the beverage served on airlines, which is called coffee, looks like tea, and tastes like dishwater.

I have become the exact opposite of the loyal customer. I am the loyally opposed customer. Even if they gave it away, I wouldn't drink it. Why would I want to drink something that is a task to finish?

Each roasting company had excellent operations and employed highly trained and qualified people. They were models of efficient operations. They aggressively fought for market share and successfully responded to the crisis of the moment. But in the process they ruined their business, lost their loyal customers, saw per capita consumption decline, and destroyed the reputation of American coffee.

An Analogy on Direction

I'd like to draw an analogy. Let's take an imaginary trip into the wilds to refresh ourselves. We travel into a wilderness park and chart a route north that should lead us out of the park in a few days. On the first day we break camp and chart the day's walk. We use our compass to sight a highly visible landmark and confirm its location on our map.

But as we start walking, we find that all kinds of obstacles hinder us. We have to walk around rocks. Some of the brush is too thick, so we walk around it. We descend a valley and lose sight of our landmark. An unmarked ravine forces us hundreds of yards eastward. Nevertheless, when we emerge from the valley we resight the landmark and walk toward it, reaching it before sunset.

Suppose another party, traveling the same route, fails to set their sights at the beginning of the day. They encounter the same problems. The brush is too thick, they have to walk around the rock. In the valley they encounter the ravine and are forced eastward. They constantly refer to their compass to make sure they're traveling north. But when they emerge from the valley, they are lost. They have no idea where they are and can't place their location on the map.

If you asked both parties how much of their time was spent solving problems, both would say 100 percent. How much time was spent planning, both would say a nominal amount. In fact the second party, which is now totally lost, is spending lots of time planning—trying to figure out what to do next.

The planning was important, of course, although it didn't take up a great deal of time. But both parties spent almost all their time attacking short-term problems. However, the way the problems were solved by the first group was somehow different. They kept correcting their direction by always aiming toward the same landmark, but they knew how and at what to aim. The second group also tried to correct themselves, always going north, but they got lost.

Purpose or Focus

In business we don't have to consider a company's purpose every day. Some managers would scoff at the idea that a business today has a purpose other than making money. Running a business on that basis is equivalent to always heading north. Of course every business wants to make money, but every organization at some point faces hard times. How they respond depends on top management's view of the purpose of the organization. If the only purpose of a company is to make money, why not sell illicit drugs, cheapen the product, or fool the customer?

Such actions eventually hurt not just the company and its customers but the whole industry. Eventually rarely means more than three years. An alternative view is, in Deming's words, "A company exists to provide goods and services which help improve the standard of living of mankind." Cheapening the product or weakening the service does not improve the standard of living of mankind.

The coffee roasters had alternatives available to them. But their concern for short-term profit was not balanced with a long-term view of their purpose. Instead of focusing on quality (from the customer's point of view), the roasters focused on margins and market share (what they perceived was in the company's best interests).

But even if direction is properly set and the intention is good, different management theories will result in different courses of action, with widely divergent results. Since we are not talking about adjusting the existing management system but a whole new way of seeing things when a Deming transformation is involved, the second of the fourteen points states, "Adopt the new philosophy. We are in a new economic age. Western management must awaken to the challenge, learn their responsibilities, and take on leadership for change."

Saying "Quality Counts" Is Not Enough

Let's look at one example. After the oil embargo of 1974 it appeared likely that demand for petroleum products would continue to increase and additional supplies were needed. The oil business looked very promising. Exxon hired many new people.

As we now know, the oil business did not grow. Instead the business contracted as businesses and consumers looked for and found ways of conserving. Energy efficiency became of prime concern. Demand leveled off and for a while declined.

When a new executive took over as chief executive of the oil giant, he embarked on an aggressive cost-cutting campaign. People were let go in droves. Some divisions suffered layoffs of one-third of their people. The people who worked in the system were paying for the mistakes of management. Management made it imminently clear that they were all expendable. Naturally, morale suffered.

Then the chief executive directed all his divisions to pursue quality. Quality was now in. The chief of Exxon had done everything in his power to destroy quality but asked his people to pursue it. What he was asking was next to impossible. But it was very difficult to tell the chief executive his actions were wrong. The financial analysts loved him; earnings were high. How can you tell someone his actions are wrong when the financial numbers are strong and he is written up in the press as a strong leader, just what the company needed?

At Exxon each division has a great deal of autonomy. Each division pursued quality in the manner they thought appropriate. One division hired a Deming consultant; in another the executives read several books. The response varied widely from division to division. But the real message from the top was not to make Exxon a quality conscious company, but to maximize short-term earnings by working on the visible numbers only.

One division where the response had nothing to do with quality was the shipping division. They did all the wrong things, at least from the Deming perspective. But they did things recommended in many business texts. They instituted a rigorous management by objective program, providing merit pay and bonuses for those captains and crews who were able to bring down the size of their crew. They insisted on giving each crew member more assignments in order to bring down the number needed to run a ship. The pressure, the amount of paperwork, and the expectations for those crew members who stayed increased. Those ships that were more successful in paring down the number of workers received higher bonuses.

Morale on the ships dropped and turnover increased. The average amount of experience per crew member declined. Exxon also avoided double-hulling its ships. They created the ideal business environment as advocated by America's best-known business consultants. From the Deming point of view, of course, it was only a matter of time before a disaster occurred.

After the *Exxon Valdez* ran aground and spilled thousands of gallons of petroleum off the coast of Alaska, Exxon and the nation found a ready scapegoat in the captain of the *Exxon Valdez* because he had alcohol in his blood the day after the accident occurred. We love scapegoats. But from my perspective, the accident was due to common causes, and those are the responsibility of management.

This example illustrates a common problem. Everyone wants better quality and lower costs, but just doing what comes naturally or what is recommended by some consultant may backfire. If you wish to duplicate the success of companies that have adopted Deming's philosophy, you have to make a choice. Everyone promises wonderful results; but not only does Deming call for certain management changes, he quite explicitly claims that many of the practices being advocated by our business and political leaders are wrong and will make matters worse. They can't both be right.

In the Deming view, certain practices are always wrong. Among these are merit pay, incentive programs, the annual review of people, any system that ranks the employees, management by objectives, setting objectives based on financial targets, quotas, searching for the cause of every problem or defect.

Other practices are either insufficient or harmful under some conditions. Among these are automation, new machinery or gadgets, best efforts or hard work. Best efforts, or everyone giving his all, can be fatal if it's not accompanied by profound knowledge. Sometimes machinery and gadgets are useful and necessary, but anyone who believes they are a cure-all or always beneficial is living in a dream world.

Competition for market share and making everyone accountable for her results are very seductive ideas, heartily recommended by business and political leaders, but Deming tells us they rarely if ever help and often are part of the problem. Every company can fight like the dickens for market share and the industry can go down the tubes.

Manufacturers of vacuum tubes kept making better and better tubes, with each company vying for market share. But when transistors were invented, they went out of business. All the coffee roasters fought vigorously for market share, and the business stopped growing.

It is silly to make people accountable for problems of the system. It is not just silly but dangerous. The vast majority of problems are problems of the system, which those working in the system are helpless to change.

Probably the largest obstacle to our accepting the new economic philosophy is a feeling in the back of our minds that "we must have been doing something right." After all, for years the United States was the world economic power. If anyone wanted to learn about manufacturing or business they came here. We considered U.S. goods the best in the world. We must have been doing something right, but Deming is telling us that we must change every important facet of management if we are to regain our former preeminence. More accurately, he is saying we ain't seen nothing yet. America has never known its true economic potential. But for us to realize it certain things must change.

The QWERTY Story[1]

I am typing this chapter on a standard keyboard. The standard used by almost everyone is called a QWERTY keyboard because the first six letters on the upper lefthand side are q, w, e, r, t, and y. Huge sums of money and time are invested in learning to type on it. I spent a year in a high school typing class, making more errors per page than I thought humanly possible, learning to touch-type on such a keyboard. So far all attempts to replace the QWERTY board have been unsuccessful. The board therefore must be pretty good, at least close to optimal, right? Wrong. It is one of the worst configurations possible. Using any one of several alternative placement of letters would dramatically lower the rate of errors and improve typing speed.

Virtually all records for speed typing have been held by an alternative board, DSK, for Dvorak Simplified Keyboard. DSK is so superior to QWERTY that the U.S. Navy concluded in the 1940s that the increased productivity from DSK would completely pay for the cost of retraining typists with ten days of full-time employment. I understand that even better keyboards have since been devised.

QWERTY, of course, had very good reasons for its awkward configuration. The QWERTY board was originally designed to slow down the human typist. It originated when typewriters were mechanical and couldn't keep up with the human typist. Slowing down the typist was essential to productivity.

The Birth of Folklore

But that was 120 years ago. In electric typewriters of today a ball or print wheel is used, making key jamming impossible. The computer I'm typing this on could easily handle a typist twenty times faster than I.

A series of events helped establish the folklore that QWERTY had a speed superiority over other configurations. In 1882, Ms. Longley, founder of the Shorthand and Typewriter Institute, developed the eight-finger typing that professionals use today. She happened to use a QWERTY board, although almost any configuration would have done just as well. Most typists of the time used the hunt-and-peck method that most of us try when we first approach a typewriter.

A crucial event in 1888 provided the dramatic victory necessary for the folklore of superiority to prevail. Longley was challenged to a contest by another typing teacher, Louis Taub. Longley chose Frank E. McGurrin, an experienced typist, who had added one particular innovation of his own, to represent her school. He had memorized the keyboard and could type without looking at it, the way all modern typists do.

In a well-advertised and well-reported public competition McGurrin trounced Taub. A crucial element of the victory must have been the method of typing, eight-finger touch-typing over four-finger hunt-and-peck. It's even possible that the QWERTY board was superior to the board used by the competition in that contest, although we now know that almost any configuration of keys is superior to QWERTY. But the QWERTY board passed into folklore as the victor in a fair match and therefore a superior board.

I'd like to draw an analogy between our keyboard and our management methods. In each case there's a natural and understandable urge to conclude that the existing way is the best way—"We must have been doing something right." But as the QWERTY story illustrates, it's not necessarily the keyboard or the management methods that led to a decisive victory. And even if they were a factor, it's possible that a better way exists.

A Tale of Two Systems

Let's do a hypothetical side-by-side comparison of two different management systems. A company has two typing pools, one located in its Russian subsidiary in Siberia and the other located in Sunnytown, U.S.A. The Russian manager, who has just graduated from the Lenin-Trotsky School of Management, gets detailed numbers. He knows the number of pages typed each day and the number of errors per page by each typist for the last year. To stimulate greater production, he sets up an incentive program. Anyone in the top third of production gets a Marx Brothers Medal. To his great satisfaction, he awards quite a few medals and finds out that speed for the group has indeed increased.

What we have in this typing pool is a stable system, just as in our red bead factory. Sure, speed has picked up, but to our manager's embarrassment the number of pages coming back to be reworked because of typing errors has increased dramatically. The work load has now increased because much of last month's work has to be redone. They all have to work even harder, if that is possible. To avoid errors, he warns everyone that black stars will be posted by the names of anyone who averages more than one error per page.

The defect rate improves, but speed goes back to its old level— even gets worse than before. Of course, some months the manager's ecstatic, when the numbers seem better than last, and other months, when a decline is posted, he's depressed. He tries putting up pretty posters urging everyone to work for the sake of the motherland, but that fails to work. He offers American cigarettes for better performance and finds himself giving out cigarettes to some, but the average for the group stays the same.

Finally, it's no more Mr. Nice Guy. He screams and intimidates the below-average workers, lets them go. He insists that the better performers take up the slack, and turns the place upside down. One day the watercooler breaks at 4:59. He asks for volunteers to help him clean up and get the place ready for the next day so that no productive time will be lost.

Guess what? No one volunteers. He's forced to conclude that people just don't want to work anymore and his country is doomed to mediocrity. I don't know of anyone who would want to work under these conditions, but I do know managers who think they're effective because they're tough SOB's.

Our second manager, in Sunnytown, U.S.A., notices that the work of her pool is in statistical control. Of course there is variation from individual to individual and from day to day, but the group's typing speed and error rate fall within control limits. She's also interested in improvement. She examines the control charts and finds that a few typists account for an extraordinary amount of errors. They're outside the system as indicated by the control charts. She delves into the circumstances surrounding each. One of them, who is by the window, tells her that at certain times of the day, he can't see the paper he's typing off because of the sun's glare. She has the eyes of several examined and finds that some need glasses. She asks for suggestions and responds to them as well as she can. She obtains a desk lamp for a typist situated in the darkest corner of the office, a shade for the one by the window.

At one point she broaches the subject of switching keyboards to increase speed and reduce the number of errors. Among groans and complaints she manages to get five volunteers to try the new keyboard on a trial basis. After several weeks of retraining they come back. They finish all their work an hour early each day. Their performance is so good that others volunteer and make the switch. Eventually everyone switches. Not one threat, not one bribe for better performance, but productivity has soared, errors have dropped, and the workers are happy to come to work. Problems are dealt with and some are even resolved. When the watercooler breaks, everyone pitches in to help.

The Russian manager knows the American subsidiary's typing pool has 30 percent higher productivity, so he knows it's possible to do better. By making simple calculations, he figures that each worker only has to handle 30 percent more. Each is given more work and pressure is applied to make sure it "gets done." But the system hasn't changed, and neither has the capability of the system. It isn't capable of producing more for any length of time.

Remember that in the red bead experiment management chose to keep the plant open using the three workers with the fewest defects. But when they did, the results were no better. Management tried to beat the law of averages. It can't be done. In my opinion, that's what Exxon was trying to do, that's what most managers try to do, when they respond to the Japanese Challenge and seek to become more competitive.

Some managers, of course, try a more humanistic approach, with pep talks and positive feedback and feel-good talk. Others try a slave-driver approach. Some talk about sustainable surge capability.

Of course, I would rather work for the feel-good manager, but if everything else is the same, they are both just trying to beat the law of averages. It doesn't pay to fight Mother Nature.

No Blame

My comments shouldn't be mistaken as accusations directed toward any one individual. I am not calling for lynching managers instead of lynching workers. Punishment is not appropriate. The culprit is not an individual but a wrong set of ideas. But no one should underestimate the difficulty of change. The very first time I heard Deming, I knew he was right. Everything he said made sense, and I began to see my past experiences in a new light. But it was two years before I realized that the power of his system was in the way of management. Like so many others, I initially looked for the techniques and methods. I thought that the power of his philosophy lay in the ability to get the numbers from the process and to interpret them properly.

It took me two years of reading, studying, and being exposed to him before I fully accepted that, while numbers and their interpretation were important, progress was incompatible with our most common and deeply held beliefs about management and work.

Even when it is impossible to measure, when a control chart can't be conceived, much less drawn, his management philosophy is applicable. We should keep in mind that the most important numbers are never known. We don't know the cost of a disgruntled customer, and we don't know the cost of a disgruntled employee. We don't know the loss to the company when the employees do everything possible to meet the numerical objective set by management. In their attempt to fit the square peg of the company into the round hole of management's objective, some part of the company and its future gets sacrificed.

Is Success Enough?

For a moment, let's go back to the manager of the typing pool in Sunnytown, U.S.A. The results coming from her department are noticed and she gets promoted and moved to a different city. A new manager comes into the typing pool and wonders what has been going on. "We're not here to have fun," he exclaims, "but to work. Who authorized this crazy keyboard?" Gradually everything will be undone unless the manager directly above the typing pool supervisor is a convert. And when he moves, it's likely that all the positive changes will be undone unless his boss in turn understands and supports the new philosophy. For change to last in a company, the chief executive must be reached.

But I'm going to reveal one of the best-known secrets. New and different ideas do not percolate up from the bottom very well in almost any organization. The newer and more different the ideas, the less likely they are to flow up. In most cases top management has to be addressed by an equal or superior.

What About 1950?

There's no reason to believe that ideas percolated up from the bottom any better in Japan in 1950. But Deming came in from the top.

He was the world's preeminent expert in quality control, and he was a member of the staff of the victorious allied forces. He was speaking directly to top management, not just one top manager but forty-five of them, at the invitation of Japan's business leaders. The Japanese did not have any natural predilection for the new philosophy, they were just as skeptical, but the order came from Japanese business leaders to give it a try, and it worked.

Crisis and Transformation

Reaching top management won't guarantee the success of the transformation in a company, but it at least gives it a fighting chance.

There's one factor that prevailed in Japan in 1950. They were really down. They had lost the war, their economy was in shambles. Their old ways had failed and they were ready for a change. As I mentioned earlier, successful companies and countries are in the best position to improve. But sometimes radical change is only accepted when disaster has struck. People just aren't ready to throw away their old ideas and take on radically new and different ones when everything seems to be acceptable or not too bad.

Summary

The first of the fourteen points calls for a company to clarify and acknowledge its purpose and maintain its focus in good times and in bad. This is hardly a moot issue. It is folly to believe that everything of importance can be justified on the basis of expected return. The impact on the financial statements and stock price of many of the most important decisions is unknown and unknowable. Investment in ideas and technologies with no immediate payoff and continual investment in a company's people are necessary ingredients for a leading company.

To try to justify long-term actions on the basis of their impact on the balance sheet is the modern equivalent of determining how many angels can occupy the head of a pin. Costs and payoffs are important, no doubt about it, but they are not enough and in many cases are just useless or deceptive. The projected return for a given course of action depends on the assumptions and inputs. Any way you look at it, it's a guess. But if a company loses sight of where it is going, which should be improvement in the standard of living of its customers, it will surely suffer along with its customers.

The second point calls for a company to accept the new economic philosophy. To try to institute methods and techniques without changing the managerial philosophy of a company will not lead to rapid results, and may even backfire. It's possible to raise the hopes and expectations of the people of a company but then disappoint them when the changes necessary to restore pride in themselves and their work aren't made. Some of the biggest barriers to individuals in a company experiencing pride and satisfaction in their work are structural in nature and often imposed by management in its attempts to "control" production, output, or results.

The meaning of the word *control* in the expression *quality control* has a very different meaning to someone who has studied with Deming and someone who is hearing it for the first time or who has studied with a hack. To the uninitiated, control means inspection, supervision, analysis, and reports to look into what went wrong. This already implies a structure to management that is inconsistent with the Deming view.

To a Deming student, control means knowledge, especially knowledge of variation and processes, continual education, training, and joy in work.

CHAPTER 11

Inspection

If you want good quality, you hire lots of inspectors, right? By now every reader should be chiming in, "Wrong."

Of course, inspection, if it's properly done, can catch the defects and prevent them from reaching the customer. But it is not improvement and does not guarantee quality. Inspection is a very limited tool, grossly overused and often misused.

Transformation in Attitude Toward Inspection

Point 3 of the fourteen points states, "Cease reliance on mass inspection to achieve quality. Eliminate the need of inspection on a mass basis by building quality into the product in the first place."

Point 3 doesn't call for the total elimination of inspection. The key words in Point 3 are *reliance* and *mass*. We cannot rely on mass inspection to improve quality, though there are times when 100 percent inspection is necessary. As Harold S. Dodge said many years ago, "You cannot inspect quality into a product." The quality is there or it isn't by the time it's inspected. Inspection provides information about quality of the end product, but the cost of the defectives has to be passed along to the customer.

A typical remark emanated from a foreman who said, "We don't need quality control. We inspect everything before it goes out." Yet year after year the level of defectives had been steady. For anyone to stay in business, all costs have to be covered. Defectives cost just as much to produce as good product. Customers end up paying for the defectives even if the products they receive are flawless. In addition they pay for the cost of inspection.

The same thing is true in service. A mechanic may say, "I guarantee my work. If there's any problem, bring it back and I'll fix it free of charge." But every car that is brought back takes him time to repair and his rates must reflect that if he is to stay in business. Customers pay for the time he works whether he charges for it or not.

In the minds of managers, politicians, judges, and the general public, inspection is associated with quality. The response of one firm to its quality problems was to add more inspectors. Almost all government efforts to prevent accidents and defects are based on increasing the level of inspection or the number of inspectors.

Limitations of Inspection

Inspection will not catch problems built into the system. The disastrous explosion of the space shuttle *Challenger* was apparently due to the failure of rubber O rings. The rings in the *Challenger* were within specifications. No amount of inspection would have prevented them from being used. But the rings tended to fail in extreme cold. It was only a matter of time before a tragedy occurred. Inspection cannot improve the level of quality that is designed into the product.

In New York City, where housing laws cover every aspect of housing, including what rents can be charged, quality housing is sorely lacking. The government's response has been to hire more inspectors to look for building violations. However, the problems of the housing market are built into the system, and no amount of inspection will improve that. Admitting the system is at fault for the massive housing problems in New York would leave no scapegoats other than the city's political leaders. But only when that is understood will any improvement become possible.

Blaming the Worker

Undoubtedly, part of the reason for the excessive reliance on inspection to ensure quality is the underlying and insidious belief that the operator or individual in the system is responsible for all the problems. The belief is quite widespread and almost universal. Dr. Joseph Juran reported in the May 1966 issue of *Industrial*

Quality Control, "There is here [in Czechoslovakia] the same widespread unsupported assumption that the bulk of defects are operator-controllable, and that if the operators would only put their backs into it, the plant's quality-problems would shrink materially."[1]

But in any system approaching stability the bulk of the problems are due to the system, and that is management's responsibility. A good sign that the problems are systemic is when "the situation has been like this for years." Working on the system, however, requires knowledge, insight, and patience. It is much easier and more comforting to believe that someone else is at fault. Adding inspectors is easy enough; it requires no thought or knowledge, and gives the illusion of working on the problem. It also provides some ready scapegoats.

What Caused the Problem?

Often, inspection is taken one step further. Why not find the cause of every defect or problem and eliminate it? Sounds like unassailable steel-trap logic, doesn't it? The vice president of a major company bragged about the strict schedule of inspection of final product. How were the data used? "The data are in the computer. The computer provides a record and description of every defect found. Our engineers never stop till they find the cause of every defect."[2] Sounds noble, even competent. How could anything be wrong with this? Why not find the cause of every problem? But doing so is not just a waste of time, it's dangerous, even counterproductive.

For years the level of defects had remained fairly steady at between 4½ percent and 5½ percent. Finding the cause of each problem had produced no improvement. We have to distinguish between best efforts and being effective.

Of course, using computers and having an explanation for every problem made management feel good. They were doing their best, in their minds being scientific. But their efforts were misdirected. This is just another case of the red beads. They were mistaking common causes for special causes. Their actions assumed there were two systems, one producing defects, the other producing acceptable product.

If management was constantly making adjustments in response to each "cause," then the exercise was decreasing uniformity, lowering quality, and substantially raising costs. Assigning a cause to each defect and then adjusting the system so that defect would not have occurred would be tampering, using either the rule of modest adjustment or the rule of extreme adjustment from the Nelson funnel experiment.

Tremendous corporate resources were employed finding the "cause" of each problem. At best these resources were just wasted; at worst they were producing an unmeasurable loss to the company. I can hear Deming's voice resounding in my mind, "I see very little evidence that anyone is interested in profit." But to the customer and to management it appears that a conscientious effort *is* being made to improve quality. They are correct, of course. A conscientious effort *is* being made. It is just misdirected and ineffective.

Rewarding Inspectors for Defects

A poor practice that makes all the other errors seem mild by comparison is the practice of compensating inspectors based on the number of defects found. The more defects, the higher the pay. What is the inspector's job in this case? It certainly isn't to help lower the incidence of problems. Improving quality is not in his best interest, and it is not part of his job. To increase his pay, he is almost sure to change his standards with time.

Good Today, Bad Tomorrow

Put yourself in the shoes of a worker whose work is examined by one of several inspectors. One day an inspector brings back some of your work, so you redo it. But another inspector tells you to redo it the way it was previously done. Your best bet is to go find the original inspector and make sure he approves the work.

The next time this happens, you just resubmit it and hope a different inspector picks it up. But what is your opinion of management? Each inspector has a different idea of acceptable work. Work that is considered defective by one is perfectly acceptable to the other. How much time is wasted with reinspection? How much loss is created by workers redoing perfectly acceptable work and walking around trying to find the right inspector? I can hear Deming's echo, "I see very little evidence that anyone in management is interested in profit."

When I first started full-time employment, I was employed by a major New York bank in their senior management training program. The program was an excellent entrée to the financial world. The bank spent a great deal of money training us. It hired well-known and well-paid professors of accounting and finance to teach us. Seminars were given on various topics so that in eighteen months each trainee had received a thorough introduction to the skills and language of the financial world. As part of the program each individual prepared credit analyses of the bank's commercial customers. Each report was read and corrected by an individual who had been in the program a little longer than we. Most of the corrections were stylistic, reflecting the reviewer's preferred way of stating a point. The reports were then redone and submitted to another person, who had been in the program even longer. This second inspector, of course, had to justify his existence. It was not unusual for the second inspector to redo many of the corrections of the first and restore the original wording.

You can imagine what we thought of management. Some wonderful talent went through that program. I know, because the copious jokes about management had us in stitches. Predictably, 95 percent of the individuals who completed the training program left the bank shortly afterward.

The inspection process itself has to be in statistical control; otherwise you don't have a system of inspection. In plain English, the results of the inspection have to be substantially the same regardless of who inspects; otherwise untold waste is created and quality suffers.

Multiple Inspection of the Same Product or Service

Another common practice often accepted as evidence of concern for quality is to inspect everything two times or more. The reasoning behind this is simple enough. Each inspector backs up the other. If an error happens to get by one, the other should be able to pick it up. Then supposedly even fewer errors will get by both.

This reasoning has its roots in mechanical systems. A nut on a bicycle wheel may loosen. Adding a second nut can make it less probable that the wheel will fall off while the bike is being ridden. Although this solution is neither elegant nor optimal, it may work.

Humans are not nuts and bolts, and it is a mistake to extrapolate human behavior from mechanical systems. When two inspectors are on the job, neither has a job. Each considers the other his backup. If he misses something, so what, the other will pick it up. When two are responsible for the same job, which either could perform flawlessly, then neither is responsible.

In a government-funded housing development the tenants found that their heating bills were enormous. When they checked their attic, they discovered a total lack of insulation, even though the municipal authority had hired three inspectors to examine and approve the project. Insulation was one of the prerequisites for approval. When the inspectors were questioned, they each admitted their awareness of the problem but each didn't wish to embarrass either of the other two inspectors who apparently had missed the problem.[3]

David S. Chambers, a consultant in quality control, was asked by a printing company to help decrease the incidence of typographical errors because of massive complaints from customers. He found that each document that went out was read by eleven different proofreaders.[4]

Inspection and Sampling

Let's look at the problem of incoming supplies. Should a given lot of incoming supplies be accepted, or rejected and sent back to the vendor?

A typical rule to determine the acceptability of a lot is to inspect 10 percent of the incoming lot. If two or more defectives are found, then the lot is rejected. Otherwise the lot is accepted and used. Suppose our supplier has a stable process, which on average produces three defectives for every hundred items made.

Most lots of one hundred have three defectives. A few have two and a few have four. When a shipment arrives at the factory door, we pick out ten items and inspect them. If we find no defectives, then we accept that lot and use it. But there are probably three defectives in the remaining ninety. Suppose, on the other hand, we find four defectives in the sample of ten. That lot would be rejected. But the remaining ninety have no defects. We have found all the defects in the lot and are in a position to eliminate them and have an excellent defect-free lot. But instead we send this lot back.

We are maximizing our costs through this system of inspection. But what about our supplier? It also seems that we're randomly punishing him. But the supplier quickly wises up. The supplier's driver calls his company with the news that the lot has been rejected. A new truck is sent out, and the truck with the rejected lot heads back to the supplier's premises. But the two trucks meet somewhere in the middle and the rejected lot is loaded onto the empty truck heading toward our factory. It is redelivered, and this time accepted.

But waste is everywhere: empty trucks moving back and forth, delay while the lots are inspected, inspectors hired to do an unproductive job.

A company using this kind of standard acceptance plan is advertising its willingness to accept a certain level of shoddy product. A telling contrast involves a Japanese company that was entering the American market for the first time. The American buyer's request was for 50,000 units with no more than three defective per 10,000. When the buyer received the shipment, a letter from the supplier explained that they were unfamiliar with American business practices and had a hard time figuring what was meant by the request for three defectives per 10,000. The fifteen defectives were attached to the letter and taped together for the buyer to do with as he wanted.

Right Practice

Deming advocates either 100 percent inspection in those cases where defect-free work cannot be produced or no inspection where the level of defects is acceptably small. The one goal of any management is improvement. Where 100 percent inspection is taking place, management should be working on the system to reduce the incidence of defectives to zero so that inspection can be entirely eliminated. In some cases it may not be possible to eliminate inspection completely, but work on the process to improve quality is no less important.

The semiconductor industry is one industry where even the best companies have yet to see a defect-free production system. When a new semiconductor is produced, fifty out of every one hundred made may not function properly. The only way to distinguish one from the other is to inspect all of them. As a company learns more about the process, yields will climb. Some companies experience yields of close to 80 percent. This still leaves twenty out of every hundred unsuitable for shipment. The only way to identify and remove those twenty is inspection of all one hundred.

The company with a yield of 65 percent and the company with a yield of 75 percent both must rely on inspection to remove their defectives. But one has a distinct cost advantage over the other. One company has seventy-five semiconductors it can sell while the other has only sixty-five with the same cost of production. The company with the higher yield can price its product lower than the other.

Both manufacturing systems are in statistical control. Both products may be excellent. Both have the same cost of inspection. The workers in each work equally hard, but in time one will put the other out of business.

It is no secret that the Japanese semiconductor companies have significantly higher yields and quality than most independent American semiconductor manufacturers. The higher quality and lower costs gave the Japanese a distinct advantage, allowing them to displace the American manufacturers. It is also no secret that IBM and AT&T, which manufacture semiconductors for their own use, have yields comparable to the Japanese.

Inspection in Service

In some areas of banking, mistakes can be intolerably expensive. Sending out $100,000 instead of $10,000 might lead to a loss of $90,000, which could completely wipe out the monthly profit of the division. Even if the funds are eventually recovered, the managerial time and interest costs involved can be enormous. But when many transactions are involved, errors are inevitable.

The best way found to date to eliminate errors is to have two individuals perform the calculations and then have the two results mechanically compared. Any discrepancy is investigated by a trained supervisor. If on average each worker makes one mistake in every thousand transactions, then the odds of their both making the same mistake is actually much less than one in a million. Of course errors that originate in a prior step won't be caught. The parallel processing may have to run the whole length of the process. Any unclear numbers, any uncertainty whatsoever, must be referred to the supervisor for clarification; otherwise both workers could interpret a smudged 6 as 8, leading to the same error being made in parallel.

In both the semiconductor factory and the bank, inspection is a necessary part of the process. Workers who are properly trained and informed realize this and welcome it as just another necessary step in the overall process to assure error-free operation. But the situation is qualitatively different when the process is error free. When every product made or every service performed can be and is flawless, inspection should be eliminated. The system and the workers are capable of delivering defective-free work, but their product is inspected nevertheless. The workers are ready, willing, and able to take responsibility for their work, but management is in effect telling them it won't trust them or give them the responsibility. This is demeaning to the workers and keeps them from experiencing pride in their work. As pride in work is lost, their attitude changes. Workers allow things to get by them because the inspector "will pick it up anyway."

No Inspection?

The idea of no inspection can be frightening. It seems like being asked to operate in the dark. But the absence of inspection does not imply the absence of information. The process should always be monitored. Control charts provide information at all stages of the process from beginning to end. Inspection just provides information at the end. When inspection is being used properly, it is like a filtering system that takes out the unacceptable and gives some information about the end product. Used improperly, it provides scapegoats and can be the source of tampering.

Control charts are much more sensitive than inspection at the end and often signal the onset of problems months before inspection could.

We already operate without inspection of supplies in much of our daily life. When we purchase a 12-ounce box of cereal, we don't weigh it to make sure we are getting 12 ounces. We don't conduct chemical analysis on the detergent we buy, and we don't count the number of toothpicks in a box labeled as containing 250. Most of the items we purchase daily are accepted without inspection or verification. It would be impossible and unwieldy to live otherwise. But we do look at everything that is purchased. We look for signs of tampering. Any opened or seriously bent box is not purchased.

If, on the other hand, our experience with a supplier is not perfect, we tend to inspect everything that comes in. If a lumberyard has sent the wrong or faulty material in the past, it is prudent to inspect every piece to make sure it conforms to the order and is of acceptable quality.

The alternative to no inspection is 100 percent inspection for suppliers whose product is less than perfect. But the long-term solution is to work with suppliers to improve quality at the source or to find a supplier who is serious about quality and improvement. The long-term solution within the firm is to improve quality by improving the product or the process.

Summary

Inspection can be a useful but limited tool if properly applied. When knowledge is used to ensure that the inspectors, gauges, and measuring devices are in statistical control, inspection can limit the risk of errors reaching the customer. Inspection, however, is not the way to ensure or improve quality. Adding more inspectors, making double or triple inspection, is a sign of a problem, not a sign of competent efforts to improve. The time will come when the courts, which now view double inspection as a sign of reasonable efforts to prevent problems, will view this as a sign of gross negligence.

Inspection cannot improve quality, and we must stop relying on it for quality. Instead we must take the necessary steps to transform the whole company so that improvement becomes a way of life.

CHAPTER 12

Attitudes Toward Suppliers

Point 4 states, "End the practice of awarding business on the basis of price tag. Instead, minimize total cost. Move toward a single supplier for any one item, on a long-term relationship of loyalty and trust."

Our Personal Purchasing Experience

All of us at one time have purchased something because it was lowest in price. Sometimes the lowest-priced items are the best for our purposes. But all of us have had experiences where purchasing the lowest-priced item has been a disaster.

When we purchase an item for ourselves, we're really looking at the total cost of that item during its lifetime. It's not the most expensive or the least expensive item that we should choose but the most suitable for our purpose. We balance initial costs with other considerations. How good is it and how much do we value our time, ease of use, quality, and so on?

If any of us were to purchase everything in our personal lives based on lowest price, we would soon go broke. In our personal lives the purchaser and the user are almost always the same. But once we enter a corporate environment, we immediately encounter the potential for a communications problem. The purchaser is no longer the user. Someone or some department may be entrusted with the responsibility of procuring supplies in an efficient and cost-effective manner. Knowing what's available outside the walls of the corporation is part of purchasing's job. But they should also communicate with the users. Purchasing should be done on the basis of lowest total cost, not just initial cost.

But when there is no communication between user and purchaser, problems quickly develop. If an item is unsatisfactory, the purchasing department may never know and never stop purchasing it.

Accountability—Assigning Costs to Departments

In a corporate environment the most visible number is price or initial cost. Accounting statements don't reflect the fact that decreasing initial cost, if it means lower quality, will increase total cost. That knowledge has to be brought along by whoever reads the financial reports. In the worst case, management starts judging and rewarding people based on the visible numbers of their departments. Only trouble can result from such a course of action.

Just Issue Good Specifications—Another Fallacy

There is another aspect to a company's relationship with suppliers that is less intuitive. Dr. Joyce Orsini uses the example of a department buying paper for its copier. One approach is to set specifications and then take bids for paper meeting the written specifications from three different suppliers.

Orsini with her seminar audience develops about twenty specifications that everyone feels adequately describe the paper. She then rattles off fifteen more key specifications no one had thought about. The point is you'd have to become a paper expert just to buy the best paper for your needs. Why not enlist the aid of an expert, your supplier?

Problems with Specifications

Let me relate a story told by Barbara Lawton, a statistician with experience in our nuclear weapons programs. As you can imagine, some pretty high-priced talent develops sophisticated models, using mathematical and statistical tools, to ensure the smooth transition of a weapons system as it moves from design to prototype and then into production. The engineers develop specifications for every item. They discover that some qualities of a product have no effect on the manufacturing process, so no specifications or just very broad specifications are written for those particular qualities.

Other characteristics are found to be critical, so tight specifications are set. But this is a government-funded operation, so the firms developing and manufacturing the systems must play by government rules. The government has a rule stating everything must be purchased on the basis of lowest price, a practice none of us could live with in our own lives. Not only that, but those in charge of purchasing receive a portion of the so-called "savings" whenever they find a cheaper source.

But all the specifications are met! How could there possibly be a problem when a different supplier, who meets all the specifications, is used? All that effort put into developing the specifications must mean they are complete, right? No. When a new supplier comes on line, the number of problems and defects rises and the whole system is thrown out of control. Even though the specifications are met, any item from a different source is different and interacts differently with the manufacturing process.

Oftentimes although the item meets all the specifications, it is sufficiently different that engineers discover a new critical variable and must rewrite the specifications. The amount of waste and loss to the taxpayer, as well as the risk to our national security, is incalculable. The government is mandating poor quality, waste, and exorbitant costs with its policy.

Why Aren't Specifications Complete?

Why aren't specifications enough? Suppose a long-lost Rembrandt painting is being unveiled in Amsterdam, but photography is not allowed. Several museums want a copy of the painting, so they enlist an art critic to describe it via phone to master painters, who will reproduce it. The critic does his utmost to describe the painting. "A woman with blue hair and a roman nose is in the middle of the painting. Her nose is 3.5 centimeters long...," and so on.

When the paintings are finished not one of them looks like any other and none looks like the original, even though all the specifications are met.

One more simple example. Suppose historians decisively prove that a given rock is Plymouth Rock, where the Pilgrims first landed in the New World. To celebrate their discovery, they want duplicate rocks made for every part of the country, and they decide to issue specifications for the duplicate rocks. This should be a relatively easy task.

If the rock is very close to a "perfect" circle, then it would seem that just one specification, the radius, is needed. Suppose, instead, that the rock, like most rocks we find in nature, doesn't even roughly approach any regular geometric shape. It is totally irregular. How many specifications would you need to get an acceptable duplicate of Plymouth Rock?

You could be writing specifications from now to judgment day and still not get it right. Any description, any set of measurements, would be incomplete. On the other hand, you could just tell a mason what you were trying to do and he could make a cast of the original. All the specifications in the world are insufficient, but showing someone the original and telling him what the duplicate would be used for allows him to do the job.

Similarly for the painting in the first example. Any master painter by setting up his easel next to the Rembrandt could make a copy that would fool most of us.

Procter & Gamble and Its Suppliers

A wonderful example of a company working closely with its suppliers involves Procter & Gamble. Procter & Gamble is one of the world's leading companies. Among their well-known brands are Tide detergent, Ivory soap, Comet cleanser, and Crest toothpaste.

Several years ago a number of engineers from the company attended Deming seminars. What they leaned at the seminars was applied to their local operations. Management were sufficiently impressed to ask Deming to work with them on a corporate-wide basis. In April 1986, Deming began a series of four-day seminars exclusively for Procter & Gamble employees. All senior management attended.

Why would a successful company like Procter & Gamble be interested in Deming's management philosophy? Tide is the leading detergent in Japan. Certainly none of us have heard of a

Japanese or European invasion of the American soap or detergent markets. P&G's earnings continue to grow. Where was the crisis? There was no crisis at the time, but P&G's management were concerned about their shrinking margins. Historically they had enjoyed profit margins of 6 percent of sales and those had gradually declined to 5 percent and 4 percent of sales. They were concerned about an impending crisis and decided to act before it was upon them. Pretty smart management, I'd say.

But what do many companies do when confronted with such a situation—when compared with a competitor or with their own past performance, they're not doing as well? Many companies start a vigorous Management By Objectives program. But of course that doesn't address the problem, so things only get worse. Companies that follow such a route find themselves streamlining, in an attempt to become more competitive, dropping some businesses, concentrating in others.

P&G took a different tack, and guess what? Margins began climbing and returned to their historical levels. But this is just a beginning. Who knows what the margins should be or how much better the company can become when the only goal is improvement?

I'd like to focus on one area where P&G adopted Deming's philosophy—its relationship with suppliers, specifically its advertising agencies. P&G is the largest advertiser in the world and probably has more advertising experience than any other company. When they did a survey of fifteen companies, some of which are competitors, they discovered remarkable consistency in the effectiveness of advertising campaigns. Among all the companies surveyed, including themselves, only about one in five of the advertising campaigns was effective.

In other words, 80 percent of the advertising was ineffective. But when they examined the situation in greater detail, they found the situation was much worse. For every advertising campaign used, five prototype campaigns are produced and tested. For every prototype campaign eight storyboards are shown to the customer, and for every storyboard shown there are two that aren't even shown to the customer.

For every successful advertising campaign six hundred storyboards or ideas for an advertising campaign are developed. Not a very efficient operation, to say the least. Why is there so much waste? One reason was that although P&G spent fortunes on consumer research, they weren't sharing the results with their agencies. They had the old attitude of maintaining an arm's length relationship with their agencies. In some circles this is known as the Mushroom Method of Management: "Keep them in the dark and feed them manure."

The agencies weren't part of P&G. Even though the company had long-term relationships with them, some going back fifty years, they were not really operating as partners.

P&G approached each of their eight agencies and explained their desire to work as partners, using the Deming philosophy and Deming methods. They received an enthusiastic response from each. Top management of the agencies, along with key personnel, began learning Deming's management methods through a seminar and written material.

A committee was established with an equal number of participants from P&G and from the agency. The company's vast resources and information on consumer research were shared with the agency from the beginning. The importance of consumer research in advertising is that the customer has certain needs. A good advertising campaign should tell the customer the product can fulfill those needs, but if the copywriters are unaware of just what those needs are, they have to guess. In the past, when they guessed right, a campaign was accepted; when they guessed wrong, it was rejected. Now that has changed: the copywriters know from the beginning what the customer's needs are.

But many managers would be appalled at the idea of sharing important knowledge with an agency, which could then be in a position to use the results to plan campaigns for competitors. But P&G had adopted the new philosophy. Their attitude was "So What!" They were out to expand the market, not just fight for market share. If a competitor's product and advertising improves as a result, the industry as a whole benefits and the customers benefit.

Procter & Gamble is very pleased with results and is enthusiastically expanding its efforts. If they can work with suppliers on a cooperative basis instead of a confrontational one, why not work with customers, such as large chain stores, on the same basis?

Procter & Gamble as the Supplier

Management decided to do just that and chose a fast-growing discount chain, which at the time was its third-largest customer. They approached the chairman, who was enthusiastic about the prospect of working together. He wanted to work on the logistical system, which involved the delivery of product.

Together these two giant organizations worked on the systemic problems of ordering and delivering, which neither could solve alone. They shared information, explored the needs of each part of the system, and worked on the system. The results were that together they were able to lower total inventory of the product by 38 percent. Volume of sales was up substantially, inventory turnover went from forty-five to seventy-five. This means inventory was turned over seventy-five times a year. The store had to pay P&G ten days after taking delivery, but it had already sold all its stock and collected its money five days after taking delivery.

Damage levels went down sharply, service levels improved, and the store became the company's biggest customer. The program was a resounding success. As P&G delved further into their logistical systems, they discovered some disturbing facts. For instance, they discovered that only 50 percent of their orders were shipped out as the customers placed them. Only 55 percent of the orders arrived on time. And incorrect or late shipments led to claims that were difficult to resolve. In 1988 the company wrote off $72 million in unresolved claims. Clearly they have quite a ways to go, but they have begun.

At what point should they be able to stop their efforts toward improvement and be satisfied? The answer, of course, is never. Here we have one of the best-run companies in the world, and when they look at their systems they realize there is vast room for improvement.

But if our best-run companies have ample room for improvement, what about our mediocre and worst-run organizations? Where are they? Our mail service is problematic at best. Our subways can change their route without an announcement. I've waited for weeks for a part to arrive, only to discover that the wrong part had been sent.

We often hear the complaint that limited productivity gains can be made in the service sectors because we can't readily invest in machinery. But in delivery, logistics, and advertising, all of which are service areas, P&G obtained startling gains in productivity. Managing the service area is no different from managing the manufacturing sector.

Reliability

Suppose your department has a copier that clogs every now and then. This creates problems and inconveniences, but management does a study and determines that all your projects are on time 95 percent of the time. Not too shabby. Ninety-five percent is considered an excellent grade in school, so it's natural to assume the same in business. But what if your department is just one of twelve in a series? Let's assume that your department takes the orders from customers and then hands over the paperwork to the factory. The factory in turn does some paperwork, and it then goes to the warehouse. From the warehouse to the shipping area and so on. All in all, there are twelve separate departments with work flowing sequentially from one to the next. Each department is on time 95 percent of the time. How often is the company as a whole on time? About 54 percent of the time. For the company as a whole to be on time, each department would have to be on time. But the odds of that happening are 95 percent times itself eleven times or 54 percent.

This is not a hypothetical situation. Procter & Gamble's products were shipped on time just 55 percent of the time, and when they investigated, they found every item went through twelve departments. Each had an on-time record of 95 percent. In business 95 percent is not good enough. But the real point I'm making is that even seemingly small quality problems can lead to significant loss for the company.

Arms-Around Relationship

Your supplier is in the best position to provide quality if he is secure and can see how his product will be used. Deming tells his clients to let their suppliers into their plants and offices. Show them how their products are used. Share knowledge and work on problems together. Make a long-term commitment to each supplier and use just one for each item.

Using one supplier for each item can lead to substantial cost savings and improvement in quality. If a supplier knows he has a long-term relationship, he can lower his costs. He doesn't need to spend time and money courting you. Those ridiculous and annoying follow-up phone calls and lunches can be avoided, and you can both concentrate on making improvements. He can invest in the relationship. Investment may take the form of plant and equipment dedicated to your needs or investment of time to understand your operations and your needs.

Supplies have to be chosen not on the basis of lowest initial cost but on the best suitability for your operation, or in other words, lowest total cost.

A close relationship with a supplier is similar to a marriage. As in a marriage, it's helpful to know as much as possible about each other before making a commitment. A marriage is much more work than the occasional fling, but it can also be much more gratifying. Even marriages do sometimes fail, but every avenue should be explored before breaking one up.

Summary

The proper way of dealing with suppliers, according to Deming, is simple and straightforward. Treat suppliers with respect. Work closely with them on a long-term relationship based on loyalty and trust. Let them see the operation and give them whatever help, assistance, and information they need to do the job right. It is not a matter of anyone working harder; it is a matter of management working smarter.

CHAPTER 13

Rebirth and Renewal

Point 5 states, "Improve constantly and forever the system of production and service."

Improvement and innovation for the people, processes, products, and services of a company should always be management's goal. I need to caution, however, that management must avoid numerical goals for improvement.

Improvement means many things to many people. No one would argue with the need for constant improvement, but some believe that focusing on results will lead to improvement. What do I mean by focusing on results? Inspection focuses on results, but it does not make any improvement. The system is left intact and the problems remain.

Sometimes a company will fire someone in charge of a department when the results are unsatisfactory. One mail-order house fired its purchasing manager because supplies kept arriving late. When he was replaced, the problem persisted.

Finding who was "responsible" for the problem is focusing on results and rarely, if ever, leads to improvement. Making people accountable for their mistakes also focuses on results without leading to improvement.

One so-called quality control expert has everyone in the company that employs him sign a pledge stating they will hereafter make no defects. This action proves that management assumes that the operator is responsible for all the errors. Companies pay millions of dollars for that kind of advice only to find several years later that there's no change. In fact, things may be worse. When the program is announced, everyone is optimistic, a superhuman effort begins, and some numbers seem to improve. But when real changes aren't made, the very same people become discouraged.

Management that tries to induce people to meet the specifications is reacting to the situation knee-jerk fashion. For management to promote real improvement, it has to take control of the situation, and that takes understanding Deming's ideas.

Just Meet Specifications

A company can go down the tubes just meeting the specifications. Point 5 is not just a suggestion to improve whenever possible, it is a call to arms. Management must aggressively and vigorously seek improvement. By improving the process, a company can make specifications irrelevant. Improvement can also be made in the design of the product or the running of the operation, both of which have nothing to do with specifications and aren't tied to yesterday's stale notion of the numbers.

The Route to Improvement

There are four ways to improve the quality of products and services.

1. Innovation in product and services.
2. Innovation in the process that creates the products and services.
3. Improvement of existing products and services.
4. Improvement of the existing process.

None of these is sufficient by itself. Slide rule manufacturers may have made better and better slide rules with ever-increasing precision. But when semiconductors were refined to the point that scientific calculators became an inexpensive reality, the slide rule people were all put out of business.

Sometimes it is very difficult to tell an innovation from an improvement. Fuel injection may seem like an innovation to the makers of carburetors, but in the overall scheme of a car's mechanics it is an improvement in the way fuel is introduced into the piston. Hewlett-Packard is known to introduce new models of its existing printers with fewer moving parts. Is this innovation or improvement? Both the product and the process are improved by such a move.

Just Meet the Competition

The company that constantly responds to its competitors already has its back against the wall. Do you think the competition will just wait for you to catch up?

How far behind can a company fall? Isn't it possible to take apart your competitor's products and discover why they work better or faster? Sometimes it's possible. Sometimes reverse engineering is useful. But matching the process may take ten years, and by then the competitor will have made radical improvements.

In some cases reverse engineering won't help at all. One company decided to manufacture copiers. So they took apart the best copier on the market and had each part duplicated. A plant was set up at a cost of over $30 million. When the plant was completed, all the parts were made to specifications, but there was just one problem: The machine didn't work.

Something was missing. I would say the missing ingredients were knowledge and skill—profound knowledge and profound skill.

The best violins are generally considered those made by two eighteenth-century masters of Cremona, Italy: Antonio Stradivari and Guiseppe Guarneri del Gesu. Their violins have been taken apart and examined for over two hundred years, and no one yet knows how to make violins that match their richness of sound.

Two hundred years later the competition is still struggling to keep up. If we needed an example of how far ahead of the competition someone can go, this is it.

Tools of the Trade

Suppose management decides that improvement must become a way of life. One good way to start is to draw a flowchart of the process. The flowchart we saw in chapter 9 is recreated here.

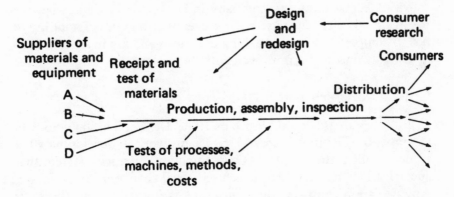

From Deming, *Out of the Crisis*

This flow chart illustrates the working of a quality-conscious company. But does the company really operate in this fashion? Does your company have a process for obtaining feedback on product and services from the customer? Is this information then made available to the engineers and designers? Do they use it? Who is responsible for delivering customer feedback to the designers? Do they actually use the information, or does it sit on the desk of the department head? Do they see the information right away or six months after it is available? A host of questions immediately come to mind when looking at a flowchart. We can start with the overall process and then look at just a part of it—at design, for example—and then draw a flowchart for that part.

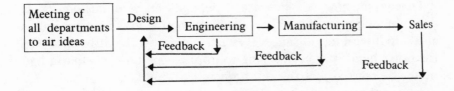

We all feel we know our company and its operations, but when we begin drawing flowcharts, we discover that our understanding is not so complete. We begin asking questions and are in a position to investigate and make improvements

Critical Variables

But what areas should we attack first? Dr. Genichi Taguchi won the Japanese Deming Prize in 1960 for his work in developing what is now called the Taguchi Loss Function. Taguchi stated that specifications as they had been used until then were out of date. Any deviation from the ideal causes a loss in quality and therefore an economic loss. The further from the ideal the greater the loss. But in some items the economic loss increased dramatically with small deviations from the ideal, while with other items even large deviations resulted in almost no economic loss. Some items were critical, with small improvements producing large gains, while other items were not critical. Where should our efforts be concentrated? We should work on the critical variables first because doing so will have the greatest impact on quality.

Here's a simple example. For cooking a pound of pasta, six quarts of boiling water may be the ideal amount. But if you use eight quarts or ten quarts, the results won't be significantly altered. It takes more time to boil eight quarts of water and more gas or electricity is used, so we do have an economic loss, but it is hardly noticeable. On the other hand, cooking the pasta for fourteen minutes instead of ten significantly affects the texture. It will be too soggy to enjoy.

Of course, how you prepare it depends on your customers. If you're cooking for the kids, you might boil it for twenty minutes and slop it with lots of sauce; they may not know the difference. On the other hand, if you're trying to impress the boss, the pasta had better be cooked just the right amount of time.

It's management's job to discover which are the critical variables and work on those.

Control Charts

Control charts can be drawn for any variable. We could draw a control chart for arrival time of a train or plane. If the plane is one minute early we would plot a $+1$ on the chart. If it were two minutes late, we would plot a -2. By plotting each time of arrival in sequence, we would generate a control chart.

A control chart has three lines on it: the average, the upper control limit, and the lower control limit. All three are derived from the data. A control chart should be drawn with no preconceived notions and without fear or pressure. A control chart gives you a picture of what's going on. As long as all the points are between the control limits and there are no trends or cycles, the system is stable.

If the lower control limit for our chart is -20 minutes, our plane may arrive up to 20 minutes late and we would have no reason to believe that anything unusual happened. Without the use of a control chart, we might be tempted to conduct a thorough investigation. We might be tempted to warn the pilot or crew or make them sign a pledge stating they will never again be more than five minutes late. But such actions, as we have seen, will only hurt. The control chart tells us that latenesses of up to 20 minutes are built into the system and will sometimes occur. We can't predict when, but we know they will occur.

Any points that fall outside the control limits indicate the existence of a special cause. Special causes should be identified and if possible eliminated.

When a special cause is indicated we may find any number of causes. We may find that the engines aren't running properly and need to be tuned up, a new supplier or new air controller may be learning the ropes, an earthquake caused a delay, or a storm forced the pilot to change course.

Once all the special causes are eliminated, or at least explained, the hard part begins. Now the system must be improved to produce greater uniformity and fewer defects. Inspection, quotas, pep talks, or threats are now all useless. Knowledge in all its forms is all-important.

Flowcharts will help clarify the company's process. But a flowchart will say different things to different people. Anyone can make a suggestion for improvement, even people who are totally ignorant of the process. A suggestion made in ignorance could be disastrous, producing problems somewhere else in the company. It is important that individuals with expertise in the various areas be present when suggestions for improvement are actually considered.

That's all a quality control circle is. A foreman or senior worker from each area form a committee, and together they examine all the possibilities.

Fish Bone or Cause and Effect Chart

A cause and effect chart looks very much like the charts used to graph sentences, and is used to help identify the possible causes of problems. In a cause and effect chart the end result is indicated to the right of the horizontal line. On the horizontal is placed the main process. All the feeder processes are placed on diagonals. These in turn have lines off them where other processes feed into them.

These charts help clarify the process and indicate possible means of improvement. An example of a cause and effect chart is shown below.[1]

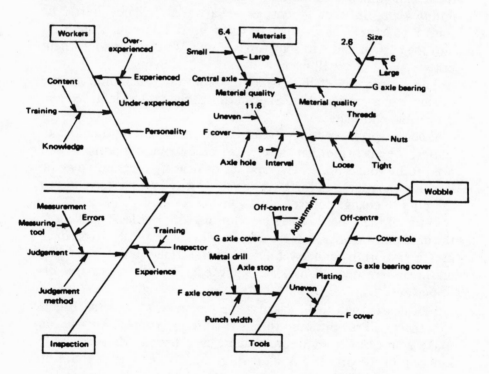

From Ishikawa, *Guide to Quality Control*

Experimental Design

A quality control circle may suspect that changing an input or part of the process may improve the end result. Guided by someone trained in experimental design, they could devise an experiment in which variables in the process are changed. They would observe the results to determine if improvement occurs. Experimental design is a highly developed discipline.

Recently, newspaper articles have reported that Taguchi's methods of experimental design are helping to improve the operations of some of our largest firms. But the bottleneck holding up American industry is not a lack of knowledge or availability of statistical methods. Many of these techniques originated here, although in many cases they have been further developed and refined in Japan. We have adequate texts and many engineers and statisticians familiar with these methods. But we cannot make a step toward improvement until management decides to take advantage of their knowledge.

Most of our management habits are inconsistent with continual improvement. Our methods, our organizational structure, our setting of priorities, our penchant for judging people, and our over-reliance on rules and clichés hamper our efforts at improvement and have to be changed. But only management, especially top management, can make those changes. That is where the real stumbling block exists today. But our managers are constantly bombarded with the wrong advice.

An essay appeared in the *Wall Street Journal* on October 30, 1986, written by one of the highest-paid business consultants in the Western world. I find the essay incredible because it is so incorrect. Consider the following:

> Each factor has to be measured separately. Indeed in the large organization—whether a business, a hospital or a university—the productivity of different segments within each factor needs to be measured, for example, blue-collar labor, clerical labor, managers, and service staffs.
>
> Ideally, the productivity of each factor should increase steadily. At the very least, however, increased productivity of one factor, for instance, people, should not be achieved at the expense of the

productivity of another factor, like capital—something American industry has been guilty of far too often.[2]

Now I will readily admit that before being exposed to Deming I would have found the above paragraphs convincing, even compelling. But now I can appreciate them as nonsense, dangerous nonsense. The numbers that the above paragraphs claim are so important are meaningless. Relying on them as an aid in business decisions will damage the corporation.

Let me use one more analogy to help clarify what I mean. Let me revert to a soccer analogy for a moment. A striker who leads the attack places himself in the right position, receives a pass from one of his teammates, and in midair kicks the ball and scores. The fans go wild. Who scored that goal? Most people would say the striker scored that goal. A good coach would say the team scored that goal.

On the other hand, a defender reads the game correctly and places himself in the correct position. When a pass goes to the opposing team's wing, the defender moves in and pressures the wing to the outside. The wing has to pass backward to keep from losing possession, and in the three seconds of delay, the defender's team completely recovers its position. A great play the equal of the flying kick that scored the goal has just been made. But the defender didn't even touch the ball. There is no roar of the crowd.

Just by being in the right position at the right time and playing well, the defender influenced—even determined—the outcome of the game at least as much as the striker who "scored" the goal.

But how do you judge the productivity of a player? You could count the number of times each player touched the ball. Each player would then be running all over constantly trying to touch the ball. The productivity of every member of the team would then increase but the team would play a lousy game and be destroyed whenever they went up against a properly coached team.

American industry is rife with critics who are judging each department and each player. What we need today is not more critics but knowledgeable coaches, real leaders to stop the judging and measuring of every form of productivity and begin leading everyone toward improvement.

Summary

The firm that continually improves is the one that stands the best chance of survival and offers the greatest security to its workers, managers, and shareholders. Attempts at improvement in this country have often been misdirected because they were aimed only at improving profit and often done without guidance from profound knowledge.

Several tools are available to managers interested in improving. Control charts, flowcharts, and experimental design can help management identify and eliminate special causes and continually improve the process.

But these tools are of little value if management refuses to do its job and change the system of management from one in which everyone and every department is judged on the basis of local numbers to one in which security prevails and people are encouraged to grow and experience joy in their work.

CHAPTER 14

The Importance of Training

Point 6 states, "Institute training."

That sounds simple enough. Don't our firms provide training. Some do, some don't do it enough, and many don't.

When I worked for a bank that lent money abroad, loans made to finance U.S. exports were insured against credit loss by an insurance consortium (FCIA). The consortium in turn had much of its credit risk sold to the Export-Import Bank of the United States, a U.S. government agency. In effect, the bank was lending abroad, with the ultimate credit risk being the U.S. government. Good, safe lending.

One young officer became concerned about the program and asked to enroll in a one-week seminar, given by FCIA, which explained the programs and the required documentation. He was turned down. There were more important things to do than attend a seminar. About a year later one of the bank's borrowers went belly up and defaulted on his loans. No problem, the loans were insured. Except that when the bank went to make its claims, all the necessary documentation was missing. The officer who turned down the request for training didn't even know these documents were necessary. How could he?

Training as an Expense

Training is often seen as an expense. It is a visible number that management can control and therefore subject to scrutiny. Training often has to be justified, but the benefits from training are often not visible.

168

When the bank was forced to take the hit and write off over one million dollars in uncollectible loans that should have been insured, they looked for a scapegoat. Someone should have known what forms to file. Of course no one was even aware of the need to file certain forms. A scapegoat was found nevertheless. But the loss was from lack of training.

Whose responsibility is training? That's management's. Training is improvement and always pays, although the benefit is not always evident.

Anyone who really wants to make improvements is better off banning the phrase *"should have known"* from his or her lexicon. To improve we have to deal with what really happened, not the hypothetical world of *should haves*.

Society at Large

How much does it cost for society to keep a person in prison for a year? $5,000? $10,000? The latest estimate I've seen is $60,000. That's a remarkable figure when we consider that the average income in the United States is less than a third of that. It costs a bundle to imprison someone, yet the most popular solution to crime is to imprison all the offenders.

There's another interesting statistic. Three-fourths of all people arrested are functionally illiterate. Of those who are functionally illiterate how many have marketable skills? Our society has not done enough to teach the basic skills of reading, writing, and arithmetic, and it hasn't even tried to teach marketable skills to many of our youth.

It is quite plausible then that providing skills to prisoners would have a real, positive return to society. But when the governor of New York was confronted with a revenue shortfall, where did he look to "save" money? He tried to cut back on the prisoner training programs and raise tuitions at state colleges.

Training for Today

Training is providing skills and knowledge for the immediate future. Skills have certain characteristics. Once a skill is learned it is very difficult, perhaps impossible to change. An example of a skill is speaking a foreign language. Once a person learns to speak a new language with a certain accent, it is almost impossible to change that accent. Notice the individuals you know who learned English as a second language. If they learned to speak English abroad, they probably picked up the accent of their teacher. After living in this country for thirty years, they still have the same accent.

How do you know someone has learned a skill? Simply, if his or her work is in statistical control, the skill has been learned and further instructions won't help. Playing golf is a skill. In an actual situation control charts were constructed for a beginning player. The charts showed his game wasn't in control. The scores were high and very inconsistent. After taking lessons, he had improved his game. His average score was lower and his game was more consistent. It was now in statistical control.

The same was done for an experienced player. His game was already in statistical control. After he took lessons, his game showed no improvement.[1]

In Japan this method is used in some hospitals to determine when additional physical therapy for accident victims will no longer help. A patient who has suffered a severe accident may have to relearn to walk. A physical therapist instructs him and records the length of time for each step over a given distance. When he has relearned how to walk, as indicated by the control chart, further lessons will no longer help. This protects the patient and helps the therapist productively allocate his time.[2]

Implications

The implication is clear. You get one chance to train someone, and you had better make it count. There is no second chance. You had better have a master do the teaching. If a hack trains your employees, the cost to your company will be unmeasurable. It is the beginner who most needs the master.

Who Does the Training?

As I mentioned in an earlier chapter, having workers train workers will lead to loss. When one person teaches the next, who in turn teaches the next, everyone will have a different idea of what to do and no one will be properly trained. One person must be put in charge of training, and he had better be a master.

In some firms the foremen or supervisors are responsible for training. On the face of it that's not so bad, but many firms use the supervisor's position as the entry level for future managers, hiring individuals right out of college to fill those positions. They know nothing about the jobs and less about the skills. Would any worker having a problem seek assistance from someone who didn't know the job?

Self-Taught

We value the ability to teach oneself. There's much to be said for this. But there are problems when someone is self-taught. The self-taught may be able to do the job or play the game, but it is unlikely they do so in an optimal fashion. We all know self-taught golfers or tennis players whose games are fine. But compared to someone of similar athletic ability who took lessons from a pro, their games are not very good. And it is too late to change. They are better off learning a different game from scratch if they want to play with the big boys.

People who are self-taught usually acquire bad habits. The best way of doing anything is rarely the way that feels most natural. High jumpers, for example, today use a technique called the Fosbury flop. Prior to Dick Fosbury's introduction of the flop, all high jumpers did a Western or Eastern roll. They would roll over the bar with their stomachs facing the bar and their backs to the sky. But Fosbury analyzed the mechanics of high jumping and developed a method that looked extremely awkward. He was going over the bar with his back to the bar and his front facing upward. He looked extremely silly high jumping, but he kept winning. He won the Olympic gold medal. Today every jumper uses his method.

Even if a self-taught person manages to figure out the best way of doing something, there is still a problem. If after fifty years of being self-taught he wanted to pass on everything he had learned in his lifetime, he would take on an apprentice. Within a few years that apprentice would have acquired the better part of the master's knowledge and would then be in a position to add new knowledge and skills. An apprentice learning under a master can learn in a few years knowledge and skills that may have taken previous craftspeople two hundred years to develop.

While renovating an apartment building, I had two master carpenters working at once. One was self-taught, the other was trained in Italy. The craftsmanship of both was exceptional. But the self-taught carpenter took about twice as long.

Corporate Attitude Toward Training

I don't think we fully appreciate the benefits of training. This is reflected in some of our common attitudes. Many firms like to hire from the outside, bringing in someone who has already been trained. That way they avoid the expense of training employees. There is also a fear that if they train someone, that person will leave and apply the training elsewhere. In general, the major benefits of training are not well appreciated.

Common Attitudes Toward Training

The attitudes we live by day-to-day are the same ones we use to run our businesses, our offices, and our schools. We don't have one set of attitudes for life and one for business.

I have observed many parents acting as coaches. Most parents run practices grudgingly. To most, coaching means coaching at the game: yelling encouragement from the sidelines, pulling players in and out, switching positions around, using strategy.

I have observed three individuals who always seem to have superior teams. The attitudes and styles of the three couldn't be more different. The one commonality is that each places great emphasis on instruction. They use the practice and the games as a vehicle to teach. But most teaching is, of course, done during practice. The super coaches believe that 80 percent of the outcome of the game is in the practice and at most 20 percent is determined during the game.

Training makes a difference in children's sports and in our factories and our offices. The firms that emphasize training inexplicably seem to have better earnings than the firms that are so cost conscious as to get rid of all training programs.

Training improves the system. It lowers costs and improves revenues.

Two Different Attitudes to Training

Let's consider two different responses to a downturn in sales. Assume that an industry's sales are down 30 percent. One company decides to close a few plants and lay off 30 percent of its work force. At first the workers are ecstatic. They get out their fishing gear, put on their hunting clothes, and head out for some serious recreation. But after six to nine months of living the hunter-gatherer life, they begin looking forward to going back to work.

When the plant finally opens, their skills are a little rusty. But they soon get into the grind and in a few months are fully back up to snuff.

The other company takes a different approach. It may cut back the work week, but it keeps everyone on. It doesn't need all its work force to produce for today's market, however, so perhaps 30 percent of its work force has nothing to do. Should they be given busy work? No. In the Deming view, there is never enough time, one never knows enough, and skills can always be improved.

This is a wonderful opportunity to improve skills and methods, and to improve the system. The welders can see what goes on in the other areas of the plant and understand the needs of the other departments. They can improve the skills needed in their own areas. They can pick up new skills. They can learn more about statistical tools and learn how to draw and interpret control charts, cause and effect charts, and flowcharts. They can learn what it means to improve the system and work aggressively to do so.

When the market recovers and sales pick up, who is in the stronger position, the company that saved money by laying off its workers or the company that invested in its people and its future?

In a real sense, this question can't be answered through rhetoric. We are conducting an experiment of this nature in real life, as one management system is going up against a completely different one. Each of us has to judge for himself which is really working out better.

Summary

Training is a critical part of improvement and is management's responsibility. Improvement always pays.

One person, a master, should be responsible for teaching everyone the same skill. Once a skill is learned incorrectly, it cannot be altered economically, if at all. Therefore, training must be done right the first time.

CHAPTER 15

Leadership

Point 7: Institute Leadership.

Supervision or Leadership?

When I first encountered Deming, Point 7 read, "Institute supervision." This was a bit confusing because, in my experience, there was too much supervision at all levels of management, people running around overseeing this or that operation, and responsible for as few as one employee.

But it soon became clear that what Deming meant by supervision had very little to do with what is often called supervision. In fact such so-called supervision often occurred in areas where Deming-style supervision was really needed. Supervision in the way he used the term required knowledge. It is different than just overseeing the work of a subordinate.

Supervision

Deming described a supervisor who at the end of each day would sit all seven of her people down to analyze and discuss what went wrong that day. Each defective was taken apart. She was doing her best trying to help each worker avoid errors and improve. All her workers liked her and felt she had their best interest at heart. It's true, she did, but for years the level of defectives had remained steady. At best, she was just wasting everyone's time at the end of each day.

Leadership

Since my first encounter with Deming, he has substituted the word *leadership* for supervision. I find it helpful to use the word *supervision* to describe the reactive and incorrect practice, and *leadership* to describe Deming's alternative.

One of Deming's client companies discovered they had a problem—a pretty serious problem. Bottles with toxic materials hadn't been labeled. The plant manager's solution was to find out who was responsible for labeling each bottle and impress upon each the importance of the job. Without the right label, money and lives were at risk.

Sounds great, doesn't it? But if the system was stable, this solution was no solution at all. This might be a case of tampering, making things worse. As it turned out, the problem had been going on for years. The system was responsible for the unlabeled bottles. The plant manager was using supervision where leadership was required. In the worst form of supervision, the supervisor is overseeing, constantly criticizing, not just building resentment but making things progressively worse. In a milder form, the supervisor recognizes superior performance in the belief that doing so will improve everyone's performance, and therefore the group's as well. Such a belief is, of course, unfounded and counterproductive.

Leadership requires knowledge of common causes and special causes. A leader has to know that the past is not necessarily a predictor of the future. He has to know the difference between a description of what happened in the past and a theory that can help predict.

Most managers, when they view their group, are supervising, judging, and ranking the performance of the individual workers. But a leader judges his own performance when he observes his group. In his mind he is determining what he has to emphasize or de-emphasize, what action he has to take to foster improvement.

A leader recognizes the individual skills, talents, and abilities of all those working under him, but to him everyone is equal. He does not judge. By equal, I mean he does not rank his fellow employees as to their performance or worth. He must be able to recognize when someone is operating outside the system, and take appropriate action. He must see that those in need of special help get it. If they need additional training, he must see they receive it. If they are beyond being helped by additional training, he must see that they are moved to positions where they can contribute and make sure they are properly trained.

Group Motivation May Be Tampering

Some managers will read the above paragraphs and nod their heads in agreement. Their response is to make everyone in the group responsible for the system. One company offered a $300 bonus to every employee if there were no accidents. Guess what? There were no accidents. At the awards assembly some employees had their arms in slings, some limped, some had their fingers in casts. There *were* accidents; they just weren't reported. Is this leadership? No.

According to Deming, "A leader works to improve the system that he and his people work in. He understands how the work of his group fits into the aims of the company. The purpose of his group is to support these aims. He works in cooperation with preceding stages and with following stages toward optimization of the efforts of all stages."[1]

Challenge and Joy in Work

A leader fosters and encourages the same understanding in those who work for him. "He tries to create for everybody interest and challenge, and joy in work. He tries to optimize the education, skill, and abilities of everyone, and helps everyone to improve. Improvement and innovation are his aim."[2]

A leader instructs. But instruction means teaching not only what to do, but why. Understanding the overall process is important. A leader should encourage education so that each employee can be thinking and working toward improvement. A leader does not threaten or plead. A leader teaches with patience. A manager without patience is no leader.

Make Sure They Think

Several years ago my wife and I acquired a Border collie. It is an extremely intelligent breed of dogs that for centuries have been bred for their ability to herd sheep. Fancying myself a gentleman farmer, I attended a clinic for dogs and their handlers, hoping to give our dog and myself an education. Luckily, my first teacher, Jack Knox, a Scot now living in Virginia, had worked with dogs all his life and had learned from master handlers. Jack's method is quite simply expressed as "Work from the mind to the foot." That is to say, ask the dog to do something, and then correct him if he needs correcting. Otherwise leave him alone. One prime lesson is that one never hits a dog or tries to beat it into submission. Doing so will ruin a perfectly good dog.

I ran across a remarkable passage in a book written by H. Glyn Jones, a Welsh national champion handler and winner of the International Supreme Championship in 1973. His first dog, Hemp, he had taught just to obey his every command, in the same way his father had trained dogs. With his second dog, Gel, he had tried something else.

> I never really understood why penning was a problem with him [Hemp] until I was handling Gel at his first trial—we were at the pen and I thought that Gel was in the wrong position so I gave him the command to move. He ignored this so I repeated the command and, when the dog obeyed me, we lost the sheep. I then realized that Gel had positioned himself...in the correct position to control the leading ewe, whilst Hemp (the dog I had taught not to use his brain) would leave it all to me....I was very careful not to make the same mistake with Gel and other dogs which followed.

A similar thing happened to me. I asked my dog to go to my right and fetch the sheep, but instead he went off to my left. I was flustered and started shouting additional commands at the dog but Walt Jagger, another master handler who was instructing me, told me to let him go. "He knows that the sheep want to head off to the left and he's going to cut them off." Sure enough, as he approached, the sheep headed to the left, toward the safety of the barn, and my dog was in a position to cut them off and control the herd, bringing them wherever I commanded. How did the dog know what the sheep were about to do? I have no idea. Perhaps the way they were positioned, or the look in their eyes. But he knew, and by not killing his ability to think we were a much more effective team than we could possibly have been if I did all the thinking.

Of course, this book is not about dogs, but my point is that if better results are obtained in working with dogs when the dog is encouraged to think, how much more so when working with people.

Years ago when I was working a summer job, an incident occurred that has gathered greater meaning for me recently. I befriended a fellow employee who worked on the loading dock. He had no title and little formal education, but anyone who spent a few minutes talking to him soon realized he was intelligent. One day a truck pulled up to unload, and he looked at the truck. He stopped the truck from entering the loading dock and began to unload it. The plant manager saw this and objected. The plant manager was very smart. After all, he was plant manager and wore a tie. The employee argued with him, but the manager had authority on his side and said, "Stop wasting our time and do as you're told." So the truck was driven into the loading dock and unloaded. But when it tried to back out, it couldn't. With the weight removed, the truck was a few inches higher and couldn't back out through the opening. It had to be fully reloaded, backed out, and then unloaded on the outside the way the employee had originally proposed.

Who Is Responsible for Improvement?

The plant manager was in a position to note that the gate was the wrong height and propose that future plants adjust the dimensions of their gates. But if he had pointed this out to his superiors, they would have responded, "What can we do about it; the plant has already been built?" In most companies no one is in charge of improvement. If a leader is not concerned with improvement, no one is. If no one is concerned with improvement, the firm might remain the same, but more likely it will decline.

In many firms anyone who complains more than once is marked as a troublemaker. Eventually the supervisor gets back at him for creating trouble. Making improvement is often a bother, but the payoff is real. But if the leader doesn't care, the people learn to live with the existing situation regardless of the number of problems. The problems may be blatant and easily corrected, but why bother? No one cares. They have been taught, conditioned if you prefer, to accept the existing level of problems. When that happens, a vital part of the company dies.

It may take a little time and effort to look for problems and correct them, but the payback is real and experienced upstream and downstream. If a firm asks that all the expenses be justified by the visible numbers of that department, some improvements might be hard to justify. But the company as a whole is the loser when the improvements aren't made.

It is the leader's job to lead the charge toward better quality. The leader can't be satisfied handling problems of today, but has to unbuckle his or her belt and go look for trouble.

A Critical Variable

There is one job that belongs to the leader alone, and that is making sure all the parts and all the people work together. It is possible to obtain the best car parts in the world, the best fuel injection system, the best tires, the best spark plugs, the best engine, yet the car built from these parts may not run very well, if at all. One can get the best and brightest managers in the world yet have a poor or mediocre operation. In a system everything has to work together, harmoniously. The parts and the people have to be optimized to work with each other toward a common goal. Improving one part alone may not help; it may even ruin the operation.

An orchestra is a good example. A person may know next to nothing about music, but he or she can hear the difference between orchestras. The conductor is responsible for making sure that everyone works together. Will the music be better if everyone does their best? If everyone tries to outdo everyone else? Of course not.

Suppose a conductor became concerned about the productivity of the individual musicians. He started paying them based on how much time they played. If a piece only has a few violin lines, the violinist wouldn't be paid much unless he played another instrument. To earn a good living, the violinist would put down his instrument and then run over to beat the drums. When that part was finished, he'd leap over the harp to play the cymbals. This orchestra would have great productivity, but who would pay to listen to them?

A leader's job is to see that everyone in his group works together and that his group works with the rest of the organization harmoniously to achieve the aims of the organization.

The Worst of Western Management

A friend of mine, with whom I disagree on a regular basis, unwittingly encapsulated Western management when he said in his inimical English accent, "We can't all be winners." He was referring to the recognition of the top performers in a group. This statement epitomizes the worst of Western management. Its corollary is "There must always be some losers." Any system where one can only rise up by pulling someone else down is already in decline.

As Deming states, "Ranking of people (outstanding down to unsatisfactory) that belong to the system violates scientific logic and is ruinous as a policy...."[4]

It occurred to me that my friend's management style may be so ingrained that, like a skill, it could not be changed once learned. Other "experienced" managers must be in the same state. Some companies with many "experienced" managers may have to wait until many of them retire before real progress can be made. But it has been my experience that if people really understand the reasons for a change, they make an effort to change. Unfortunately, some ideas strike at our core beliefs. For instance, we believe that best efforts should be rewarded. Almost everyone tries his best, and when he succeeds, the idea gets reinforced. But even when all are giving their best, some will perform better than others. Differences in performance are not necessarily a question of effort or ability. A manager who doesn't understand this can't lead.

Management is people. Most managers in the Western world, however, see management as the rules, regulations, organizational methods, and motivation techniques. But in the Deming view, all of the management structure should be directed toward one aim, allowing the individual to perform his or her job to the utmost while experiencing joy in his or her work in a manner consistent with the aims of the organization. If the organizational system gets in the way and robs people of their pride, there is something wrong. It is a leader's job to foster joy in work, harmony, and teamwork.

The leader must work diligently and conscientiously to assure that everyone is a winner.

Summary

Leaders play a crucial role in quality. The leaders have to be primary agents for improvement. Leaders must understand common causes and special causes and be able to tell the difference. Leaders have to understand the overall system and where their group fits in. They have to cooperate with those in the steps ahead of and following them.

Leaders build trust. They help but do not judge. They encourage everyone to improve. They work to create an environment where the workers can experience pride. Their efforts are directed at allowing each worker to perform his or her job to the utmost while experiencing joy in his or her work and performing in a manner consistent with the aims of the organization.

CHAPTER 16

Driving Out Fear

Point 8 states, "Drive out fear, so that everyone may work effectively for the company."

When I was ten years old, my friend Leonard and I would traverse the alleyways and backyards of Manhattan's West Side. Hopping over fences was a steeplechase and gymnastic challenge rolled into one. One day as we emerged from the alleyways to the sidewalk, a man appeared and chased after us. My pal and I were both so scared we easily outran our pursuer, but Leonard was really scared. When I stopped, I watched in amazement as he ran the next block in four seconds flat. I had never seen anyone run so fast before, and I doubt that I ever will again.

Incidents of this kind reinforce the idea that fear is a useful management tool. Most managers confuse fear and pressure. We can induce our own pressure, such as the desire to excel or satisfy ourselves, our mentor, our coach, or our boss, yet experience no fear whatsoever. Also, as I have mentioned throughout, increased effort of the individual does not translate into increased results for the company. In fact, just the opposite may occur. People are limited by the systems they work in.

In one company a new go-getter salesman was determined to get new customers. But the potential customer required immediate delivery. Using whatever was necessary, the salesman was able to arrange immediate delivery for his prospect and thereby gained a customer for the firm. He did this by taking deliveries scheduled to go to two long-time customers and redirecting them. Sure, the firm gained a new customer, but it lost two long-time customers who absolutely needed delivery, but were let down by the company.

183

Fear, even if it were to produce greater effort, will not produce greater results. But fear doesn't even produce greater individual results. Someone who is fearful takes whatever action necessary to remove the source of the fear. That may mean harming the long-term prospects of the company.

Overcoming Fear

When someone is scared in a life-threatening situation, his body may respond with a remarkable surge of strength and energy, which is immediately used to extricate himself from the threat. Everything is done to remove the threat. When fear is artificially used to improve performance, performance is not improved. Instead, much of the effort of the organization goes into dealing with and removing the threat—at the expense of performance. That may mean reporting wrong numbers or taking other action that is detrimental to the firm. A plant manager who is fearful of not meeting his quota may ship items that aren't ready to ship. The customer either ships them back or refuses to pay for them. In either case the problem is pushed into a different area of the firm. It becomes a problem for the quality control department or the credit department in the next quarter. If the customer stops doing business with the company as a result, it then becomes a marketing problem or a problem for the salespeople.

Using fear prevents people from thinking. It robs them of pride and joy in their work and kills all forms of intrinsic motivation. The thinking and creative potential of the workers are stopped cold. Most managers who rely on fear believe those working under them are incapable of thinking, and this becomes a self-fulfilling prophesy.

Fear as a Necessary Tool in the Military?

At one of Deming's lectures someone commented that many managers are trained in the military and that fear may play an integral and necessary part in the military because of the nature of its business. Frankly, my experience with managers trained in the military hasn't borne that out. Most whom I've known are at least as effective as those with only business-school training.

I also haven't found any evidence to support the theory that fear makes for a better military machine. Quite the contrary. One of the great military engagements in the Western world occurred at the battle of Marathon about 2,500 years ago. The empire of Persia was determined to conquer the city state democracies of ancient Greece. But at the battle of Marathon the volunteer Athenian army, made up of citizens of the city, defeated the involuntarily conscripted army of Persia. In *The Greek Way*, Edith Hamilton wrote:

> The Persians had gone. It was an incredible contest and an incredible victory. How could it happen like that—the little band of defenders victors over the mighty armament? We do not understand. But Herodotus understood, and so did all Greeks. A free democracy resisted a slave supported tyranny. The Athenians at Marathon had advanced at a run; the enemy's officers drove them into battle by scourging them [using fear]. Mere numbers were powerless against the spirit of free men fighting to defend their freedom.[1]

In any battle soldiers on both sides must experience fear, fear of the enemy, fear of death. But good military managers strive to have their soldiers overcome fear. On the battlefield it is courage that is needed.

What makes a great army? One answer comes from the two-thousand-year-old Chinese classic by Sun Tzu, *The Art of War*:

> War is a matter of vital importance.... Therefore, appraise it in terms of the five fundamental factors.... The first of these is moral influence; the second, weather; the third, terrain; the fourth, command; and the fifth, doctrine.
>
> By moral influence I mean that which causes the people to be in harmony with their leaders, so that they will accompany them in life and unto death without fear of mortal peril.[2]

It is clear that Sun Tzu was not only a great general but a great manager and leader. According to him fear, especially fear of the leader, detracts from the prospect of victory and hastens defeat.

Fear in Business

Fear should be eliminated from business. Fear is the cause of untold waste and loss. There are at least two kinds of fear in a corporate environment. A worker may find himself waiting on company time for supplies to arrive so he can begin his work. Of course, he's paid for the time he waits but he begins to wonder how a company with such blatant waste can stay in business. Will it be around another year? Another ten years?

Although the fear is not intentionally directed at him, he fears for his job. Some managers would like to eliminate the cause but retain the fear because they perceive fear to be a motivator. They are correct in a sense: fear is a motivator—but it does not motivate toward constructive action.

The second kind of fear is more insidious. This is the artificially generated fear consciously directed at employees by managers working according to the rules of their system: If a worker doesn't meet his production quota, he's in trouble. A salesperson had better meet his sales quota or else.

Recall the example cited earlier of the chief executive of a bank who decided to eliminate errors using fear. If tellers had errors, they would be placed on probation. All the problems suddenly disappeared. Of course, they didn't disappear, they just weren't reported. The tellers started managing the situation themselves.

Quotas and Work Standards

Among the leading causes of fear in modern corporations are quotas and numerical goals for management and the work force. Deming's advice on these issues is simple, direct, and not subject to misinterpretation. Point 11:

11a. Eliminate work standards (quotas) on the factory floor. Substitute leadership.
11b. Eliminate management by objective. Eliminate management by numbers, numerical goals. Substitute leadership.

Sales Quotas

Suppose the salespeople of a company average sales of $100,000 per month. Suppose we calculate the lower control limit to be $85,000 per month and the upper control limit to be $115,000. Anyone between these limits is to be treated the same. If one salesperson is averaging below the control limit, does that mean she's not a good salesperson? Not necessarily. The control charts are saying this is a special case, but she may not be the problem.

In one company, one salesperson regularly underperformed the group. When his area of the country was examined, it was found to include the hometown of one of their main competitors. No matter who had that area, it would regularly underperform the sales results for the rest of the country.

Loss from Quotas

Quotas shouldn't be established at all, because variation is a fact of life. Setting quotas anywhere between the control limits or above the upper control limits will lead to tampering. Suppose a well-meaning manager, wishing to inspire her people, set a sales quota of $105,000, slightly above average. Some salespeople won't be able to meet the quota in the existing system, so they'll have to work extra hard to make those additional sales. As the end of the month comes around, they find those sales. They promise customers delivery schedules the company can't possibly meet, offer unauthorized discounts, and do anything else necessary to meet the quota.

But isn't that a salesperson's job, to sell as much as possible? In many firms that is the job, and that is one cause of problems and loss to the company. The customer doesn't pay when the item arrives a month late. He won't pay until the invoice shows the promised discount. Some customers do pay but never use the company again. Management sees late receivables as a credit problem and low sales as a marketing problem, but they are the result of poor management, using quotas when leadership is necessary.

Another Example

One supermarket chain had a rule that shrinkage—the difference between what comes into a store and what is sold—must not exceed one percent. Sounds reasonable. The less shrinkage, the higher the profit. The manager of one store knew fifty-nine different ways to control shrinkage. He could direct his butchers to leave more fat on their cuts of meat. He could stop carrying those fruits and vegetables that spoiled quickly but that customers liked. All fifty-nine ways lessen quality and the customer's satisfaction with the store. Instead of improving profits, the quotas hurt profitability.

The least harmful quota would be one set at the lower control limit. Nothing would be done unless the individual fell below the control limit, in which case management would try to find out if any special cause was at work. Most people wouldn't consider this a quota at all, since most people would regularly exceed their quotas, often by 20 and 30 percent. This, however, is similar to what IBM does. It sets sales quotas that are attainable and then has awards for those who meet or exceed their quotas by 10, 20, and 30 percent. In this system everyone can be a winner. The company is trying to make the sales force feel good about themselves and their jobs and tap intrinsic motivation.

Setting Quotas

In reality how are quotas established? One way is to take last year's quota and increase it by a percentage. If you sold $100,000 last year, your quota is $110,000 this year. Sometimes quotas are just invented. In any case, no matter how they are set, whether the quotas are attainable or not, they are harmful. The more unrealistic the quota, the greater the damage that is done to the system.

Quotas for the Work Force

Quotas for the factory worker are often set at the average for the whole factory. No one is supposed to be below average. Anyone producing below quota on a given day rushes to finish. Quality suffers. But the worker who can habitually produce above the quota suffers also. If she exceeds the quota, she is intentionally hurting those people she works with. If she exceeds the quota, it will be raised. There is great peer pressure for her to keep her production down. She has no motivation to produce at her capacity unless she has a sadistic streak in her. She, too, is robbed of her inherent right to pride of workmanship.

The worker whose average performance this year is at the quota will have some days when he can meet or exceed the quota and some days when he cannot. He saves the excess production of his good days for those bad days when he isn't meeting the quota. Everyone ends up just meeting the quota and no more. These workers aren't lazy, but the system penalizes them for being above average or below average.

The worst part of quotas is that all prospects for improvement vanish. The pressure to not exceed the quota equals the pressure to equal the quota.

Controlling the Workers?

If quotas, management by objectives, and most forms of numerical comparisons of workers are eliminated, how do we control the worker? How do we keep them honest and working at their utmost so that we can compete with the Japanese? These questions already have the answers embedded in them. They imply that people are naturally beyond trust and will take you at the first opportunity. They imply that all problems are caused by people not doing what they are supposed to. If you can't trust your workers, you're already up against the ropes. The Deming view of management acknowledges the existence of trust.

Eliminating Fear

Fear is harmful to the company and to individuals. To eliminate fear, management must strive to tap intrinsic motivation.

Management may not be able to eliminate all fear from the lives of its employees but it can eliminate the source of fear built into the management structures. Management can and should eliminate all quotas, management by objectives, and any other sources of fear it can.

A Big Source of Fear

Even if management doesn't use quotas or numerical objectives, there is one significant move it can make to eliminate fear. It can change the reward system and eliminate the annual review.

Imagine yourself in the shoes of a manager who works in a corporation that annually reviews the performance of all its people and its departments. You are working as hard as you can, and despite your inability to make some changes, you feel pretty happy. Comes the annual review, and you're expecting some praise or a pat on the back for all your good work. But instead you are told that you are just above average. How do you feel? You are totally dejected. You have given the firm everything you had, and the only response is a slightly above average rating. Even worse, you may be rated average, or below average. After all, we can't all be above average, can we?

You and I thinking about this with some detachment and with the benefit of profound knowledge might see this as almost comical or farcical, but to the individual who receives the review this is real life. He is devastated. Even if he has a strong self-image, he has to keep thinking that in the corporation's eyes he's just average. He's told he's not one of the winners, therefore he's a loser, and it takes a heavy toll on him and his ability to work effectively.

The annual review of people is a major culprit generating fear and wreaking havoc in our corporations and on our people. Companies suffer untold loss because of the annual review. People emerge from their reviews shaken and destroyed, unable to function properly for months. The review artificially creates winners and losers. If you find yourself in the top half or top quarter or top tenth, you're a winner. Everyone else is a loser.

Justifications for the Annual Review

Most justifications for the annual review fall into one of these five:

1. It provides an opportunity for a supervisor and an employee to meet and discuss what's going on, to give each other feedback.
2. It provides a record of the employee's performance.
3. It provides external incentive for employees to do their best. Fear of a bad review and the hope of a good review are supposed to provide incentives for individuals to perform better.
4. When everyone tries to excel by being recognized as a top performer, it improves everyone's individual performance, and therefore the group's performance.
5. It helps management recognize the better performers and thus

provides a basis for rewarding and promoting those who are innately more talented or have worked harder.

We all understand the rationale behind the annual review. It is no different than the grading we have been subjected to since kindergarten. Some of the reasons seem self-evident. But are these reasons valid? Some of these statements can be examined and subjected to empirical studies, even if just to confirm what seems evident.

Is It So?

The reality is very different from the myths and notions we have taken as truth without questioning. Let's look at the given justifications for the annual review.

Reason 1

Reason 1 is so that people can sit down with their bosses and talk. The need to communicate is real. People have plenty of common problems to discuss with their bosses and they should sit down once a year at the very least and air them. But there is no reason to rank employees in order to accomplish this. Reason 1 doesn't justify the annual review; it justifies greater communication.

Reason 2

Reason 2 is that a record of employees' performance is necessary for manpower and staffing needs. Performance, however, is often meaningless, and rankings are absurd. This doesn't preclude companies from maintaining records on employees' experiences, training, educational background, and so on. A firm should maintain background information on its people for planning and staffing needs. But it doesn't have to rank anyone to accomplish this. Most of the difference in performance is caused by the system. Most ratings are just a lottery. Lotteries are fun, but call the results of a lottery a review and you'll have problems.

Reason 3

Reason 3 is that individuals need incentives to work. But it really goes further and says that people must be recognized for their differences in performance, otherwise they'll sluff off. If we reward everyone equally or based on the performance of the group, there is no need for a performance review of the individual. If we call everyone into our office individually and tell each that he or she is excellent and wonderful, we don't have anything resembling an annual review of people.

Suppose we conduct some studies and find that performance doesn't improve if rewards are based on individual performance? Then reason 3 would have no validity.

Morton Deutsch tested the proposition that tasks are better performed under various reward systems in a series of six experiments with Columbia University students. Among the possible reward systems were a winner-take-all system, a distribution proportional to accomplishment, and an equal distribution. When the tasks involved could be done independently without help from any of the other students, the reward system had no effect whatsoever on the performance. A competitive reward system wasn't able to squeak out even a scintilla of better performance from the individual. But when the tasks required that the students work together, which is the essence of commerce, the reward system did make a difference. A system of equal reward gave the best results and the competitive winner-take-all system gave the poorest.[3]

Reason 4

"Okay," you say, "so maybe how people are rewarded doesn't make much difference, but still people like to play the game and try to win. It adds zest to the task at hand and people just work better and harder if there's a competitive element to it." There is no empirical evidence to support this.

Most of the studies done to empirically measure the ability of a competitive environment to improve performance have to do with education. This is relevant since running a business relies heavily on knowledge and the ability to learn. In most respects the annual review is just an extension of the report cards we all received in school, and we're used to it.

The empirical record is very one-sided. Work done by Morton Goldman, Abaineh Workie, and others found that high school and college students were more effective when they were cooperating rather than competing.

A comprehensive review of the literature by David and Roger Johnson and their colleagues in 1981 examined 122 studies. In the overwhelming number of cases cooperation was found to promote higher achievement than competition or independent work.[4]

How can this be? How is it that competitiveness doesn't improve performance and in fact is less productive then cooperative behavior? A more fundamental question is really, why should we be so surprised? With the data presented and the evidence so one-sided why are they still difficult to comprehend?

The problem is not just that some deep-seated beliefs are being challenged; the problem is that our language has some hidden assumptions. We use the word *compete* to mean not just vying against someone else but to do so successfully, and to be successful, period. For instance, the term competitive schools is used to identify the more prestigious colleges and university. We instantly assume that competitive, a higher grade point average, and better are all synonymous. But are they really?

Assumptions of Language

In a previous chapter I made the statement, "Excessive competition may be hurting our international competitiveness." Here I'm using the word competitiveness (the second time), in the way it is presently being used in our national dialogue on productivity, as the ability to create goods and services of roughly equal quality and at a price comparable to what other nations, especially Japan, are able to create them for. We could call this instead commercial parity.

Let's substitute this phrase. The statement above then becomes, "Excessive competition may be hurting our commercial parity." Now all the contradictions are removed, and the sentence loses its original irony.

I can say that a company wishes to build a product or that it wants to enter a market, or what most of us would consider equivalent, that a company wishes to compete in a given market. Yet the later form of the statement implies more than the others. Is Japan our competitor or our trading partner? Which term you use immediately frames the tenor of any subsequent discussion.

Success in our lexicon too often implies beating someone else out, being better than someone else. But success need not imply competition. I can succeed at a task or fail at a task regardless of what anyone else does. It's possible for everyone in a group to succeed or for everyone to fail. If success in a college course depends on mastering the material 100 percent, then it's possible for everyone in the group to succeed.

Competitive, Independent, and Cooperative Situations

Suppose you and I hit a time warp and we find ourselves in the middle of the Roman Colosseum with swords lying next to us. A voice from the reviewing stand yells, "Pick up your sword and fight. Whoever lives will be let go." I whisper to you, "Don't pick up the sword. Let's cooperate and not fight." But our taskmaster has anticipated this and says, "If you don't fight, you'll be fed to the piranhas and both die. Quite painfully I might add." This appears to be a competitive situation where a cooperative strategy just won't help much.

On the other hand, a pickup touch football game among friends is a competitive situation. But it also has many cooperative elements. Until the players agree on the rules, there's no competition.

If the time warp were to take us to paleolithic times and dump us a thousand miles apart, we'd have to start working to survive, and we'd be in independent situations because of the distance and lack of knowledge of each other's presence. Your survival wouldn't impact positively or negatively on my survival.

Cooperative situations are substantially easier to envision. If you and I buy a business together, we're in a cooperative situation. I benefit from your work and you benefit from mine. We're also in a cooperative situation with our customers. If we provide a great product, the customer wins as well.

The point is there are different kinds of situations; some are competitive, some independent, and some cooperative in nature. Business and commerce are essentially cooperative.

Competitive, Independent, and Cooperative Reward Systems

Clearly most people working together in a company or in a department are in a situation that is essentially cooperative. Working together is better than working against each other. I'd like to introduce two different concepts that I think help clarify the situation. In addition to the underlying situation, every system has imposed structure, and individuals and organizations have systems of beliefs that aren't always written down anywhere. Work rules, regulations, quotas, and the reward system are all part of the imposed structure. The notion that competition is always best is part of our system of beliefs.

If the reward system is competitive, the people in the system will view this as a competitive situation and act accordingly, despite the inherently cooperative nature of the situation. Working against each other carries substantial risks when the situation is cooperative in nature.

An Example of a Competitive System

I heard a remarkable confession the other day from someone who always tried to be number one. He was number one academically in his high school and college classes and then became a successful lawyer. When a new syllabus was issued, he would immediately rush to the library and take out all the copies of several important books. Then no one else was able to read those books except for him, and his top grade was virtually assured.

We normally think of learning as being an independent situation, but this example illustrates that even what appears to be roughly independent is not. The actions of one person in a class can affect everyone. The performance of the class, the amount they were able to learn, the effectiveness of the teacher and the college, and the value of the education were diminished because some people were trying to be number one. But that's a possibility when we urge everyone to compete. Everyone tries to be number one.

An Alternative Approach

Consider the opposite approach. One college professor became so disgusted with grading that he told everyone in his class that anyone who mastered 100 percent of the subject matter would get an A and no longer had to attend class. Of course some mastered the material earlier than others. But they kept coming to class and helped everyone else. Everyone received an A, and the level of mastery of the subject matter was the highest of any class ever taught by the professor.

A recent magazine article presented another dramatic case. Trudy Hammer, acting principal of the Emma Willard School in Troy, N.Y., "describes a dramatic rise in the quiz scores of geography students who were organized into map study groups and told that their grades would be the average of all the group members' scores." The girls achieved "extraordinary high grades. Almost everyone got a perfect score."[5]

Now a cynic may argue that these systems disturb the natural order of things (whatever that means) because the slower students were helped by those who learned more quickly. But anyone who has done any teaching or coaching knows that one's mastery of a subject deepens considerably in trying to explain it. Everyone benefits. Everyone is better off.

Cooperation in Brokerage Service

I've been in brokerage offices where everyone works on commission and no one would pick up anyone else's phone because he or she personally had nothing to gain. I've also done business with a firm that has a team philosophy, and I could speak to any one of five brokers. The team approach provided me a much better level of service than I had experienced elsewhere.

Competition in an Employment Agency

Although the studies done in a business environment are not as plentiful as those done in schools, the results are consistent. Peter Blau in 1954 compared two groups of interviewers in an employment agency. One worked cooperatively and the other competitively. In one there was fierce competition to fill job openings. The workers were ambitious and concerned about productivity. Workers in this group tended to hoard job notifications instead of posting them as they were "supposed" to do. Members of the other group shared their information. The group that worked cooperatively "ended up filling significantly more jobs—the clear index of performance."[6]

This example shows that there is something other than the way people are compensated that helps determine how they act—their system of beliefs. People can be rewarded on a straight commission system, depending on the number and type of placements or sales that each makes. But if they believe that acting competitively, one against the other, is the best or perhaps the only way, then they will compete, with the resultant decline in results. On the other hand, if they act cooperatively, because they see that to be in their own interests, then their individual and group performances will improve.

People who have been brought up in a competitive environment have a difficult time imagining any alternatives, much less acknowledging its superiority in a given situation. The main reason the annual review is so difficult to abandon is that most top managers are products of the system and see their success as due in part to the competitive environment fostered by the system.

I'm tempted to say, "No wonder we can't compete with the Japanese," but instead I'm going to be more careful in the language I use and say: One major reason why our corporations are not as productive, innovative, flexible, and quality oriented as Japanese firms is our extensive use of merit reviews, which encourage everyone to try and outdo everyone else while they discourage cooperative behavior.

Isn't there something obnoxious and silly about the idea that a group performs better when everyone is trying to beat up on everyone else in the group? But the message that is constantly given to the American people and American firms, not just by popular consultants but by our political leaders, is that competition among people is the best, perhaps the only way of obtaining good results. This despite overwhelming evidence to the contrary.

Real Competition? Promotions

There is still one major question that you must be asking. If there aren't to be performance reviews, or annual reviews of people, whom do we promote to the top, how do we discriminate as the pyramid gets thinner at the top? I would question that performance reviews are used to promote people, even where they are used. Like so much else in life, politics, or who you like, who you know, and who likes you, is really the basis of promotions. Performance reviews just discourage people, so the turnover is greater, and maybe the choice narrows down to whoever is left.

In picking top executives of the firm, it seems reasonable to say they should have the interests of the firm at heart. Their desire to obtain good operating results should be balanced with the long-term view of the firm. But annual reviews foster a strictly short-term view. A worker or a manager may need extra results, extra output, extra profit this quarter, and he finds it. He doesn't perform a capital budgeting analysis, which might balance the value of today's profit against tomorrow's unhappy customer. He just does it because he has to in order to get a good review. Annual reviews force a short-term view of business. Even if the company's shares are in safe hands and the president issues a memo saying the long-term view is extremely important, if it uses an annual review, its employees and managers will all have a short-term orientation. And those managers who make it to the top, products of the system, will have been trained by the time they get there to think only short-term.

CHAPTER 17

Enhancing Pride and Joy in Work

In one class Deming asked his students, "What is it that kills the joy of learning?" There was general agreement among the students that grades are a major culprit.

A major barrier to people in business experiencing joy in their work is the annual review of people. This has been dealt with in the previous chapter, but we should acknowledge that it is not the only barrier. To repeat Deming's Point 12:

12a. Remove barriers that rob hourly workers of their right to pride of workmanship. The responsibility of supervisors must be changed from mere numbers to quality.

12b. Remove barriers that rob people in management and engineering of their right to pride of workmanship. This means, inter alia, abolishment of the annual or merit rating and of management by objective.

Let's conduct a small imaginary experiment. Suppose you are a worker in a large company and you are given a choice. In one subsidiary you can work on a product until you are satisfied, you alone are the judge of the product's acceptability. In the other subsidiary you have to produce the same article but are required to produce a given amount each day, regardless of any extenuating circumstances.

In which environment would you, the reader, prefer to work? In which would you experience greater pride in your work? In which

199

environment would you feel you had a greater common purpose with the management and shareholders of the company?

Someone who feels a bond with management and her company will pick up a nail in the parking lot even though it's not her responsibility. Someone else in the company who may not see the nail benefits and avoids a flat tire. She who feels a bond with the firm goes out of her way to help new employees.

The individual who experiences the firm as a numerical goal becomes alienated from the rest of the firm. He loses intrinsic motivation, which is the key to quality and improvement. He won't pick up the nail, he won't help the new employee. That's not his job, that's not his problem. Such actions won't impact on his rating. Why help someone who is potential competition?

Once intrinsic motivation is replaced by an extrinsic reward system, intrinsic motivation dies and is very difficult to revive. Something that originally would be done for its own sake, such as doing the best job possible, would require a reward once a reward system is introduced. Many young people enter firms eager to work, produce, and learn; but once they receive their first bonus or criticism based on their individual results, they lose interest in what's best for the firm and start worrying about number one.

It's true that insufficient extrinsic rewards can kill motivation too. If you have to worry about paying the mortgage and have to moonlight, you can't possibly work at your best. But after a point, extrinsic rewards become useless and may even backfire.

Barriers to Pride of Workmanship

At some of his seminars Deming asks the participants to name the obstacles that prevent them from experiencing pride in their work. A composite list of the responses is then drawn up and distributed to the participants. Here's one of those lists:

Obstacles Preventing Pride in Work
1. Lack of direction
2. Goals without the tools to achieve them: time, resources
3. Arbitrary decisions by boss
4. Lack of clear goals and objectives

5. Unclear how contribution is valued
6. Lack of expectation setting up criteria
7. Insufficient information available
8. Different organizational goals within the company
9. Too much group management
10. Deadline anxiety
11. Lack of product definition re: purpose and product arbitrarily changed by consumer/customer within company
12. Organization (staff) not valued by line organization
13. Hierarchy tries to run technology it does not understand
14. Lack of communication
    a. conflicting and unclear objectives
    b. lack of advance information
    c. inadequate information flow
    d. inadequate feedback
    e. lack of authority to do what needs to be done
15. Lack of resources: time; improper tools and equipment.
16. Short-term objectives conflict with long term
17. Nonuniform application of policy
18. Poor training
19. Specifications constrain creativity and procurement and manufacturing
20. Fear. Pressure for short-term results. Total organizational fear
21. Company and union adversarial relationship
22. Red tape
23. Unrealistic goals and objectives[1]

In Your Firm

Putting together a list of this kind in any firm would help management understand the constraints to improved quality. But management had better enter any such exercise with an open mind and a commitment to avoid anger because the most basic structural aspects of management are challenged by such an exercise. The above list, which is typical and was chosen at random, seems to me to condemn current management. Company and union adversarial relationships, fear, poor training, short term conflicting with long term, deadline anxiety, arbitrary decisions by the boss, goals without tools and resources, seem to me to be an indictment of management at its most basic level.

Slogans, Exhortations, Clichés, Targets

One seemingly harmless activity is to place posters in the office or on the factory floor urging the worker on to higher quality or greater output. Slogans such as "Quality is up to you" or "Do it right the first time" sound benign, but they're just not true. Quality is made in the boardroom. A worker *can* deliver lower quality, but she *cannot* deliver better quality than the system allows.

When the posters also demand some numerical level of production that is beyond the system's capability, the effect is to demean the workers.

Point 10: "Eliminate slogans, exhortations, and targets for the work force asking for zero defects and new levels of productivity. Such exhortations only create adversarial relationships, since the bulk of the causes of low quality and low productivity belong to the system and thus lie beyond the power of the work force."

One so-called "quality consultant" bases his whole management on just such exhortations. That this consultant has a thriving business I attribute to our unquestioned need for better quality. Exhortations not only have no long-term effect, but eventually they backfire and the companies that resort to them find themselves several years and several million dollars later even further behind than before.

And the Walls Came Tumbling Down

Point 9: Break down barriers between departments. People in research, design, sales, and production must work as a team to foresee problems of production and in use that may be encountered with the product or service.

Several years ago I decided to develop a building I owned. I planned to renovate and then sell the individual apartments as cooperative units. This was an attractive proposition for several reasons, not least of which was that I would have an opportunity to apply Deming's ideas in a small, controlled environment where the results could be observed in a relatively short period of time. I knew very little about construction and the legal and financial intricacies involved, so I spent a great deal of time talking to other developers, benefiting from their experience and knowledge.

When it came time to begin, I had neither the time nor the resources to prepare control charts. Everything was learn as you go, and I was bounding from one problem to another. But one principle that I could apply was Point 9.

A great deal of time was spent with the floor plans. Normally the architect draws up the plans after consulting the developer, and then the plans are given to the contractor, plumbers, carpenters, and electricians.

But I decided to do it differently, the way Deming advises. The people involved, including those who would sell the units, walked through the space with the architect and discussed general ideas. Input was taken from everyone, and the salespeople were called upon to lend their knowledge of the market and the customer. When the architect had a preliminary plan, everyone saw it; and suggestions, where feasible, were adopted.

By the time the carpenters, electricians, and plumbers saw the final plan, they knew it intimately. It was their plan as well as the architect's. Their job was no longer to do what someone else had requested, but to complete a project they had helped design. I'm not going to tell you I didn't have problems. My whole life was problem solving. As Deming says, "He who thinks there won't be problems is living in some other world, not this one."

But brokers, customers, and other developers who saw the finished apartments consistently remarked on their exceptional quality and superior craftsmanship. Some called them the best apartments they had ever seen. Years later I'm still getting feedback that my apartments were what cooperative apartments should be. Not bad for a first try.

Now, I'm not bragging, because I did very little. All I did was allow those people who worked on the project to use their talent and ability. I tried to remove whatever obstacles kept them from experiencing pride in their work. One way to do that was to avoid having them build something that was flawed in design simply because the designer wasn't aware of the problems at hand.

I also don't mean to give the impression that getting people who have traditionally worked at arm's length to work together is easy. It is quite difficult. I experienced major problems trying to build an L-shaped staircase. The architect said it could be built, and the carpenter said it couldn't be done as drawn. I was completely dumbfounded. Eventually we figured out a way of doing it to everyone's satisfaction.

Even in a relatively straightforward situation, problems can arise that seem insurmountable, and the will to spend the time required to understand the problem is not always present in all the parties involved. Nevertheless the benefits are real and immediate. Working together can help all parties increase their understanding, which will produce continual savings in the future.

But just imagine the problems that occur when, instead of two people, there are twenty-five who interact on a product. Their areas of expertise may even be unrelated. Furthermore, years of tradition often hamper efforts to work together. But the effort exerted to break down barriers between departments pays the very lucrative dividends of improved quality, superior performance of the product or service, greater customer satisfaction, and profit.

CHAPTER 18

Improvement and the Minds of Workers

P oint 13 reads, "Institute a vigorous program of education and self-improvement."

Point 6 deals with training. Training means the skill and knowledge necessary to do the job today. Point 13, on the other hand, deals with the need to encourage and provide resources so that people may develop. For tomorrow. Each person is responsible for herself. Each is her own judge as to what she'd like to learn. Point 13 calls for development of intrinsic motivation.

All the programs I've encountered in the financial world are inconsistent with Point 13. For instance, one bank I know had a program where they reimbursed tuition up to 100 percent, but the courses had to be "relevant" to business and had to be approved by the bank. In another program the reimbursement depended on the grade received, with only A grades receiving 100 percent reimbursement. But no one knows in advance what knowledge will be "relevant" tomorrow. Grades are irrelevant. The important thing is that each worker become enthusiastic about learning.

Two Views of Management

Most of us carry a model of management that is strongly influenced by the popular view of the work of Frederick Taylor, whose time and motion studies were conducted in the early part of this century. His book's title, *Scientific Management*, was an unfortunate misnomer that has led to great misunderstanding. Let me encapsulate the popular version of this view as the fact that any skill, job, or task can be analyzed and broken down into smaller and smaller segments. When the job gets broken down so that it can be taught in a short period of time, say a day or two, then even the most unskilled person can be taught and therefore made productive. When the skill is broken down further and further and bigger and more sophisticated machinery is used, the level of education and training of the work force becomes irrelevant. This is seen as a blessing because even the poor and ignorant can be made productive and prosperous.

In this view there are always some tasks that can't, or more likely have not, been broken down into their constituent parts, so some highly skilled labor is always required. But the experts in time and motion studies would be working on those complex skills and trying to break them down so that in time, with the proper machinery, they could be performed by anyone.

In this view, what makes management tick—what brings about increased productivity—is the machinery, the organization, and those experts and managers who are constantly bringing the ability to be productive down to the least productive members of society. We're all influenced by this view, whether we wish to acknowledge it or not. A great deal of time and effort of modern society has gone into measuring the value of machinery, land, inventory, cash, and other "tangibles." A financial statement values a corporation as the sum of its tangibles, such as factories, equipment, and receivables. Almost everyone will admit there are other less tangible items that must affect the value of a company, such as patents, and trademarks, and even some real intangibles such as customer goodwill. But hardly ever is the force sitting behind the eyes of the workers given any value—and that is the essence of productivity.

In the Tayloresque view, a corporation is a mighty wrench that can effectively leverage the force of many smaller and less powerful parts (workers), whose power is magnified beyond the sum of their individual parts by machinery and organization.

In the Deming view, a corporation may also be seen as a mighty wrench. But the wrench is alive, changing adapting, finding new and better ways of doing the same job. The constituent parts must be brought to life and their power of mind harnessed.

In the Taylor view, productivity, wealth creation, and improvement of the standard of living come from the management, organization, and machinery, which harness the brute force of the individuals.

In the Deming view, productivity and wealth come from the efforts of everyone and their harnessing of mind. Management's job is to see that the organization doesn't get in the way. Management has to eliminate barriers to people experiencing joy in their work and has to encourage each to develop himself.

In the Taylor view, the organization and its rules and structure are the key. If the people are complaining about the rules and regulations (and it should be remembered we're talking about adults, not children), that may be unfortunate, but it's a sign that the organization is effective and guiding people's efforts toward the productive goals of the organization.

In the Deming view, if the organization is the cause of discomfort and pain, it is also the cause of loss to the company. Organization and structure are important—they pull together the efforts of the individuals into a common cause—but good organization is hardly felt and hardly seen. If it is seen and felt, it is most likely the source of problems and therefore the source of loss.

In the Taylor view, the working motto may be "Divide and conquer."

In the Deming view, the working motto may be "Cooperate with knowledge and trust, and you become invincible."

The Source of Productivity: A Common Assumption

In a recent television show Peter Jennings acted as moderator of an impressive panel of government officials and business leaders from the United States, Europe, the Soviet Union, and Japan. The subject was the productivity, and relative commercial positions of the major economic areas of the world. The question came up: What happens when a plant's productivity doesn't keep up with the level of productivity of a plant in a different part of the country or even a different continent? One panel member, an entrepreneur who was one of two founders of a well-known computer manufacturer, said that management was to blame for not making the necessary changes. So far not bad. But then he went on to say that management had failed to bring in the new machinery and equipment that the other plants had and this was why the plant fell behind.

What's wrong with this? Aren't new machinery and equipment a possible source of improved productivity? Yes, they are, and if they were the only source of improved productivity, the statement would be absolutely fine. But the speaker's assumption was just that. New machinery was, in his view, the only way of improving productivity. But if that's the only way one is aware of, then it will become a self-fulfilling prophesy. If a manager closes his eyes to the other sources of productivity improvement, he will close the door on the most important source of improvement.

While new machinery can be a source of improvement, so can many other factors, such as better use of the existing machinery, redesign of the product and the work flow, improvements in the way the parts work together. One small change in one area can lead to a vast improvement in another area and an improvement in the end result. The knowledge and skills of the individuals are the real source of improvement, and these are far more central to improvement than new machinery. By emphasizing machinery as the only source of improvement, management is neglecting the major source and therefore dooming the plant to extinction.

When the subject of plant closings came up, one panel member a 1988 presidential candidate, said that management had to realize they would be paying for the laid-off workers in one way or the other. The workers would be eligible for unemployment insurance, or even welfare in some cases. If they or their children resorted to crime, all of society, including management, would be the loser. In my opinion, he was right.

Another panel member, the present secretary of commerce, said that the government shouldn't interfere. Each company had to have the right to close obsolete plants; otherwise business would be discouraged from operating in that area, and the sick plants could hurt the economic health of the rest of the company, which might still be healthy. In my opinion, he was also right.

One Japanese panel member, with a well-known consulting firm in Tokyo, said that management must not close the plant. They must work under the assumption that they cannot close the plant. If they do, they will really stretch themselves and find alternatives. In

Japan, he stated, steel plants have become chemical plants. The people have all shifted and borne the brunt equally. The result is another profitable operation for the company. In my opinion, to use the saying of an underworld chief from a Charles Bronson movie, he was more right.

It's absolutely true that we are all interconnected. In a society the welfare of one affects all. This isn't just an interpretation of chaos theory, it is just basic economics. When one of us loses his job, he stops producing for the time being, but society still has the same number of mouths to feed. Modern science, including the science of chaos, has shown us that we are much more interrelated than we ever imagined. When a plant is closed, we all suffer, including management.

It's also true that government shouldn't be dictating to management what it can or cannot do. Management has to have leeway. But plants shouldn't be closed; and employees shouldn't be randomly let go. Just because there is no item on the balance sheet measuring the value of the knowledge and cohesiveness of a plant doesn't mean it has no value. To put a successful plant together took years of the combined efforts of many people in management and in the work force. When a plant fails to keep up, it is most likely because of management. Management has failed to keep the plant alive and constantly improving.

A plant that has kept up but is failing because of market conditions, such as a rise in currency values, a decline in the market for the plant's goods, a new product, or a shift in the world economy, has a powerful resource in its people that can be redirected into other operations. To do so is certainly not easy for management, there is no obvious or easy path, but it can and must be done.

But a plant that has failed to keep improving has a more fundamental problem. They have a problem of management. Management doesn't know how to manage with a view toward continual improvement. All the legislation in the world will not help that. All the restrictions, quotas, and pronouncements of government regulations won't affect that one iota. In fact, the government regulations are based on the same outmoded view of management.

When Sony took over a U.S. high-technology company recently, the first thing they did was to reassure the employees and try to relieve fear. Even though the company was in the midst of a sales slump, not a single employee was let go. The chief executive of the firm said that if he had been acquired by an American company, their first action would have been layoffs.

When our managers sell an operation, they are evaluating it from the point of view of its present income stream or the value of all its tangible pieces. But Japanese management have an appreciation for the real creative force in a company. Its people. If you understand this, you can see that continual development of its people is of prime importance.

What Do the Experts Know?

In the Tayloresque view, an "expert" can analyze the situation and direct the best course of action. Let me give one major example to the contrary. Do customers care about quality? When it comes to actual decisions, it appears not. In fact, most often a few cents off is what seems to drive a customer's purchase. Deming, who has more experience with consumer research than anyone living, says, "In my opinion the customer doesn't give a hoot about quality." Then what's the point of this whole book if that's the case? Well, the point is that if a company offers continually improving quality, they'll capture the market—that's all. When quality is offered, customers will choose it. Quality becomes an issue after the fact.

The meaning of quality—what consumers expect—is determined by the producer. Once better quality is offered, consumers notice. Their definition changes. What was satisfactory before is now totally unacceptable. But no enumerative analysis of consumer behavior would show this in advance.

The same is true of new products. When Chester Carlson was trying to interest major corporations in his copying technology, they weren't interested, because market research showed the product would only capture a small market. But he persisted. When the product finally came to market, it became one of the most spectacular successes of the twentieth century. Companies that said they would make several hundred copies a month made tens of thousands. Once it was available, people used it—that's all.

When a new product comes to market, it changes the market, often in ways that are unknowable beforehand. What are the new products of the future? None of us know. What fields of knowledge will be of extreme importance to your business in ten years? No one knows.

The best offense, then, is not a good defense. The best offense is to tap the real source of improvement, your people, by keeping them alive, encouraging their growth and continual education, and nourishing intrinsic motivation.

Improvement

When a Taylor manager wants to determine the optimal way of performing a task, he finds someone who has mastered the task and then breaks down the steps. He does this to find the best, most efficient way. Once that's done, the "best" way has been found. It is considered unlikely that the worker can improve on it. Improvement is therefore automatically ruled out. Improvement could only come from the expert who must introduce new machinery or new capital, or make some other gross adjustment. Any organization developed along these lines is extremely inflexible. Change can only come from the expert, of which there are few. If there is one expert for each 1,000 workers, one mind out of 1,001 is being utilized.

Of course, in the Deming approach everything is different. An expert comes in and helps establish statistical control through his knowledge and understanding. Sometimes control and uniformity are improved by doing less. Stop the attempts to control by overadjusting, stop the tampering, and quality improves.

Once the system is bought under control, improvements to the system can be effected. The expert is helpless to make the necessary changes. He can and should offer his guidance, help design the tests, help avoid tampering. But many changes require intimate knowledge of the process. The people who have the greatest familiarity and are most knowledgeable of the actual workings of the system are in a position to make important suggestions for improvement that no one else can make. These would include chemists, engineers, and other acknowledged experts, but also workers and managers, who have intimate knowledge of the company.

If the people in the company have been constantly beaten up or, more accurately, beaten down and told not to think, just do it, they will require some adjustment before they are even willing to make any suggestions. Ultimately improvement has to come from the brains of those working in the system, and they have to be alive enough to use their brains.

CHAPTER 19

Basic Transformation

Point 14 reads, "Put everybody in the company to work to accomplish the transformation. The transformation is everybody's job."

Necessity of Transformation

The word *transformation* is appropriate because the individuals in a firm embarking on a path of continual improvement have to change their perceptions, not just of common business principles but of more fundamental aspects of how the world works. Most of us trained in traditional management theories, myself included, would like to dismiss many of Deming's ideas because they are so different and directly clash with what we were initially taught. Clearly either Deming or the other management experts are right, but they can't both be. We are forced to grapple with Deming's management theory simply because it works.

New Attitude: Understanding the Interactive Nature of the Company

I'd like to review some of the points that I found to be important but different in the Deming view. One essential tenet of management, which for me was never challenged by anyone except Deming, was the idea that to improve output, production, sales, profit, quality, or any other important factor, every part of the organization had to improve. Essentially we have been taught that

213

every unit and every individual in an organization is independent of the others. Improving the results in one area therefore necessarily improves the results of the whole. This view, which seems reasonable at first, is in fact wrong and leads to some very destructive practices.

A company is highly interactive. Improving the financial results of one part of a company may lead to a loss for the whole. Sometimes the financial performance of a company is vastly improved when the financial results of one department are sacrificed. When every department is out for itself, substantial performance problems occur. When everyone is out for himself or herself, the firm as a whole suffers. We can't make everyone responsible for the transformation as long as everyone has to keep an eye out for number one.

This notion that the performance of every part of a company is independent of the other parts of a company has to be replaced with the realization that any change in any part of a company affects every other part. It is management's job to help understand these interactions and to have everyone in the firm work for the common goal of improved quality and improved customer satisfaction. Loyal customers are the source of profit. Cost cutting in the more conventional sense, rating of each individual, or making each department responsible for its own results will only lead to loss.

Forget About Blame—No Problems, Only Solutions

Another idea that requires some work to understand is that we can't bring down the level of mistakes or errors by going after the offender or by punishing whoever is closest to the problem or crime. Today, in all levels of management from the lowest up to the highest government levels, the rule is find the offender, whoever was responsible, and punish him or her.

We have to understand that the individual may not be responsible in a real sense. He or she is just part of the system. The way to improve is often via changes of the system, and management has to know when a problem is due to some special cause and when the problem can only be resolved on an ongoing basis by improving the system.

Limitations of Inspection

In business, inspection is often seen as the cure to quality. One hundred percent inspection might seem to mean great quality. But it doesn't. Managers in a firm have to understand the limitations of inspection. They have to understand that quality is built in and is reflected by everyone and every department's actions and decisions.

Resistance to Transformation

The point I'm trying to make is that transformation isn't easy, and can be confusing as we learn to see the world of management in a new light.

Top management play a crucial role in any transformation simply because they have more leverage than anyone else. Their decisions affect everyone. But middle managers and entry-level managers also have to come on board, as do the workers. Sometimes the greatest resistance to change comes from middle management. A good first step for many companies is attendance by key managers at a Deming seminar.

Need for a Consultant

Deming recommends that companies hire a trained consultant to advise management. This is more difficult than it sounds because there are probably no more than a dozen people in the world with the proper qualifications and knowledge who are engaged in a consulting practice.

Why a Consultant?

Why is an expert important in making the transformation? Because problems just don't present themselves. They are often hidden from view, and our familiarity with the existing system often prevents our seeing them. There is no way of knowing what the real problems are unless the way of thinking changes, and this may take some time. Guidance from an expert who has already transformed his or her own thinking can save management from making some of the gross errors.

Train an Internal Consultant

Deming also calls for the development of an internal consultant. Almost every firm has people with training in statistics. It should be one of the outside consultant's main jobs to help some of these people develop sufficient understanding of the Deming philosophy to make them agents for change.

Complete Reeducation

Virtually everyone in a company has to be reeducated. Internal programs to teach the new philosophy should be one of the main priorities for top management. Just how the transformation proceeds is top management's job. They have to lead.

Description Versus Prediction

One point in particular has broad ramifications. That is the difference between description and prediction. Most efforts at analysis that we encounter every day are just descriptions. They may be fun to read, but they are of no use in helping us improve. One of my favorite examples is the attempt by reporters to explain the movements of the financial markets. I'll turn to the stock market commentary, which might say that stock market prices went up in reaction to a decline in gold prices. Turning to the gold page, I find that the gold market declined because of a decline in interest rates and a strengthening bond market. Finally, turning to the bond commentary, I find that the market rose in sympathy with the stock market. Aaghhh!

When the stock market fell 500 points in one day, there were plenty of experts the next day with plenty of explanations of what happened and "why." Almost all of these were just descriptions although they used the words "because" or "because of" a great deal. But how many were able to predict the event would occur beforehand? They all predicted it after the fact.

In listening to the analysis of a baseball game, we often hear that someone dropped the ball in the last inning, or someone struck out, and that cost us the game. But everyone else on the team had a chance to hit a home run every time he was up in any of the earlier innings. Statements like, we lost the game because of this play, are pure description.

This worker made so many defects, this salesperson only sold so much, are just descriptions; they don't constitute predictions and don't give us any information that helps us to improve. Improvement means in the future. Improvement means prediction.

Management is prediction. Management is not a game. Games are fun. There's nothing wrong with games. Someone wins and someone loses, and we should keep in mind that it's a game. But management requires prediction. Will making a change lead to better results? Are the results really better? That requires that we understand something about variation.

The red bead experiment, as simple as it is, helps a great deal. In the red bead experiment we were totally helpless to predict the performance of any individual worker on his next try. But a little knowledge helps us predict the way the system—all six workers— will perform. It helps us to predict that the changes made by management of employing only the "best" workers, of rewarding the "best" workers, of berating or letting go the worst workers will have absolutely no effect on the performance of the system.

There are many valuable lessons to be learned from the red bead experiment. Management in the broad sense refers to almost every aspect of an enterprise: the company's relationship with suppliers, relationship with competitors, tax strategy, educational policy, and so on. But there is one area that is common to all businesses at all levels. To most of us, management refers particularly to the way we treat our people. And it is here that I think Deming's lessons are most profound and most radical. And it is here that I believe most managers will have the greatest difficulty in adjusting.

The Annual Review—Description or Prediction?

The beauty of any rating system is that it makes the persons doing the rating feel good about themselves. It gives the illusion of creating positive change, of helping the company to do better. It also gets the problem off the desk quickly and easily. "Okay, I took care of that problem, let me get on to a serious issue, like how can I increase my loan volume, or production number, or sales?"

Unfortunately this illusion of having dealt with the problem is a dangerous one. Not only is nothing solved and improvement preempted, but the people are systematically destroyed. And this precludes real improvement from occurring.

Everyone in the company must work to accomplish the transformation, but at the core of necessary change is the need to change our way of thinking on some critical matters. The biggest challenge to our managers from Deming is in the way we treat our people. This will determine whether we really can "compete" in the future.

CHAPTER 20

Competition

U pon first being exposed to Deming's ideas, almost everyone finds one or two points that are especially difficult. In the past the idea of a single source of supply for each individual item was one of the most bothersome. Today so many individuals and corporations have been influenced by Deming, directly or indirectly, that single sourcing rarely presents a problem. It has proved its merit beyond contention among those who have tried it.

But the idea that competition can and should often be replaced by cooperation is still difficult for some to grasp and accept.

Pick up a newspaper or turn on the television, and you find messages propounding the need for more competition. President Bush, in his 1990 State of the Union address called for our people and corporations to become more competitive. Those passages in his speech were not controversial and received applause from both sides of the aisle. Economists and business consultants constantly talk about the benefits of competition as if there were no ills. Where is the justification for such a view?

Today much of the justification for competition is blurred in our language. We use the phrase "to compete" to mean our participation in almost any activity. When a company develops and offers a product, we say that company is competing in the marketplace. Is there an alternative way of looking at it? Yes. A company can offer a product, and sales of the product may not detract from the sales of other companies. A product can expand the market without negatively impacting on sales of its "competitors."

Sales of American automobiles in the United States in 1988 were comparable to their best year of past decades. Sales of Japanese brand cars, however, were also substantial. When sales of both American and Japanese cars are combined, the market for automobiles today appears a lot bigger than in past decades. But have sales of Japanese cars supplanted American cars or have they expanded the market? Would sales of automobiles remain at today's levels if all Japanese manufacturers committed hara-kiri tomorrow and stopped producing? I think the answer is no. Some buyers would buy the American product but others would resist buying, holding on to their vehicles much longer.

If we look only at market share, then the market share of Japanese autos has risen from zero to a substantial share of the market and American manufacturers' share has fallen, from close to 100 percent to a smaller share. If you frame the question this way, it seems there's no way out—Japanese companies have competed with American manufacturers and beaten them out. But there is an alternative way of looking at it. The Japanese manufacturers have expanded the market. Some consumers who wouldn't have purchased a car chose a Japanese brand because of its economy, cost, or quality. Other consumers found they could now afford a second car.

All manufacturers in a sense could be said to be winners if they each earn a decent return and satisfy their customers.

Competition as the Source of Improvement?

Now you may object. "Look," you may say, "the American producers had to scramble to make better automobiles because of competition. Their products are much better now than before the Japanese competition began." No one could argue with you about the quality. It certainly is better now. But improvement was not caused by competition. The American motorcycle companies tried to compete. But they didn't know how to change in the face of similar competition and died. The improvement of American autos came about because the companies made drastic changes in the way they conducted their business. It was the change in the way they manage that caused the improvement. In the case of autos, Japanese and American companies alike took their cues from Deming. What competition did was focus the auto manufacturers' attention on the fact that they had a problem.

Competition and Improvement

Competition may make us aware of a better alternative. Competition may help stimulate us to perform well today, but it will not make us better tomorrow. We have to work toward improvement each day. To make a quantum jump to a better system, we have to learn the alternative system. Working harder isn't going to help if we're already working our hardest and the other company's methods are superior.

In our language improvement and competition are sometimes used synonymously. But in competition in the extreme, say when the loser dies, improvement does not occur. It's hard to adopt your opponent's ideas when you're dead.

Price, Cost, and Competition

A lot is inferred about the benefits of competition. Where did such ideas come from? Sure, they appear to be ingrained in the language at this point, but is there any justification or source for this? There may be a string of philosophers responsible, or perhaps the experience of hundreds of years of European warfare, but let's stick to a more narrow source. Let's look at a few quotes from Adam Smith's classic, *The Wealth of Nations*, first published in 1776:

> The price of monopoly is upon every occasion the highest which can be got. The natural price, or the price of free competition, on the contrary, is the lowest which can be taken, not upon every occasion indeed, but for any considerable time together.[1]

This statement is saying that monopoly is always the highest price, and competition in time leads to the lowest price. An even stronger statement follows:

> The quantity of grocery goods, for example, which can be sold in a particular town, is limited by the demand of that town and its neighborhood. The capital, therefore, which can be employed in the grocery trade cannot exceed what is sufficient to purchase that quantity. If this capital is divided between two different grocers, their competition will tend to make both of them sell cheaper, than if it were in the hands of one only; and if it were divided among twenty, their competition would be just so much greater, and the chance of

their combining together, in order to raise the price, just so much the less. Their competition might perhaps ruin some of themselves; but to take care of this is the business of the parties concerned, and it may safely be trusted to their discretion. It can never hurt either the consumer, or the producer; on the contrary, it must tend to make the retailers both sell cheaper and buy dearer, than if the whole trade was monopolized by one or two persons.[2]

This statement goes even further. If two competitors are good, then twenty must be better still—the more the merrier. Now to disprove this, I just need one counterexample, since Smith isn't saying that competition sometimes works to the advantage of the community but that it always does.

Competition Driving Up Costs

As reported in the *Wall Street Journal* on January 10, 1990,[3] one of the established hospitals in Fort Wayne, Indiana, opened a new modern building at a cost of $91 million. The two other hospitals in town tried to keep up and remain "competitive." They remodeled and refurbished. Each attempted to increase its market share at the expense of the other. But the three hospitals already have more than enough capacity. The vacancy rates of the three range from 47 percent to 77 percent. Each hospital has excess capacity, which raises their average costs per patient. Patients, then, must pay higher fees than they would if the hospitals cooperated. Three hospitals offer high-technology medical services in an area where the community would be just as well served by one or two hospitals. By cooperating and avoiding duplicate services, the hospitals could lower patient costs, lower interest costs for new construction, and give their staffs more work to do, thus making them happier in their jobs.

But what would happen if one hospital should fail, a possibility that might be welcomed by the most severe proponent of competition? Massive waste would result from the bankruptcy of just one. Doctors, nurses, and administrators would be put out of work and have to spend months, perhaps years, adjusting. The hospital's bonds would be worthless, causing financial loss to the individuals, pension funds, and other institutions who invested in them. The reader will forgive me if I find it very difficult to understand how waste can lead to lower costs or better service.

But what would happen if the two remaining hospitals then kept on competing and one of them failed? The result would be more waste, and, ironically, there would then be no competition. In the extreme case, competition leads to no competition. The victor who would have been weakened by the fight would then be forced to increase revenues to refill its coffers before any improvement in services could begin.

Heaven Forbid

Would cooperation lead to higher prices? According to Smith, the answer is yes:

> People of the same trade seldom meet together, even for merriment and diversion, but the conversation ends in a conspiracy against the public, or in some contrivance to raise prices.[4]

Adam Smith's view is that competition always leads to lower prices and cooperation of any kind leads to a conspiracy of higher prices. Does he prove this proposition in any real sense? The answer is no. Nowhere does he offer confirmation of his view. This is his considered opinion. But it is simply opinion.

Yet this is the thinking being used by our leaders to justify competition as the panacea for all our economic woes. Incredible as it seems, our economic policy is guided by the unproved propositions in a classic work on political economy written over two hundred years ago.

I disagree with this and other propositions in Adam Smith's economic philosophy, but this doesn't mean I don't respect or appreciate the power of his work and his achievement in offering understanding in the area of political economy. We now know, for instance, that Galileo was incorrect in many of his scientific beliefs, but this doesn't detract from our respect and admiration for the work of this great man, one of the giants upon whose shoulder's Newton and Einstein stood. Progress in understanding often comes from discovering that a proposition which we believed to be correct has been replaced by one that is "more correct" or even contradicts the old proposition. But this shouldn't detract from our respect for the men who helped us see in the first place.

The Source of Improvement

In Smith's philosophy, competition keeps the price to the consumer reasonably low, but is it also the source of improvement and an increasing standard of living? No. According to him, "The greatest improvement in the productive powers of labour, and the greater part of the skill, dexterity, and judgment with which it is any where directed, or applied, seem to have been the effects of the division of labor."[5]

The division of labor, however, cannot occur without great cooperation. As the division of labor becomes more complex, each person's reliance on others increases.

It is not competition but cooperation that accounts for the improvement in the standard of living of people in the industrialized world over that of people in less industrialized societies. But competition, according to Smith, keeps costs and profits down, benefiting the customer.

Cooperation Leading to Lower Costs

Let's for the moment consider a hypothetical example. Suppose two full-service gas stations are located on opposite corners of an intersection. In addition to pumping gas, they offer towing and have trained mechanics. In a real sense they are competing against each other. Customers who need to fill up their gas tanks can choose one or the other. They may alternate, but at any given instance they are choosing one to the exclusion of the other.

The gas stations may cooperate. Suppose that Sunday is a very quiet day with little business. As a service to customers, however, the managers of the stations wish to remain open on Sundays. The amount of business doesn't justify two stations being open. One station may easily handle all the business. The stations could cooperate by each opening on alternate Sundays. By their doing so, the customers of both are better served and the costs to the stations are lower.

Each station may have a tow truck. On rare occasions one station may get a call from a customer needing a tow when its truck is out on the road. If the other station's truck isn't being used, why not borrow it and pick up the stranded customer? By sharing unused resources, the stations serve their customers better. Each station increases capacity without increasing costs.

But let's suppose that the two stations compete in every way and refuse to cooperate. When one opens on Sunday, the other competes and opens also. One buys a second tow truck and advertises guaranteed availability. To remain "competitive," the other buys a second truck. Now the costs of each have increased. They are aggressively fighting for market share while the market has remained the same. Their revenues are the same while their costs are higher, yet the level of service offered the customer hasn't improved in any meaningful way. Either their profits have to be lower, or their prices for gasoline and other services have to increase.

But let's take our example one step further. The two stations vigorously compete and lower prices, weakening their financial condition. Eventually one wins over the other, who leaves the business. But the winner is also close to bankruptcy and has to build up his financial condition. So he raises prices.

The lesson here is that competition taken to its ultimate conclusion leads not to lower prices but to higher prices.

Objection: Competition Keeps Them Honest

Some of us will object: "Look, we need competition because if one producer holds a monopoly, he has all the power and can charge whatever he wants. I don't want to be in a position where there aren't alternatives. I want competition so that I can check the price of one against the other. If I'm not happy with the service of one, I can use the other." In other words we'd like alternatives. But the question is, when do we have more alternatives—when there is extreme competition, or when we have cooperation? The examples I've given suggest that more alternatives are available when producers cooperate. When they share unused resources and work on common problems, not only are their costs lower, which will lead to lower prices, but more of them can survive in the market, and more alternatives become available to the customers.

The Meaning of Competition

Part of our confusion stems from the many different ways we use the word *competition*. I think we can clean up some confusion if we delineate some of the word's meanings.

Meaning 1. The first way in which we use the word *competition* is in a contest. Let's have a competition to see who is prettiest, best, fastest, and so on. There can be only one winner, and everyone else is a loser. This is win/lose.

Meaning 2. The second way in which we use the word is to imply the existence of alternatives. "I want there to be competition so that I can compare prices." This meaning is distinct from the first meaning, although the two are often used together, indistinguishably. I can go to a farmers' market where I have my choices of homemade pies. I might be able to taste several and buy one, two, three, or more different pies. I don't have to think one is necessarily better than another: they can each be different. But if they have a contest and give out a blue ribbon to the "best" pie of the fair, then we have a competition in the sense of meaning 1, with one winner and the rest being losers. Otherwise we have alternatives without any winners or losers.

Meaning 3. The word *competition* is often used to mean "as good as." For instance, when someone says she is competitive, she means her prices or features are as good as someone else's. In a previous chapter I called this meaning "parity."

Meaning 4. When the expression "I'm more competitive" is used, the meaning is "I'm better. My prices are better." In English "better" is the proper way of saying "more good." If "more competitive" means "more good," then *competitive* can be inferred to mean "good." So *competition* is also used to mean "good." This is so ingrained that few of us can think of any ill effects of competition. It is necessary that we become aware of the ill effects of competition in given circumstances.

When the word *competition* is used in the first sense of "win/lose," then meanings 2, 3, and 4, of "alternative," "as good as," or "good," are often unwittingly implied. The implication that win/lose is innately good and guarantees more alternatives is built into the language.

Meaning 5. There is one other meaning, which is a bit more

subtle in its distinction, and I'd like to use an example to bring it out.

As should be evident by now, I grew up in a fairly typical American environment and participated in competitive enterprises, including athletics. For many years I played and relished the game of basketball. I played on my high school team, but most of my play was with friends on one of many courts available to us. We would play a game, and after it was over we'd choose up sides again and play a new game. When I was thinking about this, the term *compete against* didn't fit. I was not competing *against* my friends, I was competing *with* them. If meaning number 1 is "competing against," meaning number 5 is "competing with." The two are not the same. There are subtle but very real distinctions. The two are mutually exclusive, although they may seem at first to be indistinguishable.

When we compete against, the object is winning and only winning. After years of play, the object is still winning. Statements like "Winning isn't everything, it's the only thing" and "Give me a good loser and I'll show you a loser" are the final and unfortunate response of someone who knows only "competing against."

In "competing with" the object is to have fun and improve. After years of "competing with," the end result is mastery. In "competing with," your teammates and competitors are helping each other to improve. While you're playing, each team tries to score as many points as possible, and each tries to win; but when it's over, it's over; forget about who won or lost. The play's the thing.

In "competing against," the object is to beat the other person, and the focus is the other person. In "competing with," the focus is on your play, your skill, and teamwork. In "competing against," there is little room for cooperation. Cooperation is a necessary evil.

In "competing with," cooperation is implied. It's an integral part of the process.

Which leads to better performance? In my mind there's no contest. "Competing with" leads to far superior results. One of the main deterrents to good performance is fear of losing. Fear of losing leads to desperate attempts to score, it leads to gross cheating. Fear of losing is a natural by-product of competing against.

How does this apply to business? The analogy of competing against would be management who are constantly fighting for market share, constantly judging their own performance on how they're doing compared to their competitor. Some managements want to be number one. They're concerned with having the largest market share. Some investment banks in their advertising show the relative rankings of the top five firms. So what! Merrill Lynch's stated goal is to be first in their markets. They just wrote off $470 million or about 15 percent of their equity. Seems like a funny way to be first.

A company's focus can and should be the customer. It should be looking to constantly improve its products, its people, its systems. It should be striving to improve the standard of living of society by meeting the needs of the customer. It shouldn't put its head in the sand and ignore what others are doing, but its focus isn't on beating the other guy. It should be open to any new ideas wherever they come from, including other companies, the customer, or its own employees. Naturally if it's forever improving and other companies are not, in time it may offer such superior goods and/or services that some companies, its "competitors," may find they can't "compete" and may be forced out of business. But it would be a mistake to say it is "competing against" anyone.

Help Your Competitor

At one Deming seminar I attended, someone came up from the audience during a break and told Deming, "A year and a half ago our company began instituting your methods. Quality began improving immediately. Inventory has declined by 90 percent, earnings have quadrupled, and sales are improving, with customers giving us great feedback about our product." Deming's response was, "Good. Now go back and teach everyone else what you've learned. Teach your suppliers, your customers, and your competitors."

Why would anyone want to help their competitors? One reason might be that "What goes around comes around." At one point your competitor might be in a position to help you. But an even more convincing reason is that if you help each other, you'll both be better off. Not just the companies, but the customers as well. In

America we tend to judge how well we're doing by indicators like market share. What's implied when we do this is competition against each other. But if a system of cooperation leads to lower costs for all the producers and better quality, costs, and satisfaction for the customers, isn't that more important than who wins or loses, or even whether there's a winner or loser? In the Deming view, cooperation almost always leads to lower costs, better quality, and more satisfied customers; and if that's the case, then who wins or loses is irrelevant. Everybody wins.

One view of business was expressed by Colonel F. N. Maude. He thought business was a "form of human competition greatly resembling war."[6] Such a view could only come from someone who had never tried to build up a business. Nevertheless, it has been quoted often enough that it has become a cliché. Anyone starting with such a point of view tends to interpret what goes on from that perspective. He'll ignore the interactions and cooperation evident in commerce that have no equivalence in war. War and business are two distinct enterprises. If commerce is seen as a warlike enterprise, however, it will likely be carried out as such and lead to war.

Who was Maude thinking of when he made this statement? He was referring to Andrew Carnegie, the steel magnate, who was a pacifist. He was trying to downplay Carnegie's pacifism. But what was Carnegie's business motto? Harmony.

My own experience has led me to believe that cooperation plays a much more important role in commerce than any form of warlike competition. As a banker I relied on other banks, my "competitors," when a loan was too large for my institution to handle alone. The loan would be syndicated among us and our "competitors." Banking would be virtually impossible if banks didn't exchange credit information. Cooperation makes sound lending possible. A more obvious case involves check cashing. You pay me with a check drawn on Security Pacific in Los Angeles, and I deposit it in my account with Irving Trust in New York. How long is it before I can use those funds? At present it's up to ten days. Even when both banks are in the same city, it may still take four days. Isn't that a bit ridiculous? But the only way that can be improved is with greater cooperation. It's not a problem that any bank can solve alone. When it is addressed, everyone will benefit, including the banks.

Cooperation

What is cooperation? "Some people think that by cooperation I mean taking money out of someone's wallet and giving it to someone else. That's not cooperation!" says Deming. "By cooperation I mean everybody is better off. And I mean *everybody.*"

Cooperation isn't putting a gun to someone's head and saying, do it this way. That's coercion.

Deming relates a story: "I was stuck in an airplane waiting for several hours to disembark. When we finally were able to get off, the stewardess said, 'Thank you for your cooperation.' That's not cooperation. What choice do prisoners have?" Mandatory cooperation is a contradiction in terms. Cooperation is win/win as opposed to win/lose.

Herb Cohen, a professional negotiator, in his best-seller *You Can Negotiate Anything,* says that there is a spectrum of negotiating styles from competitive to collaborative. At one extreme is what he calls the Soviet Style of negotiating, or winning at all costs.

> The competitive (Win-Lose) approach occurs when someone or some group attempts to achieve their objective at the expense of a perceived adversary. These attempts to triumph over an opponent may run the gamut from blatant efforts at intimidation to subtle forms of manipulation. I call this self-oriented strategy the "Soviet style." This term is descriptive, because more than anyone else, the Soviet Union's leaders consistently try to win at the expense of other nations or groups.[7]

On the other side, according to Cohen, is the collaborative Win-Win style that emphasizes "three important activities:

1. Building trust
2. Gaining commitment
3. Managing opposition"[8]

Winning in the collaborative style "means fulfilling your needs while being consistent with your beliefs and values. Winning means finding out what the other side really wants and showing them a way to get it while you get what you want."[9]

Cooperation may take more time than a win-lose style. It takes more energy. Sometimes the Soviet style of negotiating has some dramatic results, but most of the time, and especially if you'll have further dealings with the other side, the collaborative win-win style is, according to Cohen, superior.

If in something as apparently confrontational as negotiating a collaborative win-win style is superior to a competitive win-lose style, how much more so when the parties, such as the people of a corporation, share similar goals?

One reason why cooperation is so much more effective than a competitive style is that, in most instances, the parties have common goals and the possible gain from winning at the expense of the other is very small compared with the amount each can gain from the other. A company and its suppliers really share the same goal. If the ultimate customer is ecstatic, the company and its suppliers and the suppliers' suppliers gain greater security and profit.

In school we're taught that business is competitive because when a company negotiates price with its supplier one will win at the expense of the other. Every penny higher in the price is a gain for the supplier and a loss for the company and vice versa. But this is an incorrect and naive view of business, although some important people have accepted it as veracity. By working together, both can lower costs and improve quality. By matching the supplies to the manufacturing process, they make possible gains far exceeding the few pennies at stake in price negotiations.

Even Adam Smith portrays business as a struggle of one against the other, where one tries to win but is kept in check by counterbalancing forces, or what he called the invisible hand. But in reality, the interests of the baker and his customers are much more aligned than Smith ever supposed. The baker who cheats or impoverishes his customers won't be in business next year, and the customer who defeats the baker in competition will have to bake his own bread next year. They need each other and both benefit from cooperation.

Totally Inappropriate Competition

Perhaps a certain level of competition is inevitable. Perhaps we have developed a taste for it and consider it inevitable, but there are too many cases where competition is totally inappropriate.

One of Deming's clients told him a story concerning her three-year-old daughter. The child went to a Halloween party and wore a costume of which she was proud as Punch. Everyone was having a wonderful time until they had a contest for "best costume." The little girl was destroyed, disheartened; all of a sudden her costume wasn't so special. All the fun stopped. Of course someone may have continued to have fun. One winner and twelve losers: Why do we need such destructive competition? What gives someone the right to build up one person at the expense of twelve others? In my experience, most parents, when they give prizes in such competitions, are trying to build up their own child. And it comes at the expense of other children. But even worse, it is conditioning our children, building up a need to win—at the expense of others.

But isn't the desire to win necessary to achieve excellence? No! Try keeping up with someone who loves what he or she does. What we need to cultivate is love of learning, love of work, love of playing. Love of what you're doing is what leads to mastery and excellence.

Monopoly Versus Competition

If in business the real focus is on providing ever-improving products and services for the customer, what's the difference between the way a monopoly and a company with ten competitors operates? It's a lot less than we would first imagine.

Deming asked Don Peterson, when he was chairman at Ford, how he would operate if Ford were a monopoly. After laughing at the thought because Ford faces competition from giant domestic, Japanese, and European companies, he answered that he would continue doing things just as he's doing them now: focusing on providing ever-improving products and processes; providing an environment where people can excel and enjoy their work.

A monopoly should focus on the same things a company focuses on when facing intense competition. A monopoly doesn't necessarily translate into the highest price at the expense of its consumer.

Of course a monopoly can stagnate. So can a whole industry made up of many competitors. If either adopts a system of beliefs that calls for gains to come at the expense of customers, suppliers, and competitors, decline can come rapidly, although final failure and bankruptcy may be years away.

Monopoly and Quality

For years the Bell System provided a level of service in the communications business that was the envy of the rest of the world. But in the name of the false god Competition, the system was broken up. Has our level of service improved? Are we still the envy of the world? Anyone who maintains the affirmative has got to be kidding.

Certainly I'm not calling for an end to competition or for the creation of monopolies wherever possible. But if we have the freedom to compete, we also need the freedom to cooperate. We have to be aware of the ills of competition and not just assume blindly that it always leads to lower cost or better service.

The critical ingredient is freedom. Companies and individuals have to be free to offer their products and services. They have to be free to enter the market and offer alternatives. But this freedom doesn't imply competition against anyone. Serving the customer doesn't necessitate being number one or beating a competitor. Serving the customer best emanates from pride in work and mastery.

Cooperation at the Foundation

Do we have to go to Japan to find good examples of cooperation? One of the best and most famous examples of cooperation comes from our own history: the Constitution of the United States of America. By 1787, less than a decade after the Revolutionary War ended, it was already clear that a loose confederation of thirteen independent states wasn't an adequate way to govern. Delegates were sent to Philadelphia to amend the Articles of Confederation. Instead, however, they came back with a new form of government, as embodied in our Constitution.

The Constitution called for much more cooperation, with many functions that were being performed by the thirteen independent states becoming functions of a new central government. In the ensuing debate on the new form of government, Alexander Hamilton, James Madison, and John Jay came out squarely in favor of the new constitution. One cannot read the *Federalist Papers* without being impressed by the claims of the great benefits that would accrue to the people because of greater cooperation. Common borders between New York and New Jersey, for instance, would no longer have to be defended. Customs would become much more manageable. Little states would no longer be burdened with the cost of raising an army comparable to their larger neighbors'. A large collective army could be raised to protect against foreign intrusion, but the cost of defending each state would decrease. Trade would increase. All these benefits, according to the *Federalist Papers*, would result from the thirteen independent states cooperating closely in the framework of the new constitution.

Did it work? You have to be the judge of that. But it is pretty clear that at our foundation is the recognition of the benefits of cooperation.

CHAPTER 21

Where Are We?

Today in the United States two distinct schools of management have evolved. One, which we can call the School of Quality Control, has its roots in the work of Walter Shewhart done at the Bell Laboratories in the 1920s. It was developed with ever-broader applications by many people, the most prominent of whom is W. Edwards Deming.

The other major school, which we can call the Financial Results School, has been developed by business schools and managers with a financial view of business.

In the Quality Control School, the purpose of business is to improve the standard of living of society by offering constantly improving products and services. By constantly improving quality, improving the process, design, cost, features, and the people in the company, a company will enlarge its markets, improve its profits, and create more and more jobs.

As the principles of quality control were applied more broadly, it became clear that improvement in quality is not just the result of applying certain statistical techniques on the plant floor or the office. The most important part is how a company is run: its relationships with suppliers and customers, its organizational rules, and the way it treats its people.

The Financial Results School looks to improve results by analyzing backward. It believes managers can determine what financial results are desirable and then, through analyses of the financial statements, decide what each unit of the company has to achieve to meet these results. Quotas and objectives for each unit and each individual are derived in this way.

235

Seen from the viewpoint of the Quality Control School, the Financial Results School commits serious flaws in logic. One wrong logical assumption is that the converses of valid statements are necessarily correct. The proposition that "providing ever-improving products and services with ever-improving quality leads to higher profit and growth, and a stronger competitive position" (If A then B) does not mean that "forcing higher profit for a company leads to better quality and a stronger competitive position" (If B then A).

By examining the financial statement, we can always find ways of improving profit, but most of these are short-term in nature and counterproductive in the long run. They lead to disinvestment, poorer quality, loss of customers, and decline in the company's fortunes.

Other Assumptions

There are other assumptions made by the Financial Results School that are untenable. That each part of the company is independent of the others, that all the important numbers are contained in the financial reports, that variation does not exist, are all incorrect assumptions from the point of view of the School of Quality Control.

Let me explain some of the deficiencies of the Financial Results School with a simple analogy. To navigate the oceans of the world, we need to know about longitude and latitude. If you tried to navigate using just longitude as a guide, you'd get lost pretty quickly.

In business we need at least two sets of numbers to operate properly. We need to know about the financial numbers, such as profit, and we need to know about quality. If we just rely on one set of numbers, it's only a matter of time before we are so far off the mark as to be lost. By just relying on one set of numbers, we are hoping that luck will lead us to our desired destination, and most of us will agree that luck is rarely enough.

Quality in turn isn't just a one-dimensional characteristic. Good management requires that we investigate those quality characteristics that are important, attempt to understand them, define them where possible, and work on them. If we fail to recognize the importance of quality, we are navigating the waters of commerce without a compass. But that is exactly what the Financial Results School does.

The Financial Results School likes to describe itself using terms like logical, rational, scientific, and results-oriented; but seen from the perspective of the Quality Control School, they are devoid of logic and science.

Historical Perspective

Quality in the United States at the start of World War II was scandalously bad in many industries. A concerted effort to disseminate quality control methods in the United States during the war led to a vast improvement in quality. Unfortunately, those who were taught during the crash program were at the level of the plant managers, financial managers, engineers, and other technical people. Division managers, financial managers, marketing managers, and most importantly, top management weren't taught, and they kept viewing quality as something that is added on at the end rather than something integral to the product or service.

To most people the words *quality control* immediately bring visions of inspections. I was trying to explain to a friend of mine the importance of quality, and he told me, "Yes, but I think design is very important, too." The point is that quality is built into a product; it is never inspected into a product. And if you understand that, you understand that when those trained by Deming talk about quality control, they are concerned with everything about a company. Quality control means management, every facet of management.

Unfortunately, to most of us quality control doesn't have that meaning, and when World War II ended, top management's main job was to increase production. Any company that could produce enough would make money. Quality didn't seem critical, and top managers thought that quality and costs were mutually exclusive. As a result they forgot about quality, and much of the progress that had been achieved during the war effort was lost.

Instead, much of American management was seduced by the desire to increase production and profits as quickly as possible. But a funny thing began to happen. Many formerly profitable parts of some companies, like radio and electronics manufacturing, became unprofitable. Something was wrong, and managers and academicians with backgrounds in finance and accounting stepped in with their ideas about increasing profitability. They looked at the financial statements, saw where profits were being made or lost, and immediately took action to increase "profits." Couched in semiscientific terms about performance, achievement, and rational action, the Financial Results School seduced much of American business and captured the imagination of the American public. The union card of the Financial Results School became the M.B.A. degree.

But an even stranger phenomenon occurred. Our competitive position versus the rest of the developed world, particularly Japan, became worse, not better.

Deming in Japan

Deming, one of the leaders in the effort to improve quality in American industry during World War II, had witnessed the ready acceptance of quality control among technical managers in the United States and its ready rejection when the pressure was off. When he was invited by the Japanese to lecture on quality, he was as willing as ever and hoped they would take his lessons to heart. But during his first lecture on statistical methods of quality control in 1950, he was seized by a sense of panic. He realized he was repeating the mistakes made in the United States. He was just talking to the technical people. Once again, management was missing. He realized that Japan would repeat the experience of the United States unless he did things differently.

After that first lecture he talked to his hosts about the problem. Luckily, he reached some who not only understood what the problem was, but were able to do something about it. A seminar was quickly organized for top managers, and all who were invited to attend did so. This simple fact is a most critical difference between the United States and Japanese experiences. Who led the charge for quality in Japan? It was top management. They understood what it was all about, and they knew their responsibilities.

Our Position Today

Where are we today? What are our main exports? Heading the roster is scrap iron. In second place is scrap paper. In third place is aerospace, and fourth is entertainment. Our largest exports are waste products that are converted into cars, radios, and other manufactured products with value added and sold back to us. We're running a yearly trade deficit of more than $100 billion.

Of course there are nations that are in worse shape than us. The economic structures of the nations of Eastern Europe are collapsing under their own weight. The Soviet Union is an economic basket case. Africa is a mess. Latin America is burdened with debt that it can never pay back. Should this make us feel good?

Certainly we should be happy that tyrannical forms of government have collapsed in Eastern Europe and elsewhere. Eastern Europe and the Soviet Union represent commercial opportunities for all the companies in the world. But certainly we shouldn't feel good because they are worse off than we are.

International trade has made us aware that other developed nations have the same economic potential as we and that one nation in particular, Japan, seems to be able to produce better quality than we do and seems to be taking the technological lead in the most sophisticated industries.

It is tempting to blame Japan for our problems. After all, if someone else is first, then they have beaten us. It's a small step then to blame them for our secondary position. But being first by one measure or another is irrelevant. Such petty talk can only add to our confusion.

In some ways our position today resembles the position of a wealthy family, desperately trying to maintain its standard of living. The first generation made the fortune and passed it on to the next generation, which lived off interest and capital. The present generation, in order to maintain its style, has sold off some of the land of the family estate and then mortgaged the furniture and the house itself. We are rapidly accumulating debt, not to build up the productivity of our farms or factories, but to consume. A wealthy family can go on this way for quite a while, a wealthy nation for even longer. But sooner or later something has to give. Debt has to be serviced even if it isn't paid back. We can take stock of the situation and begin making changes, or else we can wait until a visible crisis occurs at which point changes would be forced upon us by circumstances.

What's Our Problem?

We have a problem in the United States, and that problem is not Japan. Nor is the problem our workers, our educational system, our technology, or superior Japanese government aid to industry. There is nothing wrong in wanting to improve our educational system, our technology, or the attitudes of business and government toward each other. But these are not the critical differences.

Japanese firms have taken over American plants that under American management were producing poor quality and in a relatively short period of time have made those plants as productive and quality-oriented as their counterparts in Japan. Our problem is quality, and quality is made in the boardroom. Quality is management. Our problem is the way we manage.

If Japan didn't exist, our problem would still be here. All of us remember cars that seemed to suffer nervous breakdowns in their third year, electronic equipment that would expire right after its warranty ran out, and toys that would break soon after being taken out of the box.

American quality was in serious decline during the 1950s and 1960s. Japanese competition showed us that poor quality was not inevitable and, more importantly, that excellent quality did not mean great expense. For this the American consumers and producers alike owe Japan our gratitude.

If Japan as we know it today did not exist, we might be number one in all areas, but the price might be poor quality and a decreasing standard of living for our people. Rather than looking at our relative position vis-á-vis some other nations, we should examine ourselves from the point of view of improvement of our standard of living. However, let's not look to increase our standard of living by manipulating economic aggregates but by improving the way we produce and the way we foster improvement. The way we manage.

Japan and Asia

Today many people place the emerging Asian economic centers, such as Taiwan, Hong Kong, and Korea, in the same category as Japan. They're often seen as earlier versions. I have to believe that this thinking results from our mistaken view that Japan's success is due to its people working harder than ours and that other Asians can work just as hard. But this view is misguided and incorrect.

In my personal experience, the quality of goods made in Korea or Hong Kong or Taiwan is not of the same quality of Japanese brands, regardless of where they are made. I have had too many toys and other items marked made in Hong Kong just fail to work properly right out of the box. The management style in Korea is more like an earlier version of our own style. It seems adversarial, with management and labor on opposite sides.

There is no assurance that the developing nations of Asia will become anything more than a cheap source of supplies of just acceptable quality until they change their way of managing.

We often forget just how extraordinary Japan's rise to prominence seemed at first. After the war, Japan's economic base was ruined. Japan was a defeated power, and our main concern was making sure it wouldn't pose a military risk to us again. Most of the U.S. efforts were directed at Europe. The Marshall Plan funneled huge amounts of American resources into Europe, while nothing of comparable magnitude was directed at Asia. Japan was an overcrowded island nation with few resources to speak of and little arable land. The U.S. consumer knew Japan as the manufacturing source of cheap, poor-quality items and little umbrellas that were served in fruity cocktail drinks.

If in 1950 one were to have picked the future economic power of Asia, it would have been China, with its huge land base, or India, which seemed to possess all the ingredients for success. India had people, knowledge, and resources. But India and China both lacked management.

Japan had people and knowledge but lacked resources. Japan had to import virtually all its raw material. To pay for materials and food, the Japanese had to manufacture well and sell abroad. This required management.

Is Japan perfect? No! Of course not. There is much about Japanese society that could be improved, not least of which is its educational system, which emphasizes test scores over learning. Just think how much more potential remains to be tapped.

Some Necessary Changes

As Deming says, no nation need be poor. But it isn't the desire of the people of a nation to work hard that determines its prosperity. It is the attitudes, system of beliefs, and knowledge that determine the long-run prosperity and standard of living of a nation. In other words, prosperity depends on management.

Any one of the nations of Eastern Europe, Asia, Latin America, or Africa could experience substantial increases in its standard of living. But of all the nations in the world, which is the most underdeveloped? It may be the United States. With its people, knowledge, and natural resources the United States may be the least developed nation in the world relative to its potential. Our management systems systematically destroy our people. They judge, grade, and differentiate people when all the difference is due to the system, which is management's—and only management's— responsibility. Our management system systematically proclaims that at least half our people are losers.

This has to change if we are to improve. Instead of worrying about who is number one and who is last, management has to concentrate on helping everyone. Management has to work on the system.

As a nation we have to cease this petty talk about being first in this, that, or the other category. We might be seventh but that's irrelevant. What is relevant and important is whether our standard of living is improving. Today we have for the first time many Americans who are convinced that their standard of living will not be as good as that of their parents. This is a strong indication that something is amiss, and is much more important than our relative ranking.

Deming's Basic Lesson

If we were to sum up the management lessons of Dr. Deming, what would they be? Let me first mention some things that they would not be. The lessons of Deming are definitely not that we have to set high standards and then stick to them. If you believe this, you've missed the point of this book. The lessons are definitely not that gadgets and machinery are the way to improve our quality and productivity. Sometimes they help, but they are not enough. The lessons are definitely not that we have to get tough with our people and demand the impossible. The lessons are definitely not that we have to reward excellence and punish mediocrity.

The main aim of the Deming philosophy is empowerment of the individual. The lesson is that we have to empower *all* our people with dignity, knowledge, and skills so that they may contribute. They have to be made secure so that they can contribute, trained so that they can do the work properly, and encouraged to grow so that the firm can develop and grow. The purpose of all of management, the purpose of cooperation, is to bring out the best in each of us and allow each of us to contribute fully.

The Immediate Future

Is there hope? Are we about to transform the whole nation? Well there's always hope, but hope can be our worst enemy, particularly if it keeps us from making the necessary changes and keeps us attached to our old and incorrect ways.

Deming has been working diligently to increase the number of people who understand quality management. American industry has in the past decade found a new zeal for quality. Transformations have begun in many companies in many industries. Among these are the American auto manufacturers, especially Ford and General Motors. Other companies from industries as diverse as apparel, photography, chemical, consumer goods, and service companies have begun transformations under Deming or one of the other able consultants.

But these companies remain in the minority. And the news from the front is not positive. I walked into a Wall Street bookstore that was reputed to have the best selection of business books. It was a mighty selection indeed, hundreds of business books, hundreds of books on management. Many of the books I was familiar with from my graduate studies; some I had read in preparing this book. I browsed and leafed through some of the others. I was trying to find one that had some elements of profound knowledge, that talked about the ills of merit reviews, the problems with competition, the importance of knowledge of variation. I found none.

In 1989 a memo was prepared for President Bush's signature that asked the Office of Management and Budget to exclude from consideration for government contracts any company that didn't adopt management by objectives. Could you think of anything more harmful to our industry, our government, or our people?

Every day we hear on television or read in the papers a proposed solution to our problems. Our problem appears to some observers to be our lazy people; or that people won't work for low enough salaries; or the lack of competition; or that our standards aren't set high enough; or that our people aren't educated enough or smart enough. All the proposed solutions sound so logical and well-meaning. And they are all wrong. If the incorrect ideas that have gotten us in trouble spread further and undo much of the good already done, things may get very much worse before they get better.

Isn't it time we stopped blaming the Japanese? Isn't it time we stopped blaming our people and got down to the real task of managing for continual improvement? Isn't it time we listened to the man who taught Japan?

The Deming Prize

The following description of the Deming Prize and its regulations is staken from a pamphlet called "The Deming Prize," published in 1960 by the Union of Japanese Scientists & Engineers (JUSE).

Instituting of the Deming Prize

The Deming Prize is a silver medal, with Dr. Deming's profile engraved on the surface, designed by Professor Kiyoshi Unno of Tokyo University of Fine Arts and other artists. A sum of money is to be given as a sub-prize to the recipients of the prizes. Since 1953, funds for the sub-prize have been donated by the Nihon Keizai Shimbun Sha. Incidentally, since 1954 the same newspaper company has been donating funds necessary for the Nikkei Quality Control Literature prize, which is to be awarded to the authors of recommendable literature on quality control.

Deming Prize Regulations

1. The Deming Prize is a prize instituted in commemoration of the friendship and contributions of Dr. W. Edwards Deming, who has visited Japan to instruct in application of statistical quality control methods to industry.

2. The Deming Prize shall be awarded to:

a) Those who have achieved excellence in research in the theory or application of statistical quality control.

b) Those who have made remarkable contributions to the dissemination of statistical quality control methods, and

c) The corporations, plants, etc., which have attained recommendable results in the practice of statistical quality control (the prize for application).

In the case of small enterprises, a prize for the application in small enterprises is provided too.

3. The Deming Prize fund shall be provided mainly from royalties due to Dr. Deming on his *Elementary Principle of the Statistical Control of Quality* and other works published in Japan. Public donations and others, if any, shall be accepted to cover the deficit.

4. The Deming Prize shall be awarded once a year. The awarding of the Deming Prize shall be put in the charge of the Deming Prize Committee.

5. The President of the Union of Japanese Scientists & Engineers shall assume the chairmanship of the Deming Prize Committee, and the Chairman shall commission other members.

Deming Prize For Application

1951	Fuji Iron & Steel Co., Ltd.
	Tanabe Seiyaku Co., Ltd.
	Showa Denko K.K.
	Yawata Iron & Steel Co., Ltd.
1952	Asahi Chemical Industry Co., Ltd.
	Furukawa Electric Co., Ltd.
	Nihon Electric Co., Ltd.
	Shionogi Pharaceutical Co., Ltd.
	Takeda Pharamaceutical Co., Ltd.
	Toyo Spinning Co., Ltd.
1953	Kawasaki Iron & Steel Co., Ltd.
	Shin-etsu Chemical Industry Co., Ltd.
	Sumitomo Metal Industries, Ltd.
	Tokyo-Shibaura Electric Co., Ltd.
1954	Nihon Soda Co., Ltd.
	Toyo Bearing Mfg. Co., Ltd.
	Toyo Rayon Co., Ltd.

1955	Hitachi Ltd.
	Asahi Glass Co., Ltd.
	Honshu Paper Mfg. Co., Ltd.
1956	Fuji Photo Film Co., Ltd.
	Konishi-Roku Photo Industry Co., Ltd.
	Mitsubishi Electric Mfg. Co., Ltd.
	Tohoku Works Ltd.
1957	None
1958	Kanegafuchi Chemical Industry Co., Ltd.
	Kureha Chemical Industry Co., Ltd.
	Matsushita Electronic Corporation
	Nippon Kokan Kabushiki Kaisha
1959–60	Asahi Special Glass Co., Ltd.
	Kurake Spinning Co., Ltd.
	Nissan Motor Co., Ltd.
1961	Nippondenso Co., Ltd.
	Teijin Ltd.
1962	Sumitomo Electric Industries, Ltd.
1963	Nippon Kayaku Co., Ltd.
1964	Komatsu Manufacturing Co., Ltd.
1965	Toyota Motor Co., Ltd.
1966	Kanto Auto Works, Ltd.
1967	Shinko Wire Co., Ltd.
1968	Bridgestone Tire Co., Ltd.
	Yanmer Diesel Engine Co., Ltd.
1970	Toyota Auto Body Co., Ltd.
1971	Hino Motors, Ltd.
1972	Aisin Seiki Co., Ltd.
1975	Richo Co., Ltd.
1976	Sankyo Seiki Manufacturing Co., Ltd.
	Pentel Co., Ltd.
1977	Aisin-Warner Ltd.
1978	Tokai Rika Co., Ltd.
1979	Nippon Electric Kyushu, Ltd.
	Sekisui Chemical Co., Ltd.

Takenaka Komuten Co., Ltd.
Tohoku Richo Co., Ltd.

1980   Fuji Xerox Co., Ltd.
Kayaba Industry Co., Ltd.
Komatsu Forklift Co., Ltd.
The Takaoka Industrial Co., Ltd.

1982   Kajima Corporation
Nippon Electric Yamagata Ltd.
Rhythm Watch Co., Ltd.
Yokogawa-Hewlett Packard Co., Ltd.

1983   Shimizu Construction Co., Ltd.
The Japan Steel Works, Ltd.

1984   Komatsu Zenoah Co., Ltd.
The Kansai Electric Power Co., Inc.
Yasukawa Electric Manufacturing Co., Ltd.

1985   Toyoda Machine Works, Ltd.
Toyoda Gosei Co., Ltd.
Nippon Carbon Co., Ltd.

1986   Toyoda Automatic Loom Works, Ltd.
Hazama-gumi, Ltd.

1987   Aisin Chemical Co., Ltd.
Daihen Corporation
NEC IC Microcomputer Systems Ltd.

1988   Aisin Keikinzoku Co., Ltd.
Asmo Co., Ltd.
Fuji Tekko Co., Ltd.

1989   Aishin Shinwa Co., Ltd.
Itoki Kosakusho Co., Ltd.
Toto Ltd.
NEC Tohoku Ltd.
Maeda Corporation

Deming Prize for Application for Small Enterprises

1958   Nakayo Tsushinki Co., Ltd.

1959–60   Towa Ind. Co., Ltd.

1961	Nihon Radiator Co., Ltd.
1967	Kojima Press Industry Co., Ltd.
1968	Chugoku Kayaku Co., Ltd.
1969	Shimpo Industry Co., Ltd.
1972	Saitama Chuzo Kogyo K.K.
1973	Sanwa Seiki Manufacturing Co., Ltd.
	Saitama Kiki Manufacturing Co., Ltd.
1974	Horikiri Spring Manufacturing Co., Ltd.
	Kyodo Surveying Co., Ltd.
1975	K.K. Takebe Tekkosho
	Tokai Chemical Industries, Ltd.
	Riken Forge Co., Ltd.
1976	Komatsu Zoki, Ltd.
1978	Chuetsu Metal Works Co., Ltd.
1979	Hamakako Denso Co., Ltd.
1980	Kyowa Industrials Co., Ltd.
1981	Aiphone Co., Ltd.
	Kyosan Denki Co., Ltd.
1982	Aisin Chemical Co., Ltd.
	Shinwa Industries Ltd.
1983	Aisin Keikinzoku Co., Ltd.
1984	Anjo Denki Co., Ltd.
	Hokuriku Kogyo Co., Ltd.
1985	Uchino Komuten Co., Ltd.
	Comany Co., Ltd.
	Hoyo Seiki Co., Ltd.
1986	Sanyo Electric Works, Ltd.
	Nitto Construction Co., Ltd.
1989	Ahresty Corporation
	Toyooki Kogyo Co., Ltd.

Deming Application Prize for a Division

| 1966 | Matsushita Electric Industries Co., Ltd., Electric Components Division |

1976   Ishikawajima-Harma Heavy Industries Co., Ltd.,
            Aero-Engine & Space Operations

1981   Tokyo Juki Industrial Co., Ltd., Industrial Sewing
            Machine Division

1985   Texas Instruments Japan Limited, Bipolar Department

1988   Joban Hawaiian Center, Joban Kosan Co., Ltd

Deming Application Prize for a Factory

1973   Mitsubishi Heavy Industries Co., Ltd., Kobe
            Shipyard

1975   Sekisui Chemical Co., Ltd., Tokyo Plant

1976   Kubota Iron & Machinery Works, Ltd., Engine Tech-
            Research Department
            Kubota Kron & Machinery Works, Ltd., Sakai Works

1977   Japan Aircraft Manufacturing Co., Ltd., Atsugi Works

1979   The Japan Steel Works, Ltd., Hiroshima Plant

1980   Kobayashi Kose Co., Ltd., Manufacturing Division

1981   Matsushita Electric Works, Ltd., Hikone Factory

1983   Fuji Electric Co., Ltd., Matsumoto Plant

1988   Musashino Brewery, Suntory Co., Ltd.

1989   Kobe Steel Ltd., Chofu Kita (Iron & Steel Plant)
            Division
            Maeta Concrete Industry Ltd., Main Plant

Deming Application Prize for Overseas Companies

1989   Florida Power & Light Co.

William Edwards Deming: A Brief Biography

William Edwards Deming was born in Sioux City, Iowa, on October 14, 1900. Shortly thereafter, when free land became available in Wyoming, his father, William, succeeded in obtaining some and moved the family out there, first to Cody and then to Powell, where their first house was a tar paper shack about the size of a freight car. It was a hard life. Deming remembers "his mother taking him and his brother by the hands and praying for food."

His mother had studied music in San Francisco, and she gave piano and voice lessons in Powell. Some students who could not pay for lessons brought food or other commodities the family could use in exchange.

The first school Deming attended in Powell had pupils ranging from the first to the sixth grade. All the students were in one room with the same teacher. When he was twelve, he took his first job for $1.25 a week.

After graduating from high school in a class of eleven students, he entered the University of Wyoming in Laramie in 1917. There was no tuition fee, and Deming subsisted on $50 in savings, money earned working, and periodic supplements from his family.

He graduated from the University of Wyoming in 1921, receiving a B.S. with a major in physics. He stayed on for a year to study mathematics and help teach engineering. He then accepted a position teaching physics at the Colorado School of Mines, where he stayed for two years. He also enrolled at the University of Colorado

251

at Boulder and graduated in 1924 with a master's degree in mathematics and physics.

Because Deming had distinguished himself in his studies, one of his professors suggested that he go to Yale University. He would later say, "I thought Professor Lester had lost his mind." Nevertheless, Professor Lester, who had studied at Yale himself, wrote the university on Deming's behalf. He was offered a scholarship plus a part-time job as instructor at $1,000 a year. He graduated from Yale in 1928 with a doctoral degree in mathematical physics. His dissertation was on the packing of nucleons in the helium atom.

While studying for his Ph.D., he worked during the summers at the Western Electric Hawthorne plant in Chicago, doing research on telephone transmitters. He came into contact with a number of scientists, mathematicians, and statisticians who greatly influenced him, including Walter A. Shewhart, who would later be recognized as the father of the statistical control of quality.

Deming's first full-time job was in the Fixed Nitrogen Research Laboratory of the United States Department of Agriculture (USDA). He was also a special lecturer in mathematics and statistics at the Graduate School of the National Bureau of Standards from 1930 to 1946. From 1933 to 1943, Deming was head of the Department of Mathematics and Statistics of the Graduate School of the USDA. During this period Deming and others were conducting much of the basic research on sampling and other aspects of modern statistics. He had many of the great names in the field appear as guest lecturers at the graduate school of the USDA. Almost all of the thirty-eight scientific papers he wrote through 1938 were on physics and physical properties of matter, but his range of lecturing and the application of statistical methods was broadening to other fields.

In March 1938, Deming's longtime friend Shewhart gave four lectures at the USDA; with Deming's editorial assistance he published a book covering the material of these lectures, *Statistical Method from the Viewpoint of Quality Control*. Deming wrote the preface for the manuscript. In 1980, when Shewhart's pioneering work *Economic Control of Quality of Manufactured Product* was republished to commemorate its fiftieth anniversary, it was Deming who wrote a new dedication.

In the late 1930s the United States Census Bureau began toying with the idea of sampling rather than relying on a full count. The Census Bureau needed the best experts available, so they asked Deming to join them, which he did in 1939 as head mathematician and advisor in sampling. The advantages of sampling turned out to be greater than expected. Not only was it reliable and cost-effective, but the swift return of the results made census figures much more effective as a business and policy tool. Today we consider sampling in both the private and public sectors as commonplace, but then it was revolutionary.

It was at the Census Bureau that Deming began using quality control methods in a nonmanufacturing environment. Building on Shewhart's work, he employed statistical methods of quality control to provide quality and reliability. The Census Bureau is one of the real success stories of government service. It provides accurate information on a broad range of areas at a cost that no other organization, public or private, can match. Deming also began lecturing on quality control in the United States.

In 1946 he left the Census Bureau to establish a private practice as a consultant in statistical studies. He also joined the Graduate School of Business Administration at New York University. As a consultant to the War Department he first visited Japan in 1947 and returned in 1950, 1951, 1952, 1955, and 1956. The Deming Prize was established in Japan in December 1950.

In 1955, W. Edwards Deming received the Shewhart Medal, which is awarded annually by the American Society for Quality Control. His scientific papers today number over 170. He has written seven textbooks and countless articles.

In 1980 an NBC white paper—"If Japan Can, Why Can't We?"—prominently featured Deming, outlining his role in Japan's economic transformation. That brought his name to the attention of chief executives in the United States who previously had not been aware of his contribution to management and quality. His already lively consulting practice became even more so, and today his schedule is booked up to three years in advance. Each year he gives more than twenty four-day seminars to managers in the United States, and he travels every summer to Japan for the awarding of the Deming Prize. He continues to teach at NYU, sponsors clinics for statisticians and other technical people, and consults leading companies worldwide.

Some National Implications of the Deming View

During all the time I have known him, Deming has emphasized that his teachings apply to any process. His management philosophy can be applied in a corporate environment or a government agency, regardless of size. Even the way we run our economy or institute social policy must be guided by profound knowledge to be effective. I mentioned to him once that certain policies may be tampering and he strongly agreed and encouraged me to pursue that line of reasoning. In what follows I examine certain government policies and try to show how our lack of profound knowledge has probably cost all of us dearly.

In Chapter 5 I mentioned that the Federal Reserve's attempts to "control" the money supply were forms of tampering, only making things worse. This shouldn't go without further explanation, particularly since most of us take it on faith that the actions of the Federal Reserve are beneficial.

One of the outstanding characteristics of financial markets, even when they are relatively stable and calm, is their movement. Even in stable times the markets bounce around a lot. As one observer stated when asked for an opinion of the stock market, "The market will oscillate." If the movement of an economic variable is random, then, as demonstrated by the experiment with the Nelson Funnel, it is impossible to lessen the amount of variation by making adjustments to the system. But there are other possibilities. What if instead of random variation the market's movements (or other

254

economic variables such as the money supply) are oscillations of a cyclical nature?

Oscillations Versus Variation

The markets may be moving away from some central point and then being pulled back by a corrective force. Economists claim that there are market forces pulling prices and other economic variables back toward some central point, an "intrinsic value" or "natural level." The argument usually runs something like this: As the price of a commodity falls, buyers enter the market and bring support to the price. As it falls further, other users of the commodity will find the price more attractive and buy some more. This buying supports the price and then brings it back up to a "natural" level. The same thing happens in reverse when the price goes "too high." Sellers begin to sell and take profits until the buying exhausts itself. The selling exerts a downward pressure on price and acts as a stabilizing force.

What we have just described is an oscillating system, rather than random variation. One characteristic of an oscillating system is that if you knew the forces involved, you could predict with accuracy its movement over time, that is, you could predict future results, in this case future prices. This alone is enough to indicate that something is greatly amiss with this idea because the predictive record of the economic profession in general and the members of the Federal Reserve Board in particular is not enviable.

But let's follow the reasoning further. The argument might run that with an oscillating system one only need resist the market whenever it rises "too high" or falls "too low." In theory, at least, it's argued that the oscillations could be dampened. We have a lot of examples of systems where dampening of similar oscillations occurs. The shock absorbers in your car, for instance, do just that. Whenever you hit a bump, the shock is absorbed by the springs, which continue oscillating, slowly losing energy, until the next bump. If your car hit several bumps in a row, the springs could oscillate so much that they would break. But the springs are linked to shock absorbers, which absorb the energy of the bumps. A liquid in the shock absorbers resists the action of the springs. The harder the bump, the more they absorb. Even a series of bumps is just taken in stride without any damage to the springs or the passengers.

My point is that there are mechanical systems in which dampening of oscillations takes place and it's not theoretically impossible to dampen such oscillations in a financial system. It just happens to be near impossible.

One of the problems with trying to dampen an oscillating system is that if it isn't done exactly right the amplitude of the system will get larger and larger, eventually exploding or breaking down completely. In order to lessen the amount of oscillation, you have to know the frequency and phase of the system exactly, something we obviously don't know about economic and financial markets.

Let's imagine we have some economic variable, such as the money supply, which is oscillating smoothly between 90 and 110. On January 1 it's at 100. Thirty days later it's at 90, thirty days after that it's back to 100, thirty days after that at 110, and so on. This would be a perfectly smooth harmonic function. The force bringing money supply back to 100 would be linear. As the money supply went further from 100, the force pulling it back would get stronger in direct proportion to the difference. In other words, at 90 the upward pull of economic forces would be twice as strong as at 95.

Suppose now the Fed tries to stabilize the money supply. Whenever it gets below 95, the Fed intervenes, putting strong upward pressure on money supply. Let's suppose the money supply with Fed interventions only falls to 92 and the Fed keeps intervening until it gets back up to 95, at which point the Fed relaxes. Will that make things better or worse? The Fed would justify its actions by the fact that this time around the money supply only dropped to 92 instead of 90. But by keeping the pressure on from 92 to 95, it has added energy into the system. On the up side the system will now tend to go well past 110, perhaps to 115. If the Fed now intervenes at 105, trying to keep the money supply down, it might keep the money supply from rising to 115. It may only now rise to 112. But as the Fed keeps up the pressure until it gets back down to 105, it is adding still more energy into the system and the oscillations are becoming more extreme.

On the downswing, even with the Fed intervening at 95, the money supply gets down to 85. The Fed is in a sense right to be helping on this particular swing because if it didn't intervene, the money supply would reach 80. But because of the intervention the swings are getting worse—if the Fed just did nothing, the system in a few cycles would settle back to its old pattern. By intervening, it is making things better this time but worse the next.

But what about the dampening effect on mechanical systems? Why can't we do the same thing in financial markets? Shock absorbers exert a force in a direction opposite to the movement of the springs. In the economic analogy it would be okay to dampen the market by trying to pull it back up if it were falling below 95, for instance, but as soon as it turned at 92 and started heading up we would have to start exerting a force downward, even though it was well below our target. We would have to keep pushing it down as long as it were traveling upward to take energy out of an oscillating system. But this is counterintuitive, just the opposite of what's actually done.

A system that dampens in a mechanical system acts in a direction opposite to the movement, regardless of the position. That means it is opposing the motion, whether the motion is up or down, regardless of whether the system is considered "too high" or "too low." By doing just the opposite, the Fed is making things worse if the markets are indeed oscillating.

Actually the situation is worse than I've painted it so far. By intervening at certain levels, the monetary authorities could be turning a predictable system with a linear stabilizing force into a very unpredictable system. In this simple example the returning force is linear, except that with intervention, when it goes below 95 or above 105, other forces kick in, making the returning force exponential. The system goes from predictable and cyclical to chaotic. The periods or frequency along with the amplitude will change. And this is a best case scenario. If the "normal economic force," which tends to return the money supply to some mean, is not itself linear—if we don't know the frequency and amplitude of the oscillations—we aren't even theoretically able to dampen the oscillations. Once in a while by luck our actions may work out to be beneficial, but when we aren't successful and instead make the oscillations worse, we can create a crisis or panic.

But it would be naive to expect that random variation isn't also at work even if there is a strong cyclical element to the market. So a combination of both random and cyclical factors would be even more impossible to control by adjustment. Once in a while, you'd get lucky, but most of the time attempts to adjust a system without perfect knowledge of the system would be tampering, making things worse. In real life we never have perfect knowledge of a system.

State of the Art

All right, you say, sounds fairly reasonable, but surely such questions have been addressed by economists and others who study these matters and are charged with developing monetary and fiscal policy? Unfortunately, that's not the case.

A more typical view of the situation can be found in *Inflation and Deflation*, an essay written in 1919 by John Maynard Keynes. As a way of controlling prices, and avoiding the injustice of inflation and the inexpediency of deflation, Keynes states unequivocally, "The remedy would lie, rather, in so controlling the standard of value that whenever something occurred which, left to itself, would create an expectation of a change in the general level of prices, the controlling authority should take steps to counteract this expectation by setting in motion some factor of a contrary tendency."[1]

The underlying assumption in the above passage is that to do something, to do anything, must be better than doing nothing. Keynes also assumes that the actions he proposes must necessarily have a positive effect. I want to suggest that there are alternatives to either doing nothing or tampering. A deep understanding of variation would be a useful start. Of course there was no way in 1919 that Keynes could have known about tampering and the interrelation of parts of a system. We should view his statement in a historical context. He was doing his best trying to understanding the trade cycle.

But this is 1990 and policymakers today have no such excuse, yet the Federal Reserve Board is still trying to "lean against the wind," only tampering, making things worse. It's possible that some economists and policymakers have addressed and written about these issues and I'm not aware of it. But the point isn't whether I'm aware of them or not. The point is that they haven't had any effect on the people who make policy and who are still trying to regulate our country at all levels of government in ignorance and without any awareness of profound knowledge.

For the Record

All of this so far is just theoretical. What does the record show? The Federal Reserve was opened for business in November 1914. (We had a central bank established by Alexander Hamilton when he was secretary of the treasury under George Washington, but Thomas Jefferson dismantled it when he became President. We seem to have done pretty well without one; by 1914 the United States was already one of the great economic powers of the world.) When the Fed opened its doors, it was limited in its scope, being unable to offset gold inflows until later. It could turn on the tap, so to speak, but couldn't turn it off or drain the system of money or purchasing power. Initially it had no portfolio of securities (bonds and notes) to sell. It could print money, Federal Reserve notes, but had no way of taking money out of circulation. So it was led to acquire portfolios. In addition, at the outbreak of World War I the Fed became in large part the bond-selling arm of the Treasury. The actions of the Fed during its start-up period of 1914–20 were roundly criticized at the time. It zigged when it should have zagged, but every institution is expected to have special problems when it first begins.

But by 1921 optimism that a new age was dawning and that the Fed was now in a position to stabilize the business cycle and offer continual advancement in the quality of life of our citizenry prevailed. This was called the Golden Age of the Federal Reserve. The Fed took and was given credit for the generally stable conditions that prevailed. From 1920 to 1929 the Fed was tampering with the financial markets. If you or I took credit for the success of an enterprise, we would naturally be forced to take the blame for any major disaster that took place during our watch. But in the ensuing collapse of the economy that took place from 1929 to 1933, the Fed generally escaped severe criticism and instead speculators of all kinds were blamed.

A stock market collapse and three banking crises all took place during the Fed's watch in this period. The great contraction of 1929–34 was followed by five more years of depression. The whole period was called the Great Depression by those who lived through it. Isn't it ironic that with the dawning of a new era in economics, when government could control key interest rates and regulate the supply of money to avoid banking panics and instability, we had the worst depression in our history? It's not really ironic, it's more accurate to say it was predictable. When engineers began building longer and longer bridges, they were surprised to find that the major problems were not in the strength of bridges but in their stability.

It's relatively easy to make an oscillating system go out of control by overadjusting but relatively difficult, almost impossible, to dampen a system by guesswork. What I'm suggesting is that while it's possible that a depression might have occurred if the Fed didn't exist at the time, it had neither good theory nor good data to guide it properly and its actions in all likelihood made the business cycle much more extreme. It caused a depression to become a great depression, lasting several times longer than any other in our history. This is the best case. It's also possible that in the absence of the Fed's attempts to "control" the economy we might have avoided many of the excesses of the 1920s and the depression of the 1930s.

The real irony is that some economists, notably Keynes, felt that the protracted nature of the depression was due to built-in deficiencies of the economic system. In his terminology, the marginal efficiency of capital tended to fall below the market rate of interest during a boom because of the market psychology of individuals, forcing disinvestment. However, as long as people saved too much of their incomes, it wasn't possible to make any meaningful recovery, according to him. But if in fact the severity of the bust that started in 1929 was due to the misguided tampering of the Federal Reserve, Keynes was making a fundamental mistake. He was mistaking the crash and its severity as being a common cause of the system, when in fact it was a special cause of tampering by the monetary authorities. If this is the case, his landmark and influential book *The General Theory Of Employment, Interest and Money*, while interesting, would have no scientific or intellectual basis.

Please don't misconstrue these comments. I have nothing but respect for Keynes's intellectual prowess. In reading his work I am impressed with his depth of understanding, particularly regarding financial markets. But he was operating without the benefit of profound knowledge.

Around the same time Keynes was tackling the problems of the business cycle, Shewhart, working in the Bell Laboratories, was given a similar problem, the problem of uniformity in manufactured products. AT&T advertised the uniformity of their phones. But they were running into a problem: the more they tried to obtain uniformity, the more they adjusted the system, the worse it became. Shewhart tackled the problems and developed the notion of control limits. He discovered that rarely, if ever, is adjustment a means for obtaining greater uniformity. His work culminated in his landmark book *Economic Control of Quality of Manufactured Product*.

There is one striking difference between the works of these two men, perhaps representing the differences in their two fields. Keynes wrote in his introduction to *The General Theory*, "It is astonishing what foolish things one can temporarily believe if one thinks too long alone, particularly in economics (along with the other moral sciences), where it is often impossible to bring one's ideas to a conclusive test either formal or experimental."[2]

Shewhart, on the other hand, wrote that men in industry must have more exacting standards of knowledge and workmanship than the pure scientist:

> [A]pplied science, particularly in the mass production of interchangeable parts, is even more exacting than pure science in certain matters of accuracy and precision. For example, a pure scientist makes a series of measurements and upon the basis of these makes what he considers to be the best estimates of accuracy and precision, regardless of how few measurements he may have. He will readily admit that future studies may prove such estimates to be in error. Perhaps all he will claim for them is that they are as good as any reasonable scientist could make upon the basis of the data available at the time the estimates were made. But now let us look at the applied scientist. He knows that if he were to act upon the meager evidence sometimes available to the pure scientist, he would make the same mistakes as the pure scientist makes in estimates of accuracy and precision. He also knows that through his mistakes someone may lose a lot of money or suffer physical injury, or both.[3]

Those of us who are involved in building houses, cars, or radios, lending money, or flying planes have a special obligation because if we make a mistake, people can get hurt. How much greater must be the obligations of government officials and regulators at all levels. When they make a mistake, hundreds of millions of people suffer.

So far I have been talking about conceptual and policy errors during the 1920s, a long time ago. That was then and this is now. Surely our understanding since then has grown and we are now able to control the economy. At least that was the argument that was given in the 1960s. We knew enough, it was claimed, to prevent the errors of the past. Using fiscal policy, or by adjusting or "fine-tuning" the expenditures and revenues of the federal government, we could have a sustained boom like Keynes had suggested.

The Fed, in this scenario, had a major role to play by controlling interest rates, keeping them low during booms. But a funny thing happened. The more the economic advisors tried to fine-tune the economy, the more volatile it became. In 1966 the prime rate reached 6½ percent before receding. In 1974 it got up to 12 percent. At this point fine-tuning as an instrument of policy was being renounced, and the Fed switched its policy from controlling interest rates to controlling inflation. In 1980 the prime rate went as high as 24 percent. By using the new science of economics to fine-tune the economy (or tamper if we use Deming's terminology), we successfully managed the economy into the highest peacetime rate of inflation and interest rates in our history.

But what's worse is that before the great economic experiment we considered 4 percent or 5 percent unemployment to be an un-satisfactory level. Today we consider the current 5.3 percent unemployment rate about as low as we can safely go without creating more inflation.

Big Deal!

All right, so interest rates went up and inflation rose. What's the big deal? To answer that we have to understand something about our financial systems.

A Short Course in Banking

There are, or at least used to be, a group of financial institutions called savings and loans or thrifts. For many Americans these institutions were the only way of obtaining mortgages. They were set up to provide mortgages and did so when there were no other organizations to do so. They were highly regulated and limited in the scope of their activity. In some respects they were like banks because they took deposits, at first just savings deposits but later checking accounts as well. These deposits are in effect loans from individuals to the thrifts. Banks and thrifts are highly leveraged organizations. A typical conservative institution would have perhaps ten dollars of deposits and other borrowings for each dollar of equity. Today a typical bank has substantially more leverage than this, maybe thirty dollars of debt for each dollar of its own capital.

But for our purposes a ten-to-one ratio of debt to capital will illustrate the important characteristics of the thrifts. All banks are financial intermediaries taking customer's money via deposits and relending them in loans. This is an efficient way of recirculating capital and allowing those who save to obtain some return from their savings and those with ideas and energy but with little capital to obtain additional funds.

Thrifts were always in a special and precarious position, because their mission, highly regulated by the government, was to borrow short-term through savings deposits and lend long-term, up to thirty years, through mortgage lending. This is a highly treacherous position, which any sophisticated banker would abhor. Its success depended on a stable environment. As long as savings accounts paid 1 or 2 percent and mortgages returned 3 or 4 percent, the business was able to make paper profits but was at risk should rates rise significantly.

Heads You Win, Tails I Lose

What happens when rates change? Suppose interest rates go up. The bank has made a thirty-year fixed-rate mortgage loan at 3 percent when it was paying 2 percent on deposits, but all rates rise by 2 percent, so short-term rates rise to 4 percent. It begins losing money on the loan. It might make new mortgage loans at rates of 5 percent, but it is losing money on all its old loans. Its portfolio is a money loser.

But suppose that instead of rising, interest rates decline by 1 percent. The 3 percent mortgage the bank made is now being financed with 1 percent deposits, giving it a higher than expected spread. Except that mortgage rates have also fallen by 1 percent and all its competitors are offering 2 percent mortgages. At the first opportunity the borrowers will come in and refinance their mortgage loans at the new lower rate. The bank can lose with a change in rates but it can't really win, at least not for long.

Increasing rates are often accompanied by increasing prices, or inflation. The prices of the borrowers' houses tend to increase under these circumstances. The bank, along with other fixed-rate lenders and people on fixed incomes, tends to lose purchasing power and wealth. Inflation tends to transfer wealth from those holding fixed-rate notes to those holding real assets.

But while deflation, which I'll define strictly as a general decline in the price of goods, tends to transfer wealth from those holding real assets to those holding fixed-rate obligations, the savings and loan associations don't benefit much from deflation either, and may also lose when prices are declining.

If the bank lends against 80 percent of the value of a house and there's a recession accompanied by falling prices, the borrower may lose his job and default on the loan. The bank, when it forecloses, may find that the house is now only worth 75 percent of the original value. When it resells the property, it may end up taking a loss.

If interest rates rise, the bank loses. If rates drop, it can't gain. It's a situation of heads I lose, tails you win—certainly not a favorable game for the bank. It will only work if rates and prices are relatively stable. Who's responsible for stable rates? Is it the management of the bank? The members of the board of directors? If anyone, it is the elected leaders and appointed experts who are supposed to maintain stable prices and stable monetary conditions. Let's consider what happens to one bank when rates increase. Let's consider a typical bank with one billion dollars in assets. Who owns those assets? Let's suppose the bank has $90 million of its own money or equity in the business and $910 million is financed through deposits.

Of the $1 billion of assets 30 percent, or $300 million, is in short-term investments and cash while the balance of $700 million is in mortgages. The portfolio's average maturity is, let's say, twenty years and its average interest rate is 3 percent. While long-term rates stay at 3 percent, everything is fine. But what happens if long-term rates go up to 9 percent? The bank will, of course, lose money every year, but there is a way of estimating the value of the existing loan portfolio based on the higher market rate. It is called present value analysis. Using a computer spreadsheet, I calculated the value of the original $700 million portfolio now to be $431.5 million. In other words, the bank has lost $268.5 million because of the increase in rates, if we were to revalue its portfolio based on the higher long-term interest rate.

This means that not only has the bank lost its own $90 million but it has also lost $178 million of its depositors' money.

The loss had nothing to do with the managerial ability or honesty of the bank's management. It was built into the system. Every bank would be affected. The loss is directly the result of the lack of stability in interest rates, and that is the responsibility of those who run the economy, our congresspeople, our presidents, our bureaucrats, and the officials at the Federal Reserve Board.

Of course, if rates rise to the 9 percent level or even higher in one year and then drop back down to the 3 percent level, the bank could weather the storm just by holding on. The portfolio's value would return to its old level, and the bank would just have one bad year due to high rates in that year. That was the hope of regulators and savings bank managers alike when rates began to soar, but hope is not sufficient to bring rates back down. Today, more than fifteen years after rates first started to move dramatically upward, long-term rates are around 9 percent and the prime is 10 percent.

Books have been written about the mismanagement in the savings and loan associations and congressional hearings have been held to investigate wrongdoing, yet all of it is silly nonsense. The problems of the S&Ls were built into the system. All of them suffered huge losses. You try running a bank with negative capital and see how good you look. Everything is easy until you try it. The S&L fiasco *is* an example of incompetent management, but not at the level of the chief executives of the banks. It is gross incompetence of the chief executives of our financial markets, our elected and appointed officials.

Variation, Oscillations, and Chaos

To illustrate the negative effects of adjustments to the system, let me bring in a hypothetical example. Let's assume we have a nine-story building with a fairly old heating system and a thermostat located on the fifth floor. The heating system is less than perfect, but it gets the job done. When the heat is first turned on, the boiler takes some time to heat up. It's giving off heat, but the water in the system hasn't reached the boiling point. Only when the water in the tank boils does the steam start to rise. When it does, the pipes in the first floor apartment get hot first, then the second floor, and so on. The ninth floor is the last to get heat. The thermostat on the fifth floor is set to 70 degrees Fahrenheit. When the temperature on the fifth floor reaches 70 degrees, the thermostat shuts off the boiler, but steam in the pipes continues to rise and the radiators continue to radiate heat. In addition, heat from the lower floors rises toward the higher floors. The lower floors become warmer quickly, but the higher floors get heat flowing into them after the lower floors are cooling. Most of the time the average temperature difference is one degree per floor with temperature dropping by one degree with each higher floor.

But the temperature differences vary greatly, and at times the higher floors may be slightly warmer, depending on the weather outside and other aspects. This is a fairly simple system, but the relationship of temperature between floors is already quite complex. The behavior has a cyclic characteristic to it but is also dependent on the weather outside, which may seem totally chaotic. On very cold days the system works differently than on mild days.

There's one more aspect to the system. When the temperature on the fifth floor reaches 70 degrees, the boiler is shut off by the thermostat, but heat continues to rise. Because of this the temperature on the fifth floor may reach 72 degrees. As the heating system cools and heat is lost to the outside, the temperature starts to drop. When the temperature gets to 69 degrees, the thermostat turns on the boiler. But the heat doesn't come up immediately. It may take some time before the heat rises, and when it does, the temperature may have fallen to 67 degrees.

There are four important characteristics of this system: 1. There is a temperature gradient from the lowest floor to the highest floor, and the actual temperature differences vary over time. 2. There is variation in the temperature of every floor over time. There is a cyclical aspect, and a random aspect to this variation. 3. The temperature inside is also affected by the temperature outside, which seems to behave chaotically. Chaotic changes are neither random nor cyclical. They just seem to change without any noticeable relation to yesterday's temperature. 4. This is a system, and what happens in one part affects conditions in the other parts even though we don't have the ability to predict just how, why, or to what extent.

A Change, but Keep It Warm

Suppose the residents on what is normally the warmest floor, the first floor, go on vacation for a week. While they're away, some children accidentally break a window in the apartment. When the residents come back, they notice that the apartment is cold. This apartment, which normally averages 75 degrees, is now 67 degrees. The residents are understandably upset. They feel they're being robbed. The system is unfair. Something is wrong and must be corrected. If they could only get their hands on the lousy landlord, coop board president, or whoever runs the building, they would get some satisfaction. Someone is to blame for the cold, of course.

Let's assume the first-floor residents have political pull in the building or through threats are able to control the setting of the thermostat. They have the thermostat raised to 80 degrees and their apartment is now comfortable again at 75. But the neighbors just one floor above them are suffocating at 84 degrees, so they open the windows. Everyone who was comfortable before is now miserable. And what about the cost? Heating bills may double, triple, or quadruple. What used to be a happy building is now filled with hostile and angry people. The solution is simple, of course. Fix the window. When the window was broken, the system was changed. If it were to be fixed, the system would undergo a fundamental change, even though it seems small in nature. Raising the thermostat is not a change in the system but a case of adjusting to deal with a different system. It's a form of tampering.

Let's consider some instances where this type of tampering actually occurs. To keep from getting political, I'm going to refer to a rather old example. During World War I, in order to finance the war, England left the gold standard. When peace came, the British political leaders wanted to restore the old state of affairs, which had worked so well. They wanted to restore the gold standard with the British pound at the old level. That meant revaluing the pound upward by about 10 percent. All of a sudden British goods in foreign markets were costing 10 percent more. To restore a reasonable trade balance, British prices had to fall. The way prices fall in most economies is for sales to decline, layoffs to occur, and orders for supplies to be canceled and delayed. In other words, the transition to lower prices is normally a recession or a depression, depending on the severity and how these terms are defined.

The consequences of a higher value for the currency relative to gold were lower domestic prices and high unemployment—at least this is one economic theory. But we need not know anything about any economic theory to know that holding any economic variable at last year's or last decade's levels will have consequences somewhere else. The more drastically we try to enforce the quota, the more important the variable; and the more effective we are at doing so, the worse the consequences elsewhere. Nothing is really solved or improved by quotas or rigid rules of this kind. Examples in recent history abound: the Fed's attempts to keep interest rates down in the 1960s; a brief and disastrous experiment with price controls during Nixon's administration; a long but equally disastrous experiment with rent controls; all kinds of restrictions on trade, the United States today having replaced France as the industrialized nation with the most restrictions on trade.

On this aspect most economists will be shaking their heads in agreement, perhaps saying, "Tell me something I don't already know." But let's go back to our hypothetical example, our nine-story building. Suppose we fix the window and restore the thermostat to 70 degrees. But we notice that the temperature in the fifth floor and, in fact, in each floor varies about five degrees. This is intolerable. We're Americans and we know how to solve this problem. We take a hands-on approach. First we create a banner saying temperatures below 70 degrees will not be tolerated. When that doesn't work, we pass a law; and when that doesn't work, we take direct control of the thermostat and establish the Building-Wide Heat Reserve Board. Our motto is zero tolerance of cold. When the temperature on the fifth floor gets to 69 degrees, we jump into action.

We're going to be scientific about this; and looking over past records we see that there's a tendency for the heat to fall to 67 degrees, so we raise the thermostat to 73. When the temperature rises to 72, we lower the setting to 68; when it goes to 74 before the pipes cool, we lower the setting down to 66. We're already well on our way to the Milky Way.

On this point there is a fundamental disagreement with, as far as I know, all economists who feel it is possible to provide additional stability by making constant adjustments. The most notable cases are adjustments to the monetary variables by the Fed and using Federal deficits and surpluses to smooth out the recessions and booms of the economy. But other cases are the constant changes to the tax code to help one industry or another. The industry that was too strong in one year has some tax breaks taken away; the one that is suffering is given some tax breaks. Several years later the position of the two industries may have reversed, and Congress then adjusts the tax code again. This is just more tampering, and it brings a terrible price tag with it. Is there any case where an adjustment is justified? Yes. In the case of our hypothetical building, if the outside temperature drops substantially, the heat loss may be so great that the thermostat may have to be raised just to keep the building comfortable. In current affairs, the crash in the stock market in October 1987 was an extraordinary and identifiable event, a special cause; and the Fed was justified in adding liquidity into the system and trying to restore confidence and maintain calm. These are responses to special or assignable causes.

Let's return to our example. Must we live with a five-degree variation in temperatures? This is a cyclical system, and it is possible to lower the difference between the high and low temperature. Replacing the old thermostat with a modern one would do the trick. New ones have a run-time cycle, which has to be adjusted once when first installed. The boiler is turned on and off in a continuous cycle before the temperature drops to 69 degrees. In effect, the thermostat attempts to mimic the effect of a constant input of heat to make up for the heat loss in the building.

But once that's installed, the heat will still vary randomly. It is impossible to decrease the difference between the high and the low by adjustment at this point, since statistical control has been achieved. Does that mean that improvements aren't possible? It does not. But improvements will only come by changes in the system. Add insulation, rebuild the windows, put in a new boiler or a whole new heating system, new radiators, and so on. Not only will these effects make it possible to lessen the variation in each apartment, but it will lessen the disparity in heat between the first and ninth floor and it will improve equity between floors as well. And it will lower costs. And herein lies an economic paradox. If the system is improved, the standard of living will increase but gross figures, such as GNP or the cost of heating the building in our example, may decline. On the other hand, tampering leads to higher costs—higher GNP figures but a lower standard of living—which is to say, lower quality.

Let me sum up the main points covered here:

1. Attempts to force an economic variable to a certain level will cause a distortion somewhere else in the system. In time the distortions will affect the variable being controlled and will backfire. This doesn't mean that the goal isn't desirable or honorable. It may very well be a desirable objective. But whether expressed as a quota, a numerical objective, or as a strict rule, the objective can't be obtained by adjustments or strict adherence to some rules. It requires a change in the system.

2. Attempts to lessen the amount of variation due to random variation by adjusting the system are impossible and will only backfire. Attempts to lessen the amount of variation (more accurately, the amplitude of oscillation) due to a cyclical cause might in theory be successful if perfect knowledge of the forces creating the oscillations is available. In other words, in real life it isn't possible and will from time to time lead to huge increases in the amplitude of the swings.

These two points alone cover much of what we call regulation. Regulations falling into either of these two categories is not only expensive but counterproductive. But this doesn't mean that the policy tools (fiscal policy to control demand and monetary policy to control interest rates or money supply) used to adjust economic variables aren't powerful. They are probably very powerful tools. But they cannot lessen the "swings" or the variation in the system. The more powerful these tools are, the more damage they're capable of doing.

This also shouldn't be interpreted as claiming that all regulation is unhelpful. What it means is that poorly conceived laws and actions, based on poor theory, can be disastrous, and we may not even know it until our understanding improves.

Labor and Capital

Most economic theory assumes that production depends on at least three variables, labor, capital, and a third variable such as the state of technical efficiency and knowledge. This third variable, which might include such factors as the degree of specialization of labor (as per Adam Smith), is often taken as a given—nothing can be done about it. As a result, economic analysis is solely concerned with capital rates, levels of output, number of employed people, and so on. It is understandable, then, that in seeking improvement in the way the economy operates, those who have been guided strictly by economic theory would revert to adjusting or manipulating such variables as the interest rates and exchange rates.

If I had to use a brief phrase for Deming's management teachings, I would call it the Science of Improvement. As such, it deals not only with visible figures such as labor and capital but with the third variable, which might be called knowledge, organization, and mind. But one of the conclusions of the science of improvement is that manipulating the visible numbers, the economic variables, doesn't lead to improvement, regardless of our ability to do so and regardless of the amount of money thrown into the effort.

Once a system has obtained a certain level of stability, only changes in the system can improve it; and one has to be careful that what looks like a change in the system is not tampering. Any change in the system at the government level should take into account the need for fairness and equity. But fairness and equity cannot be enhanced when ignorance is the main tool.

This third variable is the most powerful of the three. Keynes did some rough calculations in one of his essays and estimated that the net worth of Great Britain at that time was just the value of the gold that Sir Francis Drake had stolen from the Spanish Galleons and returned to England, reinvested at 3 percent interest compounded yearly.

In 1950, on the other hand, Japan's net worth was probably negative. There was no input of funds from the outside, just some knowledge and ideas. Today Japan's net worth would by all accounts far exceed Great Britain's and by some accounts exceed that of the United States. This third variable, which we can call harnessing mind, is by far the most powerful of the three. While capital and labor are essential, knowledge, initiative, cooperation—those elements that we might call elements of mind—are the powerful impetus for growth and improvement. The amount of labor and the amount of capital are important measures, but improvement comes not from trying to control these visible variables but by encouraging and allowing the minds of all individuals in society to flourish.

Use of Control Charts in Interpreting Economic Data

Could a random chance cause system actually exist among economic variables? The idea might seem an anathema to economists who make a living by explaining every glitch in economic variables, but let me show one example. Our balance of trade figures have been negative for some time. In October 1988 official imports exceeded official exports by $9.2 billion. From that month until December of 1989 our trade deficit ranged from $7.2 billion to $10.8 billion. I computed control limits for this series of numbers of $6.0 billion and $12.8 billion and graphed the series of numbers. The graph looked like a typical control chart of a stable process with no point falling outside the control limits. Yet every month when these figures come out, the newspapers run articles and headlines announcing that the deficit has either increased or decreased, and lots of explanations follow.

But the control charts tell us that all the variation is best explained by chance and we shouldn't attach any significance to these fluctuations. The chart indicates that this is a constant chance cause system with no single cause predominating.

Another example is the silver markets. I drew a control chart for silver starting with April 1975, using monthly data. The charts indicated the presence of a special cause in early 1979. Silver for years had traded between $4 and $5. In 1979 it started the year at just over $6 and then had a spectacular run up in price until it traded at over $40 an ounce in January of 1980. It took an equally spectacular fall and closed in 1980 at about $16 an ounce. Today it's trading at close to $5 dollars an ounce again.

The control charts indicated the presence of some cause or causes that had a dramatic effect on silver prices. Under these conditions it makes sense to try and find or assign a cause for this price movement. One or another set of causes was swamping the random price fluctuations and creating a distinguishable price move.

We can speculate about the possible cause of the price run-up. Some possible causes might be the rampant inflation of that time, the run-up in oil prices due to the concerted action of the oil producers, and even the heavy silver buying of some very rich Texans. But are these really "causes" or are these just symptoms of a deeper, perhaps systemic cause?

At the time that silver was skyrocketing, gold was also having a spectacular run. The Federal government was intent on wringing inflation out of our system. One of the main leaders in the fight was the Fed, which was taking liquidity out of the system. Interest rates went to record levels, and the bond market lost close to one trillion dollars in value. A shift in wealth seemed to be occurring, with savers and holders of paper assets losing and holders of hard assets winning. The stock market also declined in value.

From the point of view of the thesis of this appendix, the root cause appears to be the result of continual tampering in the economy. Even though the intent is to lessen the swings in the economic cycle in the absence of good theory and perfect information, tampering increases the amplitudes of the swings. Have we learned our lesson?

We've seen some spectacular price changes in the 1980s. Real estate in some sections of the country collapsed; in other sections it soared. The bond markets partially recovered and the stock market, which as measured by the Dow Jones Industrial Index traded as low as 777 in 1982, is at this writing trading at over 2900. A society that attempts to control itself using inadequate or incorrect theory needs a lot of people employed in certain professions. Large numbers of accountants, lawyers, and police are needed. But the profession that becomes most profitable is speculation. In fact, almost everyone becomes a speculator, although we don't call them such.

An economy with wide swings in its booms and busts creates large opportunity for profit for some people and companies and large losses for others. Fortunes have been made in real estate speculation in the last decade. Everyone involved in leveraged buyouts is essentially involved in a form of speculation or even arbitrage. Markets that move dramatically reward those who position themselves correctly and cause havoc for others. Anyone who bought a house prior to 1975 and held on for a few years in the Northeast has a large paper profit. Holders of bonds, those living on fixed incomes, and those working for thrifts have suffered.

To blame speculators for the swings in the markets and the profit potentials large swings create is silly. The large swings are created by tampering, which means adjusting and attempting to control in ignorance. Ignorance is the most expensive commodity in the world.

But are we tampering today? It seems to me that the large federal deficits, although justified on the basis of supply-side economics, are completely consistent with Keynes's ideas of keeping the boom going through government action. If such action can be continued indefinitely, then we have nothing to worry about. But at one point the interest payments on the debt can become so large as to become onerous. Any attempt to pay back the debt then has to create a new swing in the economy. The government might chose to sterilize the debt through inflation, or it might attempt to pay back some debt or at least keep the debt from increasing further. If the thesis of this appendix is correct, then the next swing, when it comes, will be very painful to many people who cannot position themselves to take advantage of it or mitigate its effects.

Further Reading

For those readers who have an interest in exploring further some of the ideas covered in this book this short list of additional readings may be helpful.

W. Edwards Deming. *Out of The Crisis*. Cambridge, Mass.: Institute of Technology Center for Advanced Engineering Study, 1986.

William W. Scherkenbach. *The Deming Route to Quality and Productivity*. Milwaukee: Ceep Press, 1986.

On the Life of Dr. Deming

Nancy R. Mann. *The Keys to Excellence*. Los Angeles: Prestwick Books, 1986.

On Competition

Alfie Kohn. *No Contest*. Boston: Houghton Mifflin Company, 1986.

On Statistical Methods

Walter A. Shewhart. *Statistical Method from the Viewpoint of Quality Control*. Washington, D.C.: The Graduate School, U.S. Department of Agriculture, 1939. And Dover, Del., 1986.

On Revolutions in Knowledge

Thomas S. Kuhn. *The Structure of Scientific Revolutions*. Chicago: University of Chicago Press, 1970.

On Win-Win Negotiations

Herb Cohen. *You Can Negotiate Anything*. Secaucus, N.J.: Citadel Press, 1980.

Notes

Chapter 1

1. *AutoWeek*, 25 August 1986.
2. *Fortune Magazine*, 18 August 1986.
3. *New York Times*, Saturday, 28 November 1987.

Chapter 2

1. Harold Geneen and Alvin Moscow, *Managing* (New York: Avon Books, 1985), 35.
2. Ibid., 2.
3. Ibid., 3.

Chapter 3

1. W. Edwards Deming, *Out of The Crisis* (Cambridge: Massachusetts Institute of Technology, Center for Advanced Engineering Study, 1986), 141.
2. Peter Drucker, *Managing for Results* (New York: Harper & Row, 1964), 87.
3. Geneen and Moscow, *Managing*, 117.
4. W. Edwards Deming, *Quality, Productivity and Competitive Position* (Cambridge: Massachusetts Institute of Technology, Center for Advanced Engineering Study, 1982), 2.
5. "Forum: Quality Is Not Enough," Daniel P. Finkelman, *New York Times*, Sunday, 14 May 1989.
6. Yoshi Tsurumi, "American Management Has Missed the Point—The Point Is Management Itself," *The Dial*, September 1981; excerpt appears in *Out of The Crisis*, 146.

Chapter 4

1. Deming, *Out of the Crisis*, 69.

Chapter 5

1. Michael Porter, *Competitive Strategy: Techniques for Analyzing Industries and Competitors* (New York: The Free Press, 1980).
2. Ibid., 123–24.
3. Ibid., 125.

Chapter 8

1. Deming, *Out of the Crisis*, 307.

Chapter 9

1. Nancy R. Mann, V. Charles Charuvastra, V. K. Murthy, "A Diagnostic Tool with Important Implications for Treatment of Addiction: Identification of Factors Underlying Relapse and Remission Time Distributions," *The International Journal of the Addictions*, 1984: 25–44.

Chapter 10

1. The facts for this section come from Stephen Jay Gould, "The Panda's Thumb of Technology," *Natural History*, January 1987. Gould, in turn, cites Paul A. David, "Understanding the Economics of QWERTY: The Necessity of History," *Economic History and the Modern Economist*, edited by W. N. Parker (New York: Basil Blackwell, Inc., 1986), 30–49.

Chapter 11

1. Deming, *Quality, Productivity*, 69.
2. Ibid., 157.
3. Ibid., 81.
4. Ibid., 70.

Chapter 13

1. Kaoru Ishikawa, *Guide to Quality Control* (Tokyo: Asian Productivity Organization, 1983), 21.
2. Peter Drucker, "If Earnings Aren't the Dial to Read," *Wall Street Journal*, Thursday, 30 October 1986.

Chapter 14

1. Deming, *Out of the Crisis*, 252–54.
2. Ibid.

Chapter 15

1. Deming Osaka Paper, delivered at meeting of Institute of Management Sciences, Osaka, Japan, 24 July 1989.

2. Ibid.
3. H. Glyn Jones, Barbara C. Collins, *A Way of Life: Sheepdog Training Handling & Trialling* (Farming Press, Ltd., 1987), 43.
4. Deming, *Out of the Crisis*, 117.

Chapter 16

1. Edith Hamilton, *The Greek Way* (New York: New American Library, 1948), 126.
2. Sun Tzu, *The Art of War*, translated by Samuel B. Griffith (Oxford: Oxford University Press, 1963), 63–64.
3. Alfie Kohn, *No Contest* (Boston: Houghton Mifflin Company, 1986), 49.
4. Ibid., 47.
5. Francine Prose, "Confident at 11, Confused at 16," *New York Times Magazine*, 7 January 1990, 40.
6. Kohn, *No Contest*, 52.

Chapter 17

1. Deming Seminar in Cincinnati, 16 September 1986.

Chapter 20

1. Adam Smith, *The Wealth of Nations* (New York: Modern Library, 1965), 61.
2. Ibid., 342–43.
3. "Medical Waste," *Wall Street Journal*, 10 January 1990.
4. Smith, *The Wealth of Nations*, 128.
5. Ibid., 3.
6. Col. F. N. Maude, Introduction to Carl Von Clausewitz, *On War* (London: Penguin Books, 1988), 87.
7. Herb Cohen, *You Can Negotiate Anything* (Secaucus, N.J.: Citadel Press), 120.
8. Ibid., 163.
9. Ibid., 201.

Appendix C

1. John Maynard Keynes, *Essays in Persuasion*, (New York: W. W. Norton & Company, 1963), 102.
2. John Maynard Keynes, *The General Theory of Employment, Interest and Money* (New York: Harcourt Brace & World, 1965), vii.
3. Walter A. Shewhart, *Statistical Method from the Viewpoint of Quality Control* (Washington, D.C.: Graduate School, Department of Agriculture, 1939), 120–22.

Index

Acceptable defects level, 38
Accidents, 65
Accountability, 56–57, 59, 93, 101, 150.
   See also Responsiblity
Achievement, cooperation promoting,
   193
Adjustments. *See also* Tampering
   constant, 75
   extreme, 71, 73–74, 142
   just-like-the-last, 73–75
   modest, 68–71, 72, 142
   negative effects of, 265–67
   overadjustments, 66, 75, 211
Alaskan oil spill, 22, 129–32, 135
Alternatives, 225–26
"American Management Has Missed
   the Point—The Point is
   Management Itself" (Tsurumi
   article), 46
American Society for Quality Control,
   253
Annual reviews. *See* Performance
   reviews
Antitrust laws, 111
Apple computer, 123
Art of War, The (Sun Tzu), 185
AT&T, 5, 15, 43–45, 146, 233, 261. *See
   also* Bell Laboratories
Attitudes
   Japanese industry vs. American
     industry, 42
   old vs. new, 32–33, 64
   toward suppliers, 149–57
   toward training, 172–73
Audits, quality, 41, 42, 116
Audit trails, 57

Auto industry, American, 3–4, 219–20.
   See also Chrysler Corporation;
   Ford Motor Company; General
   Motors Corporation
Auto industry, Japanese, 21, 220. *See
   also* Honda; Mazda; Nissan;
   Toyota
Automation. *See* Technology and
   mechanization
Autoweek (periodical), 4
Axioms of quality, 113

Backup systems, 37–39
Bakken, James, 110
Banking industry
   cooperation with competitors
     example, 229
   importance of training example,
     168–69
   inspection in service example,
     146–47
   management by control example,
     27–28
   and savings and loan problems,
     262–65
   tampering example, 100–101
Basketball analogy, 227–28
Bell Laboratories, Shewhart's quality
   and uniformity work in, 6, 49, 51,
   122, 235, 260
Bell System. *See* AT&T
Best efforts, 61
   fallacy of, 31–32, 71
   plus knowledge, 131
   vs. effectiveness, 141
Bethlehem Steel Company, 110

Blame, 65, 136, 140–41, 214
Blau, Peter, 196
Boardroom, quality emphasis in, 117, 202, 240
Bonuses. *See* Incentives; Merit system; Reward system
Brazilian external debt, 27–28
Burlington Industries, 15
Bush, George, 219, 244

Carlson, Chester, 210–11
Carnegie, Andrew, 229
Cause and effect chart, 164
Causes. *See also* Common causes; Special causes
    working backward to, 28–30, 32
Census Bureau, U.S., 7, 18, 252–53
Challenger disaster, 22, 140
Chambers, David S., 144
Chance, 55–56, 57, 58, 62, 95
Change, transformation vs., 121–22
Charts. *See* Cause and effect chart; Control charts; Flowcharts
Chrysler Corporation, 3, 45, 111
Coffee analogy, 126–27
Cohen, Herb, 230–31
Common causes, 62–63, 66, 94, 95, 97, 131, 141, 176, 182. *See also* Special causes
    interaction of, 101
Compaq Computer Company, 102
Competition, 113, 116–17, 217, 219–34
    Adam Smith's views on, 221–24
    benefits of, 219
    cooperation replacing, 192, 211, 224–25
    cooperation vs., 113
    in cooperative framework, 83, 85, 90, 105–12, 194, 230–31
    counterproductive, 93–94
    destructive, 60, 231–32
    in employment agency, 196–97
    fear of losing as byproduct, 227–28
    helping competitor, 228–29
    and honesty, 225
    as improvement source, 220–21, 224
    and intrinsic motivation, 200
    lack of, 244
    meaning of, 226–28
    mistaken view of, 93, 102, 131, 224, 244
    and monopolies, 232
    and price-cost issues, 221–25
    purchasing theory of, 86–87
    and quality, 5
    responding to, 160
    and reward system, 194–95
    situations, 194
    standards as basis of, 109–10
    with/against comparison, 227
    worker, 60
Competitive Strategy: Techniques for Analyzing Industries and Competitors (Porter), 86
Computers
    competition and standards, 110
    IBM policies, 42–43, 110
    inventors of, 123
    and management, 93, 114
Constitution, U.S., 233
Consultants, 215–16
Consumer Reports (periodical), 3
Continual improvement, 213
    Deming-Shewhart cycle of, 114–15, 119
Control charts, 80, 167, 203
    and improvement, 162–64, 167, 170
    and inspection, 147–48
    for interpreting economic data, 272–74
    for training results, 170
    for variables, 162–64, 167
Control limits, 57–58, 77, 80, 95, 135, 261
Cooperation, 101, 102
    in brokerage service, 196
    and competition, 85, 192–93, 230–31
    competition vs., 113
    of competitors, 83, 105–12
    as Deming basic axiom, 113, 207
    European-American example, 85
    foundation in U.S. history, 233–34
    and improvement, 82
    intra-company, 90–91
    in Japan, 83–85
    management-worker, 93–104
    promoting higher achievement, 46, 193
    purpose of, 243
    quality control circles, 91–92
    resulting in lower costs, 224–25
    and reward system, 194–95
    situations, 194
    as source of strength, 89–90
    and standards, 108–11
    with suppliers, 87–90, 112
Corporations. *See* Boardroom; Managment; specific names
Costs
    competition affecting, 221–23
    cooperation affecting, 224–25
    cutting, 9, 214

of lack of quality, 14, 40–41
purchasing at lowest, 149–50, 151
and quality, 13–20, 38, 42, 113
quotas raising production, 60
Creativity, 27, 184
Crisis, and transformation, 137
Customers
complaints of, 66
confidence of, 9
costs of disgruntled, 14
dissatisfied, 14, 21, 44–45
feedback from, 161
loyal, 8–9, 12, 41, 206
preferences vs. quality, 37
satisfied, 8, 14, 120
Cycle of continual improvement. *See*
Deming-Shewhart cycle of
continual improvement
Cyclical factors, 257

Darwinism, 93–94
Defects
acceptable fallacy, 38
arbitrary, 40
blaming workers for, 65, 140–41
control limits, 58
cost of, 22, 40, 139
and inspection, 142–43
and intra-company cooperation, 90–91
recognizing vs. improving, 79
special causes, 77, 163
worker motivation and, 101, 102
as worker performance measure, 52
zero, 33–34, 145
Deflation. *See* Inflation/deflation
Deming, William Edwards
association with Shewhart, 7, 51,
252–53
axioms, 113
basic management lesson summation,
242–43
biography, 251–53
compared with Taylor, 206–7
flow chart, 119–21, 160–61
14 Points for Management
Transformation, 33, 124–25
in Japan, 6, 137, 238
organizational beliefs compared with
conventional companies, 17–18
Red bead parable, 53–58, 59, 60,
61– 62, 77, 80, 94, 135, 141, 217
view of management, 115–17,
242–43, 254–74
view of quality control, 138, 237
Deming Prize, 6, 8, 18, 22, 33–34, 67
162

establishment of, 253
regulations, 245–46
winners listing, 246–50
Deming-Shewhart cycle of continual
improvement, 114–15, 119
Deming view
control charts for interpreting
economic data, 272–74
labor and capital, 271–72
national implications of, 254–74
oscillations vs. variation, 255–58
Departmental barriers, breaking down,
202–4
Description, prediction vs., 216–18
Design
importance of, 119
overdesign fallacy, 37–39
Deutsch, Morton, 192
Direction analogy, 127–28
Dodge, Harold S., 139
Dog analogy, 177–79
Dow Jones Industrial Index, 272
Drucker, Peter, 11, 38
Drug use and rehabilitation, statistical
study of, 121–22
DSK. *See* Dvorak Simplified Keyboard
DuPont, 5, 122
Dvorak Simplified Keyboard, 132

*Economic Control of Quality of
Manufactured Product* (Shewhart),
51, 252, 261
Economic data, control charts for
interpreting, 272–74
Education, 205, 211, 216. *See also*
Training and retraining
Effect. *See* Cause and effect chart;
Improvement
Effectiveness, 141
Efficiency studies. *see* Time/motion
studies
Effort. *See also* Best efforts
and improvement, 81-82
Employees. *See* Work force
Errors. *See* Mistakes
Experts, 210–11
Extrinsic motivation, 103–4
Exxon, 22, 129–32, 135

Fear
as antithesis to quality, 121, 202
driving out, 183–8
of losing, 227–28
as management by control
byproduct, 27, 78, 80, 95
and meeting quotas, 186–89

Fear (*Cont'd*)
　as military tool, 184–85
　as motivator, 186
　need to eliminate, 117, 124, 184–86,
　　189
　and performance reviews, 189–93
　two business-related types, 185–86
　vs. pressure, 183–84
Federal Aviation Administration, 65
Federalist Papers, 233–34
Federal Reserve Board, 71, 254,
　255–62, 265, 269, 273
Financial results school of management,
　138, 235–37, 238
Firestone, Harvey, 123
Fish bone chart. *See* Cause and effect
　chart
Flowcharts, improvement, 160–62, 163,
　167
Focus, 128–29
Folklore, 133–36
Ford, Henry, Sr., 38
Ford Motor Company
　monopoly vs. competition, 232
　quality and profits rise, 32
　quality program, 3–4, 5, 7, 15, 117–
　　18, 243
　research on customer response, 14
　suppliers policy, 87
　transmissions quality study, 40
　voluntary standards, 110
Fortune (periodical), 4
Fosbury, Dick, 171
14 Points for Management
　Transformation, 33, 124–25
Funnel experiment, 67–69, 71, 72, 73,
　75, 142, 254

Geneen, Harold, 22–23, 27, 38
General Motors Corporation, 47–48,
　70, 103, 111, 117–18, 243
*General Theory of Employment, Interest
　and Money, The* (Keynes), 260, 261
GM *See* General Motors Corporation
Goldman, Morton, 192
Gold standard, 267–68
Gorbachev, Mikhail, 65
Government, and plant closures, 208–9
Greek Way, The (Hamilton), 185

Hamilton, Alexander, 233
Hamilton, Edith, 185
Hammer, Trudy, 196
Heating system analogy, 265–70
Hewlett-Packard, 5, 33–34, 159–60
Honda, 15
Hospitals, 115, 222–23

IBM, 5, 15, 27, 42–43, 46, 110, 123
　146, 188
"If Japan Can, Why Can't We?" (TV
　program), 8, 253
Improvement, 158–67
　cause and effect chart, 164
　and competition, 220–21, 224
　continual, 213
　control charts, 162–64, 167–70
　cooperation causing, 82
　critical variables, 162
　Deming-Shewhart cycle of continual,
　　114–15, 119
　Deming's management teachings as
　　science of, 271
　and effort, 81–82
　experimental design, 165–66, 167
　flowcharts, 160–62, 163, 167
　and just meeting competition, 160
　of process and products, 64
　responsibility of leader, 179–80
　route to, 159–60
　short-term, 236
　and specifications, 159
　and workers' outlook 205–12
Incentives. *See also* Merit system;
　Performance reviews; Reward
　system
　and competition, 93, 194–5
　drawbacks of, 51–52, 59, 71, 98–100
　　118, 119, 131
　example, 94–96
　external, 190, 200
　Exxon shipping's use of, 130
　Ford's retention of, 118
　and management by objectives, 11,
　　23, 25
Independence, fallacy of, 30–31
Individuals
　knowledge/skills of, 208
　restoring, 122–23
Industrial Quality Control (periodical),
　140–41
Inflation/deflation, 264, 274
Inflation and Deflation (Keynes), 258
In Search of Excellence (Peters), 29
Inspection, 139–48
　associated with quality, 140, 237
　attitude toward, 139–40
　and control charts, 147–48
　eliminating, 145–46, 147–48
　as ineffective quality control method,
　　63, 64, 116–17, 140, 163
　limitations of, 140, 215
　multiple, 143–44
　and reward for defects, 142
　and sampling, 144–45

in service, 146–47
and stable system, 143
Interaction, company, 213–14
Interest rates, 262, 265, 272
Internal Revenue Service, 7
Intrinsic motivation, 103, 184, 189, 200, 205, 211
ITT management, 22–25

Jagger, Walt, 178
Japan
auto industry, 21, 220. *See also specific companies*
compared with other Asian countries, 241–42
cooperation in, 83–85
Deming Prize award in, 6, 253
Deming's quality lectures in, 6, 137, 238
management in, 210
net worth, 271
plants in, 208–9
Japanese Union of Scientists and Engineers (JUSE), 6, 43, 245
Jay, John, 233
Jennings, Peter, 207
Job security, 47
Johnson, David and Roger, 193
Joiner, Brian, 22
Jones, H. Glyn, 178
Joy in work, 117, 138, 167, 181, 184, 207, 2323. *See also* Pride of workmanship
barriers to, 104
and leadership, 177
ways to enhance, 199–204
Juran, Joseph, 140–41

Keller, Norb, 103
Keynes, John Maynard, 258, 260, 261–62, 270, 274
Keys to Excellence, The (Mann), 121–22
Knowledge. *See also* Profound knowledge
and accountability, 56–57, 95
and quality, 47–48
of variation, 77, 258
Knox, Jack, 178

Language, assumptions of, 193–94
Lawton, Barbara, 150–51
Layoffs, 22, 26, 46, 129, 208–9
Leadership, 96, 175–82
compared with supervision, 175–76
defined, 176–77
encouraging cooperation, 180–81
and quality, 182

and responsibility for improvement, 179–80
Limits. *See* Control limits
Longley (touchtyping inventor), 133
Loyal customers, 8–9, 12, 41

Madison, James, 233
Maintenance, 26
Management
boardroom setting quality policy, 117, 202, 240
and changing system, 31, 165, 242
and computers, 93, 114
by control and fear, 27, 78, 80, 95
conventional literature on, 101–3
cooperation with workers, 93–104
crisis of, 89
Deming's view of, 115–17
eliminating barriers, 207
Japanese, 210
layers of, 73–74
methods folklore, 133–36
"mushroom" method of, 154
need for profound knowledge, 49
no-blame, 136
and prediction, 217
and problems, 104, 209
purpose of, 243
and quality, 3–18, 49, 92, 237, 238, 240
Red bead parable, 53–58, 59, 60, 61–62, 77, 80, 94, 135, 141, 217
responsibility for quality, 4–5, 49, 237
responsibility for training, 95
and training, 95
two schools of, 235–37, 238
variation in, 51–66
visible numbers only (VNO) manager, 10–11, 130
by walking around, 61
worst of Western, 181–82
Management by objectives, 11–12, 22, 25, 29, 30–31, 116, 118, 125, 130, 131, 153, 189, 199, 244
Managing (Geneen), 22, 38
Mann, Nancy, 121–22
Market research, 14
Market share, 9
Matsushita (Panasonic), 109–10
Maude, F. N., 229
Mazda, 45
McGurrin, Frank E., 133
Mechanization. *See* Technology and mechanization
Medicine analogy, 115–16
Merit pay. *See* Incentives; Merit system

Merit system, 13, 81, 93, 98–100, 102. *See also* Incentives; Performance reviews
Merrill Lynch, 228
Mistakes
  solutions not blame for, 214
  types one and two, 65, 95
Monopolies
  and quality, 233
  vs. competition, 221, 225, 232
Morale, 81, 130
Mortgages, 262–65
Moscow, Alvin, 23–24
Motivation, 32, 101–3. *See also* Incentives; Merit system; Performance reviews; Reward system
  extrinsic, 103–4
  fear as, 186
  of group, 177
  instrinsic, 103, 184, 189, 200, 205, 211
"Mushroom" method of management, 154

Nashua Corporation, 64
Negotiations, 230–31
Nelson, Lloyd, 67
New technology, 37
New York City Transit Police, 13
New York Times, 43
New York University School of Business Administration, 253
Nissan, 15
No-blame management, 136
Nonexistent standards, 109
Nuclear Regulatory Commission, 81

Oil spill, Exxon, 22, 129–32, 135
Orsini, Joyce, 78–79, 150
Oscillations, 255–58, 265–67
Ouchi, William G., 108–9
Overadjustments, 66, 75, 211
Overdesign, 37–39

Panasonic. *See* Matsushita
Panhandle Eastern Corporation, 97–100
Parity, 226
Peer pressure, and quotas, 60
Performance reviews, 29, 55, 101, 116, 118, 125, 197, 199, 214, 244. *See also* Incentives; Merit system; Reward system
  creating winers and losers, 190
  as description or prediction, 217–18
  fear and, 189–93

justifications for, 190–93
  and promotions, 197–98
Peters, Tom, 29
Petersen, Donald, 4
Peterson, Pete, 232
Phantom problems, 66
Philips, N.V. (Dutch electronics firm), 109–10
Philosophy, quality focus, 126–38
Piecework, 60. *See also* Quotas
Piketty, Robert, 35
Plan. *See* Prediction
Planning, 128
Plant closures, 208–9. *See also* Layoffs
Porter, Michael, 86–87
Prediction, 114, 115, 267
  vs. description, 216–18
Preferences, 37
Pressure
  confused with fear, 183–84
  for results, 26–27
Price. *See* Costs
Pride of workmanship, 15. *See also* Joy in work
  barriers to, 125, 200–201
  enhancing, 199–204
  inspection hampering, 76
  profit relationship, 47
  and quality, 43–45
  quotas hampering, 188
Problems
  causes of, 104, 141–42
  with competition, 244
  and management, 104, 209
  phantom, 66
  solutions, 61–62
  solutions, comonly proposed, 59–61
  solutions not blame for, 214
  special in nature, 59, 214
  symptoms vs. causes, 79
  of the system, 59, 102, 131
  U.S. management, 240
Problem solving, 79–80, 128
Process, quality improvement, 64
Procter & Gamble, 5, 153–56
Productivity, 101
  and management by control, 27
  and quality, 5, 19–20
  quotas and, 60
  source of, 207–10
  and workers, 15
Profits
  loyal customers as source of, 8–9
  management theory working backward from, 21–22
  maximizing, 20

and quality, 5, 9–11, 19–20, 21, 33,
47
short-term, 91
Profound knowledge, 190, 244, 258. *See
also* Knowledge
adverse effects of improvement
attempts without, 75, 81, 131, 160,
167
defined, 49
Keynes's lack of, 260
and real improvement, 75
Promotions, and performance reviews,
197–98
Purchasing. *See also* Suppliers
lowest-cost basis of, 149–50, 151

Quality 19–34
acceptable level fallacy, 38
ambiguous definitions, 38
backup systems/overdesign fallacy,
37–39
as boardroom policy, 117, 202, 240
and competition, 5
consequences of, 42
and costs, 19–20, 38, 42, 113
defined, 35–50
as first priority, 32, 45
historical perspective of, 237–38
improvement methods, 63–64
and inspection, 63, 64, 116–17, 140,
163
as ITT's problem, 24
Japanese attitude toward, 42
and knowledge, 47–48
and leadership, 182
and management, 3–18, 92, 237, 238,
240
measuring, 35
and monopolies, 233
negative impact of quotas on, 186
price of, 13–18
price of lack of, 40–41
product improvement, 64
and productivity, 5, 19–20
and profits, 5, 9–11, 19–20, 21, 33,
47
and quotas, 27
rethinking definition of, 36–39,
118–19
and sales, 5
and specifications, 39–40, 41,
118–19, 150–52
and uniformity increasement, 39–40
and worker responsibility, 15, 16
Quality control. *See also* Statistical
control

audits, 41, 42, 116
Deming's lectures in Japan, 6, 137,
248
Deming view of, 138, 237
diminished consciousness of, 4–5, 16
meaning of, 237
misconceptions of, 38, 41, 66, 139,
237
Shewhart's work in, 51, 122, 235,
252
specialists, 49
Quality control circles, 91–92, 164,
165
Quality control school of management,
235–37
Quotas
counterproductiveness of, 60, 125,
131, 163, 187–88
and customers, 44–45
and fear, 186–89
in financial results school approach,
235
insidious characteristics of, 60
loss from, 187–88
and profits, 21–22
and quality deficiencies, 27
sales, 22, 186–88
setting, 188
in Soviet system, 28
work force, 22, 49, 60, 188–89
and work standards, 186
QWERTY analogy, 132–36, 137

Random variation, 65, 254, 255, 257,
266
RCA, 20–21
Real estate market, 273–74
Red bead experiment, 53–58, 59, 60,
61– 62, 77, 80, 94, 135, 141, 217
Reeducation. *See* Education; Training
and retraining
Regulation, 270
Reliability, 156
Responsibility. *See also* Accountability
of leader, 179–80
management, 4–5, 49, 57, 95, 237,
238
worker, 15, 16
Results. *See also* Quotas
cause and effect chart, 164
pressure for, 26–27
working backwards from, 28–30, 32
Retraining. *See* Training and retraining
Reward system, 194–95. *See also* Merit
system
as tampering, 177

Sales
  and quality, 5
  quotas, 22, 186–88
Sampling, 144–45
Sarnoff, Robert, Sr., 20
Savings and loan associations, 262–65
Scherkenbach, William W., 70
Scientific Managment (Taylor), 205–7
Scott Paper Company, 5, 15
Semiconductor industry, 146, 147
Shewhart, Walter A. *See also* Deming-
    Shewhart cycle of continual
    improvement
  association with Deming, 7, 51, 252–
    53
  at Bell Laboratories, 6–7, 49, 51,
    122, 235, 252, 260–61
  compared with Keynes, 260–61
  and control limits, 57–58, 261
  as father of statistical quality control,
    49, 51, 252
Shewhart Medal, 253
Short-term improvement, 236
Silver markets, 272–73
Slogans, 129–32, 202
Smith, Adam, 221–22, 223–24, 231
Soccer example, 96–97, 166
Solutions, 214
Sony, 109–10, 209–10
Soviet Union, 28–29
Special causes, 62, 77, 79, 94, 95, 141,
    163, 176, 182, 214. *See also*
    Common causes
Specialists, quality control, 49
Specifications
  and imrpovement measures, 159
  problems with, 150–52
  as proposed quality solution, 39–40
    41, 118–19
  and rethinking quality concept,
    118–19
Speed typing analogy. *See* QWERTY
    analogy
Stability. *See* Statistical control
Stable systems. *See* Statistical control
Standard of living, 240, 242
Standards, 108–11
  nonexistent, 109
  quotas and work, 186
  voluntary, 110–11
Statistical control, 62, 64, 94, 134–35,
    141, 211, 271. *See also* Control
    limits
  inspection system as, 143, 146, 148
  overadjustment of, 75
  practical example, 58–59

Shewhart's inception of, 7, 49, 51,
    252
  stable systems, 67–82, 113
*Statistical Methods from the Viewpoint
  of Quality Control* (Shewhart), 7, 51,
    252
Statistics, 7, 49, 51, 80–81, 252, 253
Stock market, 273
Sun Tzu, 185
Supervision, compared with leadership,
    175–86
Suppliers
  attitude toward, 149, 157
  cooperation with, 62, 89, 112
  Procter & Gamble example, 152–56
  relationships with, 116, 149–57, 217
  and reliability, 156
  single sourcing, 87–89, 124, 157, 219
  and specification, 150–52
Survival of the fittest theory, 93, 94
Systems. *See also* Merit system; Reward
    system; Statistical control
  changing, 31, 165, 242
  competitive, 195
  control limits, 135
  improving, 31
  low quality, 202
  oscillating, 255–58
  problems, 59, 102, 131
  responsibility for, 57
  stable or unstable, 67–82, 113, 143
  tampering in small, 76–77

Taguchi, Genichi, 162, 165
Taguchi Loss Function, 162
Tampering, 75, 211, 258–60, 267,
    269–70, 271, 274
  and acting without knowledge, 81
  and assigning causes, 142
  examples in dealing with variation,
    77–79
  group motivation as, 177
  improper use of inspection as, 147,
    148
  in small system, 76–77
Taub, Louis, 133
Taylor, Frederick, 205–7, 210, 211
Teamwork, 97, 196
Technology and mechanization, vs.
    quality, 37, 47–48, 60, 131, 206,
    207, 208, 211, 243
Telephone system, 6–7
Testing, 61
Thrift institutions. *See* Savings and
    loan associations
Thriving in Chaos (Peters), 29

Time/motion studies, 205–6
Toshiba, 120
Townsend, Lynn, 45
Toyota
  and General Motors, 47–48
  quality concept, 5–6
  worker input, 15–16
Trade deficit, U.S., 5, 29, 239
Training and retraining, 26, 47, 124,
    176–77
  attitudes toward, 172–73
  for immediate future, 169–70
  importance of, 168–74
  management's responsibility for, 95
  poor, 202
  seen as expense, 168–69
  self-taught, 171–72
  worker training worker method, 74,
    170–71
Transformation, 113–25, 129
  of attitude toward inspection,
    139–40, 215
  basic, 213–18
  change vs., 121–22
  consultants, 215–16
  and crisis, 137
  description vs. prediction, 216–18
  interactive nature of companies,
    213–14
  need for, 121, 213
  and performance review, 217–18
  and reeducation, 216
  resistance to, 215
  solutions instead of problems, 214
Tsuda, Yoshikasu, 42
Tsurumi, Yoshi, 46
Type one mistakes, 65, 95
Type two mistakes, 65, 95

Unemployment rate, 262
Uniformity, as quality component, 113

Variables, 270–72
  and control charts, 162–64, 167
  critical, 162, 180–81
  wrong ways of dealing with, 77–78
Variation, 49, 94, 113, 244, 270. *See
    also* Uniformity; Variables
  knowledge of, 51, 77, 258
  lessening, 63
  in managment, 51–66

nature of, 79
oscillating, 255–58, 265–67
random, 65, 254, 255, 257, 266
sources of, 49
special, 65
Visible numbers only (VNO) manager,
    10–11, 130
Voluntary standards, 110–11

Wall Street Journal (newspaper), 97–
    100, 165–66, 222
Wealth of Nations, The (Smith), 221–22
Western Electric Company, 6
Wooden, John, 98–100
Work, joy in. *See* Joy in work
Work force. *See also* Joy in work;
    Performance reviews; Pride of
    workmanship
  competition among, 60
  controlling, 189
  cooperation with management,
    93–104
  excessive testing of new employees,
    61
  improvement and outlook of, 205–12
  as individuals, 46, 122–23, 208
  investment in, 138
  layoffs, 22, 26, 46, 129, 208–9
  morale of, 41, 81, 130
  quotas for, 22, 49, 60, 188–89
  responsibility for quality issue, 15, 16
  as scapegoat for accidents and
    defects, 65, 140–41
  and special help, 76–77, 80, 81, 96
  tampering with, 76–77
  treatment of, 46, 218
  unemployment rate, 262
  worker training worker method, 74,
    170–71
Workie, Albaineh, 192
Working backward, 28–30, 32
Workmanship. *See* Joy in work; Pride
    of workmanship; Quality
Work standards quotas and, 186

Xerox Company, 123

You Can Negotiate Anything (Cohen),
    230

Zero defects, 33–34, 145